Teardown

Teardown

Memoir of a Vanishing City

Gordon Young

UNIVERSITY OF CALIFORNIA PRESS

Berkeley · Los Angeles · London

University of California Press, one of the most
distinguished university presses in the United States,
enriches lives around the world by advancing
scholarship in the humanities, social sciences, and
natural sciences. Its activities are supported by the UC
Press Foundation and by philanthropic contributions
from individuals and institutions. For more
information, visit www.ucpress.edu.

University of California Press
Berkeley and Los Angeles, California

University of California Press, Ltd.
London, England

Library of Congress Cataloging-in-Publication Data

Young, Gordon, 1966–
    Teardown : memoir of a vanishing city / Gordon
Young.
        p.   cm.
    Includes bibliographical references and index.
    ISBN 978-0-520-27052-7 (cloth : alk. paper)
    1. Flint (Mich.)—Social conditions.   2. Flint
(Mich.)—Economic conditions.   3. Plant shutdowns—
Michigan—Flint.   4. Urban renewal—Michigan—
Flint.   I. Young, Gordon, 1966–   II. Title.
    HN80.F54Y68   2013
    307.3'4160977437—dc23

                                        2012039951

Manufactured in the United States of America

22   21   20   19   18   17   16   15   14   13

10   9   8   7   6   5   4   3   2   1

In keeping with a commitment to support
environmentally responsible and sustainable printing
practices, UC Press has printed this book on Rolland
Enviro100, a 100% post-consumer fiber paper that
is FSC certified, deinked, processed chlorine-free, and
manufactured with renewable biogas energy. It is acid-
free and EcoLogo certified.

For Pat, Traci, and Leone

Memory fades, memory adjusts, memory conforms to what we think we remember.

—Joan Didion, *Blue Nights*

It's a dismal cascade of drek, but it's still home.

—Ben Hamper

We shall not cease from exploration
And the end of all our exploring
Will be to arrive where we started
And know the place for the first time.

—T. S. Eliot, *Little Gidding*

Contents

Photographs follow page 116

Prologue

Summer 2009

The sticky summer weather had finally overpowered the cold, rainy spring, and I was sleeping on the floor of a vacant house across the river from downtown Flint, Michigan, in a neighborhood called Carriage Town.

Festive Victorian-era homes in various stages of restoration battled for supremacy with boarded-up firetraps and overgrown lots land-scaped with weeds, garbage, and "ghetto palms," a particularly hardy invasive species known more formally as *Ailanthus altissima,* or the tree of heaven, perhaps because only God can kill the things. Around the corner, business was brisk at a drug house where residents and customers alike weren't above casually taking a piss in the driveway.

Hardwood floors were as advertised, but my camping pad and L. L. Bean sleeping bag weren't nearly as comfortable as they had looked in the catalog. A loud thud—either real or imagined—had woken me with a start at two in the morning, and I finally drifted back to sleep snuggling what passed for my security blanket—an aluminum baseball bat. A siren served as an alarm clock just after dawn.

Awake, I wanted to call my girlfriend, Traci, back in San Francisco, but I knew she was still asleep. I figured Sergio, our aggressive twenty-pound cat, would have reclaimed what he considered his rightful spot in our bed by now, as he always did when I was out of town. I grabbed my cell phone. Maybe Traci was up early for work. At 4 A.M. West Coast time? Not a chance.

I tossed the phone down, got dressed, and ventured outside for what had become my morning routine. Each night, someone unfettered by bourgeois concerns about recycling deposited an empty pint bottle of Seagram's Wild Grape in the front yard of my temporary residence. For the uninitiated, it's "Extra Smooth Premium Grape Flavored Vodka." I dutifully picked it up before breakfast, arranging it with all the others in a corner of the front room, figuring I'd throw them out once the pattern was broken. Years of Catholic school had made me unwilling to depart from ritual.

This was my old hometown. Birthplace of General Motors. The "star" of Michael Moore's tragically funny *Roger & Me*, the unexpectedly popular 1989 documentary that established Flint as a place where desperate residents sold rabbits for "pets or meat" to survive. A city that continually challenged the national media to come up with new and creative ways to describe just how horrible things were in a place synonymous with faded American industrial and automotive power.

In 1987 *Money* magazine ranked Flint dead last on its list of the best places to live in America, and the city's reputation hadn't improved much over the ensuing years. *Time* called it the country's most dangerous city in 2007. *Forbes* named Flint one of "America's Most Miserable Cities" and one of "America's Fastest-Dying Cities" in 2008. (Alas, the clever editors at *Forbes* keep no such tallies for magazines.) The next year, Flint was on the magazine's compendium of "Worst Cities for Recession Recovery" and "Worst Cities for New Jobs." Though these labels angered locals and Flint expatriates alike, the numbers didn't lie.

The Flint area had lost more than 70,000 GM jobs since peak employment in 1968. The official jobless rate hovered around 30 percent, but if you counted the people who had given up looking for work it was closer to 40 percent, maybe higher. When the auto factories were booming, it had one of the highest per capita income levels in the country for a city its size; now more than a third of all residents lived in poverty. But given Flint's dismal high school graduation rate, it might make sense to dispense with the facts and figures and describe the city in more direct terms, the way a guy had summed it up for me the previous night in the Torch, a bar hidden away in a lonely downtown alley that had somehow managed to survive Flint's socioeconomic swan dive: "What can I say?" he offered with a shrug of his shoulders. "This place is fucked up, man."

It goes without saying that such devastation has led to population loss. Flint has become the ultimate "shrinking city." My family moved out, along with what seemed like everybody else, in the mid-1980s. As the B-52s used to sing over the sound system at the Our Lady of Lebanon dances I attended in high school—after overindulging in illegally obtained Boone's Farm and/or Mickey's Malt Liquor—"Don't feel out of place/'Cause there are thousands of others like you." In fact, Flint has lost half its residents, plunging from 200,000 to just over 100,000 in five decades. As a result, roughly one-third of Flint is abandoned. If all the empty houses, buildings, and vacant lots were consolidated, there would be ten square miles of blight in the city.

The decline has had a devastating impact on local schools, perhaps the most powerful symbols of happier times, the brick and mortar repositories of childhood memories. In 1968, Flint schools had 46,557 students attending kindergarten through high school. By the fall of 2008, there were just 14,056 kids left. Enrollment is projected to dip to 10,432 students by the fall of 2013—a 78 percent decline.

Throughout the city, abandoned schools suffer the same fate as empty houses. They are torched by arsonists and ravaged by thieves, known as scrappers, in search of any metal they can resell—doorknobs, radiators, aluminum siding, but especially copper wiring and plumbing. Despite these indignities, you can sometimes peer through the gaping holes once framed by windows and see old American flags and weathered bulletin boards filled with tattered assignments decorating the classrooms. Four of the schools I attended as a kid are now closed.

It was clear that after fifteen years in San Francisco I had drifted uncomfortably far from the town my grandparents had moved to from the cornfields of Iowa at the turn of the twentieth century. How did I know? I sometimes fretted over the high cost of organic avocados. I went to Belgian beer tasting parties. Once an investigative journalist, I was now a freelancer who wrote meandering travel essays and sappy feature stories in college alumni magazines. I also taught journalism at a Silicon Valley university where the tuition tops the yearly income of many Flint residents and BMWs are easy to spot in the dorm parking lots. After growing up driving a silvery blue Buick LeSabre and a bamboo cream Buick Electra 225—that's a "deuce and a quarter" in local parlance—I owned a dull gray 1990 Toyota Camry, a car that was once officially banned from the city hall parking lot in Flint and still isn't welcome on UAW property. Embarrassingly, it's only a four-cylinder. And then there was the fact that I was so jittery that I was bedding down with a baseball bat.

I had returned to my troubled hometown on a quixotic mission.

I was there to buy a house.

That was the most concrete aspect of my plan. I wasn't sure if this would be a permanent residence, an improbable "vacation home," a low-cost rental for a needy family, or a rehab project that Traci and I would give to charity. Those were details I could figure out later. I was worried that if I did too much thinking, I'd talk myself out of all this. And I didn't want that to happen.

It's difficult to explain why I would want to spend time away from the quaint little house Traci and I had somehow managed to buy in San Francisco, let alone consider moving to Flint and giving it up forever. Although it's characterized by what the housing inspector charitably called "light construction"—the place shakes when you walk through it too quickly—our five-room bungalow in the heart of the Bernal Heights neighborhood is just a short stroll from a used bookstore, a wine bar, an organic market, a great Peruvian restaurant with dishes I can't pronounce, and two taverns with names that wouldn't be out of place in Flint—Skip's and Wild Side West. It has a front *and* back yard, a rarity in San Francisco, albeit only because it is so small at seven hundred square feet that it doesn't take up much of the city lot. Unlike numerous Flint residents, it's a safe bet that most of my neighbors don't feel the need to own firearms or police scanners. Why would I leave the City by the Bay, sometimes described as forty-nine square miles surrounded on all sides by reality, for a city where violence and heartache were all too real? And why would I try to convince Traci to do the same?

It's complicated.

PART ONE

1

Pink Houses and Panhandlers

I had arrived in Flint in early June of 2009 after listening to the Tigers game in my rental car during the ninety-minute drive up I-75 from the Detroit airport. I thought baseball on the radio would snap me into a Michigan frame of mind, but the legendary Ernie Harwell, whose distinctive voice had mesmerized me as a kid, was no longer calling the games. It wasn't quite the same. But the game did remind me to stop at a thrift store and buy that baseball bat, a handy accessory for any extended stay in Flint.

I eventually made it to Saginaw Street, the city's main artery, which roughly divides Flint between east and west. As I crossed the river into what was once the thriving shopping district in the heart of downtown, the first of several black metal arches harking back to the early twentieth century spanned the thoroughfare, announcing that this was the "Vehicle City." The rumble caused by the uneven, old-timey bricks that still lined several downtown blocks gave me a jolt of nostalgia, a rush of the familiar that tapped into memories of numerous trips down this bumpy street with my mom, my grandparents, and my friends. It felt reassuring. And although no one would describe downtown as bustling, with its empty storefronts and boarded-up buildings, I saw signs of hope.

There was a crowd at Blackstone's, a new restaurant located in the former home of a fashionable men's clothing store that had folded decades earlier. (Spotting a new business in downtown Flint is as rare as seeing someone driving a new Buick in San Francisco.) The Art Deco splendor of the sixteen-story Mott Foundation Building, scrupulously maintained with the financial legacy of a fabulously wealthy industrialist once referred to as Mr. Flint, would draw attention in any city. There were enough people out and about to chase away the eerie sense of emptiness pervading so many other parts of the city. A few construction projects generated a reassuring racket that indicated something was happening here. The city wasn't dead yet.

I was headed to a vacant house owned by a friend of mine named Rich. Like me, he had grown up in Flint and eventually moved to San Francisco, where we met. He owned three "investment" properties in Flint, although the fact that all of them were empty indicated they weren't exactly generating a lot of income. He had happily agreed to let me crash at one of them. "It's good to have it look like there's someone actually living there," he had told me. "It keeps the thieves from stealing the plumbing."

It took me a while to find the house because downtown still had an inexplicable number of confusing one-way streets, an unnecessary remnant of the days when growth and good fortune meant traffic congestion. I'd also never spent much time in the Carriage Town neighborhood. It was unfamiliar terrain when I lived in Flint, a neighborhood to avoid unless you were in the market for drugs, hookers, or an ass kicking.

Rich's sister, Berniece, was there to greet me when I finally arrived. She still lived in Flint. Although we'd never met, she showed me around the house like I was an old friend, presenting a very practical housewarming gift—a four-pack of toilet paper. She seemed worried about me, offering advice like "Don't let anybody you don't know into the house" and "Be careful who you talk to on the street." I tried to reassure her that I knew how to take care of myself. I was from Flint, after all. But I sensed that my San Francisco pedigree, the new Patagonia shirt with lots of snaps and pockets that I'd bought for the trip, and my teal-striped Pumas were undermining my street cred.

Before I try to pawn myself off as a minor-league George Orwell writing a Rust Belt version of *Down and Out in Paris and London*, I should point out that Rich's house wasn't as rundown as many in the neighborhood. It was the well-preserved former home of Charles W. Nash, the president of GM in 1912 and founder of Nash Motors. It was just across the street from the Durant-Dort Office Building, the beautifully restored birthplace of GM. Unlike many of Flint's empty structures, the Nash House had luxuries like plumbing and electricity. The water heater was broken, but a cold shower would be better than nothing. Inexplicably, the place was painted pink, destroying any chance I had of establishing myself as some kind of tough-guy writer, a Buick City Bukowski.

The wood floors, wraparound porch, handsome stained glass window, and high ceilings oozed Victorian charm. There was no sign of habitation other than an awkwardly modern glass table in the dining room, a couple of folding chairs, and an expensive-looking Persian rug in the living room. Our voices echoed in the empty space. The bulk of the tour was devoted to the house's four doors and eight locks. The kitchen door had been nailed shut from the inside with a two-by-four after a break-in. The side door was locked and seldom used. If there was a fire, Berniece advised, the front door was my best option, other than the windows.

"I'll try not to burn the place down," I joked.

"It's not you I'm worried about," she answered. Like any city with a lot of abandoned property, Flint houses regularly went up in flames.

I decided to bed down on the nice rug. Besides adding a little padding, it was close to the fire exit.

I walked Berniece out to her pickup truck, suddenly feeling lonely and wishing she'd stay for a while. As she was driving away, I saw my two closest neighbors, a man and a woman who looked to be in their thirties, playing with two dogs in their massive yard, which took up about five city lots. I wanted to introduce myself, but it looked like they were heading inside. I started jogging across the wide expanse of lawn that separated the two houses. "Hey there!" I yelled, for some reason deciding to wave both arms over my head to get their attention. "Hey! Hi!"

I immediately realized this was not the way to introduce yourself in Flint. In unison, the couple and the dogs swung around to face me. A consistent and unmistakably hostile look animated the faces of both humans and canines. "What do you want?" the guy demanded, as one of the dogs started to growl. I skidded to a stop, still a good fifteen yards away, far enough that I was almost yelling as I awkwardly explained who I was and offered up a rambling history of my relationship to Flint dating back to 1972, dropping every local name and cultural reference I could muster. I'm not positive, but I may have recited the names and addresses of all my high school girlfriends. "I used to be an altar boy at Saint Mike's, right over there on Fifth," I trailed off.

The dogs were still intent on ripping me to shreds, but the couple turned and looked at each other, apparently trying to decide if I was a harmless oddball, a potentially dangerous criminal, or just fucking crazy. "Sorry about that," the guy said after a long pause. "When someone we don't know runs up on us like that, we're not sure what to expect." We shook hands, but the dogs continued to eye me warily.

Nathan and Rebecca told me they had purchased their cornflower blue, two-story house seven years earlier for $90,000. I was shocked by the high price tag, and they admitted that they'd paid way too much. It was a great place, nevertheless. We walked over to their back deck, complete with a hot tub, and they pointed out their herb and vegetable garden, compost heap, and the fruit trees and berry bushes scattered across their half-acre property.

They had good jobs. Nathan commuted to Lansing, where he worked as an environmental policy analyst with the Michigan Senate Democrats, and Rebecca was the executive director of the Flint Watershed Coalition. "I grew up in Lansing, and when I told people I was moving to Flint, they were like 'Are you frickin' kidding me?'" Rebecca said. "But we never had a lot of apprehension about moving here. When we lived in various suburbs we were never engaged in our community at all. Now we know everybody. You have a hard time getting your yard work done because people stop by to talk. You really feel like you're part of something."

They pointed out that although they'd dealt with crackheads, panhandlers, and various shady characters, the only thing that had ever been stolen from their property was the small metal sign planted in their front yard warning intruders that they had a burglar alarm.

I was growing suspicious. I wondered if these two were operatives planted by the real-estate agents I was planning to meet later in the week. Aside from an abandoned brick building casting a long shadow that nearly reached the healthy clusters of rhubarb in the backyard garden, the conversation could have been taking place in San Francisco, although in that scenario Nathan and Rebecca might become millionaires simply by selling off a portion of their yard. Here was a couple who seemed to prove that you could have a meaningful, fulfilling life in Flint.

Right on cue, a loud, exuberant yelp of either agony or ecstasy cut through the quiet, followed by what sounded like a board breaking and laughter. Rebecca giggled and shook her head. "Ah, that would be the drug house across the street," Nathan said calmly as he continued to survey his property, a smile of satisfaction—or was it resignation?—on his face.

After I said my goodbyes, I cut across the yard to my empty pink house. I didn't exactly know what to do with myself, so I started organizing, attempting to create a makeshift bedroom by sorting stuff from my suitcase into carefully arranged piles on the living room floor near my sleeping bag. That's when I heard a strange, ghostly voice floating through the house. "Oh luke aht this window, so bootiful!" a woman said in what sounded like a German accent.

I slowly pulled back the curtain of the window closest to the voice and was face-to-face with a meticulously made up elderly woman who was peering intently into the house. She had on lavender-tinted glasses and was wearing a long cotton nightgown and slippers. With her bright red nail polish contrasting with flashy gold rings and bracelets, she reminded me of an aging Hollywood legend padding around the grounds of her mansion. She tapped on the window with a well-manicured index finger. "Oh, hello there!" she said and unsteadily weaved her way toward the backyard.

I'm ashamed to admit that I briefly considered grabbing my bat before I ventured outside to investigate. Sure, she appeared to be a sweet little old lady, but she was wiry, and those polished nails looked sharp. What the hell was wrong with me? I needed to cool it with the security measures. I went outside—unarmed—and introduced myself.

It turned out to be Rich and Berniece's mom, out for a drive with a friend. They had stopped to look at the purple and yellow irises blooming in the yard. I gave them a tour of the house and told them my plans. I mentioned that I had gone to grade school at Saint Mary's, and I could tell that the connection meant something to Rich's mom. It was her parish. Before she left, she gave me a hug in the front yard. "You woot be happy if you came back home," she whispered to me.

Once again, I was in the front yard waving goodbye, this time as my two unexpected visitors drove away. A shirtless guy down the street saw me, waved back, and made a beeline down the block. I considered hustling into the house to avoid the encounter, but he was fast. "My man, you have to help me out," he said, rubbing his head with one hand and imploring me with the other. "I just got robbed. You know what it's like to get robbed on your birthday? That shit is messed up!"

I was used to being panhandled in San Francisco, but it had never happened in my front yard before. Rich had warned me to *never* give anyone change in the neighborhood, but I didn't want to be too harsh with this guy since he knew where I lived. "Happy birthday," I said, trying to sound firm yet friendly. "I don't have any money."

"Come on, man!" he said, taking a step toward me, suddenly angry. His face was inches from mine.

"Sorry, but I can't help you out," I said, getting a little pissed off myself and regretting the decision to leave my bat in the house.

"Cheap-ass muthafucka," he yelled before abruptly turning, crossing the street, and cutting through the parking lot behind the Durant-Dort building, no doubt covering the same ground that GM's creator, Billy Durant, had traversed numerous times about a hundred years earlier.

I took a deep breath, found a shady spot on my front steps, took out my phone, and called Traci in San Francisco. She reported that our cat, Sergio, had invaded the neighbor's house again, peeing in their basement, then sacking out on one of their beds and refusing to leave. He was relentless in his quest to acquire new territory, an impulse I was beginning to understand. The previous night Traci had gone to a party filled with other writers and reporters that had degenerated into the typical group lament over dwindling jobs, bad editors, and low pay—the sort of unrestrained bitching that often defined our lives as journalists.

I tried to explain how one day in Flint contrasted with the cold, superficial friendliness of San Francisco, where I sometimes felt like I could go long stretches without making a real connection with anyone besides her. I'd already been fretted over by Berniece; confronted, scrutinized, and ultimately accepted by Rebecca and Nathan; embraced by Rich's mom; and called a muthafucka by the birthday boy. It was all a visceral reminder that the anonymity of big-city life in San Francisco and the stereotypical laid-back character of California had their drawbacks. If you weren't careful, you could float along on a sheen of lovely views and trendy pop culture distractions. Ironic roller derby matches at the Kezar Pavilion, graffiti masquerading as art in the Mission, and the mesmerizing fog rolling over Twin Peaks. At the risk of sounding like a touchy-feely Californian, somehow Flint felt more real, like I had permanent ties here that I could never make in San Francisco. This must have come off as an overly enthusiastic endorsement, because Traci cautioned me to give Flint a few weeks before I came to any big conclusions. "I miss you," she said before we hung up. "The house seems empty without you."

I lingered on the front porch, resisting the urge to go inside and needlessly rearrange my belongings. There was nowhere I needed to be. I tried to sit back and appreciate the fact that after all the planning, worrying, and soul searching, I was really in Flint, well on my way to buying a house. But I couldn't quite silence the small voice in the back of my head whispering that this was a very bad idea.

2

Bottom-Feeders

Looking back, the desire to own property in Flint was rooted in my decision to buy a house in San Francisco. Despite the yawning economic, geographic, and meteorological gap between the two places, they were united by one thing: I didn't have any business owning property in either place. By nature, I am deeply skeptical when it comes to most things that involve spending money. A few friends have jokingly used terms of endearment like "cheap bastard" and "tightwad" to describe me. (At least I think they're joking.) But my frugality seems to disappear when it comes to real estate.

Traci discovered this six months after we gave up our respective apartments and moved in together in 2003. We had a nice two-bedroom flat up a steep flight of stairs on the western slope of Bernal Heights, with built-in bookshelves, an elegant nonfunctioning fireplace, and a back deck, all set to a soundtrack of muffled salsa music that drifted up from the bars on nearby Mission Street. At $1,850 a month, it was reasonably priced by the outrageous local standards. We were happy. We were in love. Why mess with this arrangement?

Well, I couldn't help thinking about all the money I'd handed over to the landlord of my previous apartment on Potrero Hill, roughly $130,000 in rent over a decade. And I'd always felt a little like a visitor to San Francisco. I liked the idea of Traci and me becoming official residents with a real stake in the city. I was in my forties, and I wanted to be a homeowner. I foolishly believed that by combining the meager incomes of two journalists we might have a shot at owning in one of the world's most expensive markets. Our household income was around $90,000. Starter homes in the San Francisco neighborhoods we found acceptable started at around $500,000. Neither of us did that well in math back in school. We were writers, after all.

Our friendly landlord at the time, Michelle, was a real-estate agent who was, of course, very encouraging. She thought my plan was brilliant, especially since we wanted her to be our agent. Her husband was a lawyer who grew up in Muskegon and wore U of M T-shirts, so there was a Michigan connection. Already I was basing housing decisions on extraneous emotional attachments.

In the spring of 2004, Michelle put us in touch with a mortgage broker named Ralph, who called to set up a meeting after we'd submitted our financial information. He was a calm, conservative-looking guy with a brush cut, a mustache, and a suit. After congratulating us for having good credit scores and living entirely debt-free, he politely said he couldn't imagine how we'd ever be able to afford anything in the city. He half-heartedly said a studio condo might be a possibility. That's right, one room for me, Traci, and our two cats—Sergio and Purdy. "I can't see you getting a loan big enough for anything larger, and even if you got it the payments would eat up more than half your take-home pay every month," Ralph said in a sympathetic but firm tone. "Now's just not the time for you to buy."

I had an instant flashback to my grandfather sitting at the wooden desk in the corner of his dining room back in Flint. He was a real-estate agent, and he would often work from home when he wasn't at the office, making calls on the hulking black rotary phone and filling out paperwork while my grandmother and I watched TV in the living room after dinner. In my memory, he frequently talked people out of buying houses. "I think you'd be much better off if you saved your money and kept renting," he'd say. "You'll be a lot happier with money in your pocket. You don't want that mortgage hanging over your head, young man."

Ralph was saying the same thing. He was being straight with us. Now wasn't the time. I was momentarily disappointed, but when I left his office I felt a huge sense of relief. I'd given it a try, and it hadn't worked out. Now I could stop worrying about it and enjoy the summer. Traci took it in stride. "Oh well," she said. "We've already got a great apartment." It was a different story when I called Michelle. "He told you what?" she said, clearly annoyed. "I don't think that's accurate at all. Let me give you the name of another mortgage broker."

The new guy, let's call him Jimmy, was down in San Jose, the sprawling city an hour south that languished in the shadow of sophisticated San Francisco. He called after we sent him another thick batch of financial info and told us not to worry; we were already preapproved for a $551,000 loan. He sounded confident, if not a little giddy. I had more or less resigned myself to not buying, so his breezy disposition made me uneasy. I told him what Ralph had said. "No idea why he'd tell you that," Jimmy replied. "That seems a little unprofessional, but I'd never criticize another broker."

Thus began the summer of house hunting. Make that the summer and fall of house hunting. Traci and I spent every Saturday deciphering the property listings like code breakers. Sundays and numerous Tuesday afternoons were devoted to open houses. That was our routine for six months. At first we tried to look presentable, but after a while the long slog wore us down, and we opted for comfortable clothes—cutoff shorts and T-shirts. We told ourselves we might appear to be anticorporate Silicon Valley entrepreneurs who had struck it rich creating a useless bit of software or a doomed website. Besides, looking fancy wouldn't do us any good when we got outbid on a house. And we got outbid five times. Or was it six? Once by $129,000. And once by someone who made an all-cash offer. (Probably some dude in cutoffs.)

We started to recognize the other bottom-feeders as we made the rounds of anything priced at $499,000 or below. Knowing that everyone overbid, this was the only price point we had even a remote chance at. It appeared that the same forty people without enough money to buy were looking at the same low-end properties every week. I started exchanging the manly chin lift of acknowledgment with guys and friendly hellos with women. They were our competitors for these properties, but the fact that they kept showing up meant they were as unsuccessful as we were. I developed a low-key camaraderie with them, although we seldom said more than a few words to each other.

There were times when well-dressed yuppie couples—women in dresses, men in suits minus the tie—would roll up in a Mercedes or an Audi for an open house, and you could feel the collective despair and resentment ripple through the rest of us as we checked out a bedroom closet or ran a hand over a kitchen countertop. We knew that if they could afford the car and the lifestyle that involved suits outside of funerals, job interviews, or weddings, then they could outbid us. It was pointless to even bother with a place if they wanted it.

Traci and I worked to maintain the veneer of low-key positivity when we were at the open houses. We wanted to look like people who were there to seriously check out the property. We tried to seem like a couple who had options. We'd complain about the utter hopelessness of the search back at our apartment, when I'd rant and rave about wasting my life looking at houses we could never have, or houses that we wouldn't want to live in even if we could afford them. But one fellow bottom-feeder, with black curly hair and a perpetual five o'clock shadow, stood out because he didn't bother to conceal his darker emotions. He'd walk into a tiny bedroom the size of a closet and let out an exasperated sigh before saying out loud to no one in particular, "Hey look, a bedroom for our pet hobbit! Bilbo will be so happy." A bathroom with crumbling tile would prompt a response dripping with sarcasm: "Hey, I'm in the public bathroom at the Mission Playground. Awesome!"

He became increasingly bitter as the weeks ticked off. He was giving off such a poisonous vibe that the other couples—and it was always couples, both gay and straight—maintained a five-foot buffer from him at all times. He had his own personal force field of disgruntlement. He was always with a fairly chipper woman who was his wife or girlfriend, but even she began to keep her distance. We thought he'd finally lost it at a two-unit condo that required the owner to walk through the living room of the downstairs neighbor to reach the backyard, which was considered common property shared by everyone in the building. Whoever bought this tiny place would need permission to do a little gardening or have a cookout. If that wasn't bad enough, the two condos shared a washer and dryer. A coin-operated washer and dryer. "You're fucking kidding me," the voice of all our fears yelled out, desperately trying to make eye contact with someone, anyone, so that he might properly convey his rage. "I'm going to pay half a million bucks for this dump, and I'll still have to pump quarters into the washing machine?"

The laundry room quickly cleared out. I figured the other house hunters, like me, were in a fragile emotional state, wavering between delusion (Yes, we can buy a house!) and despair (No, we can't buy a house). Some guy shouting the obvious might send us all over the edge. We saw him the next week at a house in Noe Valley, a blandly prosperous neighborhood that was proving to be way out of our price range. He was sitting in a lawn chair on the back patio with his head in his hands. He may have been silently crying, but I didn't want to get close enough to find out. He wasn't even bothering to look at the houses anymore. I worried that I could end up just like him in a few weeks if I wasn't careful.

In desperation, we finally resorted to considering a TIC, or tenancy in common, a strange bit of San Francisco real-estate exotica that involves teaming up with someone else and buying a property together. Typically, you join forces with strangers, even though you'll be cosigning a loan with them after paying an attorney to draw up an elaborate legal document that spells out the solution to everything that could possibly go wrong with the arrangement. Of course, it's often a very long document, a testament to all the potential pitfalls. Michelle told us she was working with another couple who was in a situation similar to ours—not enough money—and that we might be able to work something out. Traci and I met them for coffee in Dolores Park. It was like some sort of couples blind date, where we all tried to act casual despite the fact that we were deciding whether to enter together into what might be the biggest financial transaction of our lives. (Traci warned me not to discuss my love of Morrissey, an '80s musical icon, or my propensity to scream at the referees while watching meaningless NBA regular season games on TV.) He had a British accent. She was from Ohio. They rode around the city on a scooter. They seemed normal. Hey, what else did we need?

Now we were simultaneously looking for two-unit buildings with our TIC partners and regular houses or condos for us. This was even more exhausting and somewhat awkward because we often ran into our partners at one house, indicating we might be competing against each other for it, before meeting them to look at another property that we might bid on together. None of it mattered, though. Even when we bid on TIC properties with the combined incomes of four well-educated professionals, we still got outbid.

Our housing odyssey may have been frustrating and time consuming, but it didn't become truly weird until we connected with a sophisticated music composer from Norway and his wife, a red-haired documentary filmmaker from an equally exotic locale—Flint, Michigan. Her mother worked at the public library where I had spent countless hours goofing off in high school. Unlike most San Franciscans, who actively disdained American-made cars, she had actually ridden in a Buick, albeit years ago. They already owned a two-unit building in the Mission District and were searching for TIC partners to occupy one of the flats and become co-owners with them. We made a bid. They accepted. It seemed like fate had finally intervened in our favor. Flint synergy was flowing.

Nothing could go wrong now. I was ready to crack open a Stroh's beer, a Michigan favorite, in celebration.

All that remained was a run-through of the building with Michelle, our real-estate agent, the couple, and the housing inspector we hired. A mere formality. We were all strolling through the basement, checking out the storage space, when we came to a door with a homemade sign taped to it: "Rosa's Room. Do Not Enter."

"Who's Rosa?" Michelle asked, immediately suspicious.

The couple glanced nervously at each other. A look of panic came over the face of my compatriot from Flint. She was about to speak, but her husband shook his head to silence her. "It's really nothing," he finally offered, stroking his beard and looking at the floor. The thick accent that had once been so endearing now made him sound like a double agent about to betray his best friend in a spy thriller. "It's not a problem."

The door opened suddenly and an elderly woman, clearly pissed off that we were making a racket, scowled at us. Behind her I could see a bed, a dresser, and other telltale signs of habitation. She amped up the dirty look to make sure we fathomed the depths of her displeasure and slammed the door shut.

"That was Rosa," the composer said softly, a note of defeat in his voice.

"Is she living in there?" Michelle demanded, not softly at all.

"Well, in a way, I suppose," he said. "But you don't need to worry about it. We've got it all taken care of. It's fine."

"Let's get out of here," Michelle said to me and Traci as she turned and headed for the stairs leading out to the street. Apparently, the inspection was over.

We were about to discover a new San Francisco real-estate term, one that has killed many a promising deal in the city: "protected tenant." Over the next few tortured days we learned that Rosa had lived in the building when the couple bought it years earlier. At one point they had attempted to get her to leave. She filed a complaint with the San Francisco Human Rights Commission and received a favorable ruling. She now had the right to live in the building as long as she wanted, a situation that not only dramatically lowered the value of the property but also opened us up to all sorts of legal entanglements if we became co-owners. Worse, as Michelle emphatically pointed out, the couple tried to hide this information from us and their real-estate agent, who quickly dropped them as clients. Not exactly the way to start off a TIC partnership. The deal was off.

"I thought Midwesterners were supposed to be wholesome and honest," Traci said when it was clear we were headed to more open houses.

"Flint's not really the Midwest," I answered feebly. "Neither is Norway."

Eventually, even my competitive spirit, stoked in the gyms and on the football fields of Flint, was overwhelmed. Traci and I decided we'd look at one more batch of houses on Sunday, then call it quits. We didn't expect to find anything. It was more of a token gesture. We checked out a cool little place in Bernal Heights. The flyer called it a "tranquil and magical cottage!" ("Cottage" is San Francisco real-estate jargon for incredibly small.) It had fish ponds in both the well-landscaped front yard and the backyard, a privacy fence covered in climbing passion flowers and trumpet vines, and a front gate with a Zen-like copper hand from Nepal for a handle. The place was crawling with house hunters, and the list price was $519,000. Given that virtually every place we had bid on went for at least $50,000 over asking, we figured we didn't have a chance. I wrote my name and number on the sign-in sheet just for the hell of it, and we went back to our apartment. We had put up a good fight, made a noble effort, but we were beaten. It was hopeless to keep trying. We accepted our fate. We were renters.

A few weeks later, we got a call from Michelle. The owner of the house, who was sometimes referred to as the unofficial "Mayor of Bernal Heights," had allegedly only gotten offers from contractors who wanted to tear the house down and dramatically transform it into a McMansion. She had rehabbed the place herself, had close relationships with her neighbors, and didn't want to see her baby become a soulless giant on a street of modest homes. She'd spotted my name on the sign-in sheet.

We wrote a syrupy letter gushing about how we fell in love with the house the moment we saw it and that we'd be honored to live in a place so lovingly restored. (We didn't mention the $25,000 in foundation work we knew it needed, or that the "new" roof had five layers of shingles on it, or that the so-called plaster walls were really just poorly installed drywall.) I wanted to put in a low-ball offer, but after our long ordeal Michelle recommended bidding everything we had.

And it worked.

The instant we gave up trying, a house was presented to us. It made me wish we had quit six months earlier. Now all we had to do was arrange financing.

We made an early morning appointment to meet with Jimmy the mortgage broker at his office in San Jose. But it was deadline day, and

Traci couldn't show up late at the small magazine where she worked as an editor, so she dropped me off in the forlorn parking lot of a cinder-block office park, circa 1950, where Jimmy did business. I planned to walk to the university where I taught, located about a mile away, after the papers were signed.

"Is this place even open?" Traci asked after I kissed her goodbye. She was reluctant to leave me there in the parking lot. The nearby streets were clogged with early morning traffic and a greenish-yellow smog was already collecting around the distant hilltops, bolstering my theory that San Jose possessed all the unsavory attributes of Los Angeles without the glamour, money, or excitement of the movie industry.

"It'll be fine," I said, trying to sound confident. "I'll call you later and let you know how it goes."

The door to Jimmy's office was locked, so I knocked and a secretary opened it almost instantly, startling me. I turned and waved to Traci, who was looking back at me from the edge of the parking lot, a worried expression on her face. She waved tentatively and nosed the car into traffic. Inside, the office had the feel of a fake place of business in an infomercial—a collection of bland, brand-new office furniture, a suspicious absence of papers, files, or clutter of any sort that might indicate actual work being done. It smelled like plastic. It's the sort of office you might assemble if you had three hours to set it up. I felt like I was in a David Mamet movie, about to get conned.

The secretary picked up the phone and announced that a client had arrived. A harried-looking guy in a black suit, a red shirt, and a loud tie burst out of a nearby door. He looked a little like Conan O'Brien gone to seed. This would be Jimmy. "Hey, man, it's too late now," he said, his reddish hair flying around in the flurry of activity. "You snooze you lose. You were supposed to be here an hour ago."

I had a moment of panic. I thought I was early, not late. Had I somehow ruined our chance for a house because of tardiness? "I'm Gordon Young and I thought I had a 9:30 appointment," I said, my voice quavering.

"Oh, Gordon, yeah, yeah, yeah. Sorry about that. You're early. I thought you were my other appointment, who's late. Come on in."

I glanced at the secretary and she smiled reassuringly, just the way a seasoned grifter would smile in a Mamet film. I noticed Jimmy's face was glistening with sweat. I thought of Ralph, the responsible mortgage broker with his sober calmness and his woody, well appointed office near city hall in San Francisco. Now I was out in the sticks of San Jose dealing with shady characters. I seriously considered walking out, but I told myself that Michelle had recommended Jimmy, so he must be legitimate.

We were working our way through a stack of loan application documents that I had only a rough understanding of—Jimmy pointing and talking rapid-fire and me signing—when he let out a low groan. I looked up, and he was grimacing and clutching his chest. Sweat dripped off his chin. I have to admit that my first thought was selfish annoyance: Don't have a heart attack now, you inconsiderate bastard! I'll have to find another mortgage broker. But my humanity overrode my lust for home ownership. "Jimmy, are you all right?" I asked, standing up and putting my hand on his shoulder. "Should I call 911?"

He offered up a weak smile and shook his head. "No, it's okay," he gasped. "This happens all the time. It's just acid reflux." He pointed to another spot with his free hand, the one not planted on his sternum. "Just initial here," he croaked. His face was still contorted, like a marathon runner toughing out that last five hundred yards before the finish line. I would have signed anything at that point just to get out of there. We finally finished up, and Jimmy rose unsteadily to his feet. He offered his hand, which was wet and clammy. "Piece o' cake," he said. "I'll be in touch when I hear back from the lender."

I stepped outside into the nearly empty parking lot. I heard the door click behind me, no doubt the secretary locking it. I imagined Jimmy and the secretary celebrating, like Paul Newman and Robert Redford in that scene from *The Sting* when they pull off their big scam. I told myself not to be so paranoid. With the bright California sun shining down on me, I wiped my hand, still slick with Jimmy's sweat, on my pant leg. I was one step closer to home ownership.

In the end, Ralph and Jimmy were both right. It was not a sound financial move for us to buy a house in San Francisco, but that didn't mean we couldn't get a loan to do it anyway. We moved into our new home shortly before the Thanksgiving holiday in 2004. Sergio, our big cat, inspected the place while Traci and I stood in the living room holding hands. He cautiously sniffed every corner, then calmly turned and sprayed a wall in the living room. He was marking his new territory. Thus, our first truly domestic act as new homeowners was screaming at the cat and mopping up pee. Too late to back out now.

We were surfing a wave of dubious, if not toxic, mortgages that would eventually help bring the world financial market to its knees. At least the lender bothered to verify our incomes, an annoying step that many would eventually dispense with altogether. But Traci and I certainly had a financing package that would have made my grandfather shake his head in disgust. No money down. An interest-only adjustable first mortgage for $446,000 with a low teaser rate that would balloon after two years, plus a second home equity loan at 7.25 percent that was instantly maxed out at $105,000. The plan was for the property to appreciate on paper enough for us to refinance before the two years were up. The $25,000 that would have traditionally been part of the down payment went toward shoring up the foundation of our magical unicorn cottage where fairy sprites danced on the banks of the fish ponds, which almost immediately began to crumble, the picturesque river stones sliding into the murky water to reveal the black plastic liner beneath them. Discolored drywall chipped off the bedroom walls because that section of the house was rotting from the ground up, a result of the foundation problems.

Every few months we'd get a letter in the mail announcing that our mortgage had been sold or that a new servicer would be collecting payment on the loans. There was Aurora Financial Group, CitiMortgage, Sierra Pacific, and a highly reputable outfit called No Red Tape Mortgage. I'm leaving out a few others because I lost track of them all after a while. But our original plan did come to fruition. In May of 2006 our house was reappraised at $705,000, which just happened to be the exact value we needed to get a new thirty-year fixed rate mortgage serviced by Wells Fargo Bank, albeit one with a ten-year interest-only grace period before the real payments kicked in. The appraiser who somehow hit that magic number was hired and compensated by our new mortgage broker, named Justin, also suggested by Michelle. (Jimmy was apparently no longer in the picture; I imagined him singing songs like "Poison Ivy" in the lounge of a casino in downtown Las Vegas, slugging Maalox before he went on stage, hoping to land a better gig on the strip.) The appraiser knew exactly the valuation Justin needed to make the new loan work, but I'm sure that didn't influence him in any way.

So we had lucked out. I guess. We had managed to buy just before prices climbed out of our reach. And we had a locked-in rate of 6.625 percent, which was higher than the prevailing rate because this was considered a jumbo loan. The good news was that we didn't have to worry about the interest rate skyrocketing when a teaser rate expired. The bad news was that we had an interest-only monthly payment of about $3,050, which was more than half our take-home pay, without making a dent in the principal. Don't forget the $600 a month to cover taxes and insurance, not to mention the maintenance costs. Basically, we were in the very situation that my grandfather would have cautioned us to avoid at all costs.

Traci and I altered our lifestyles in accordance with the financial demands of home ownership. Despite the rainy winters and the chilly fog of the so-called summers in San Francisco, we rarely turned on the heat in our house. Eating at the city's famed restaurants became as rare as making a deposit to our IRAs. Our fleet of luxury cars—my aging Camry and Traci's banged-up Hyundai Elantra—would not be upgraded anytime soon.

This wasn't a huge adjustment for me. Despite frequent bailouts from my grandparents, I'd grown up in a household in Flint constantly in the throes of financial crisis. A minor repair to one of our unreliable GM cars was a calamitous event. I learned early on how to misdirect bill collectors when they called our house, often employing a fake British accent. We regularly ate breakfast for dinner—pancakes, bacon and eggs, or waffles—when money was especially tight. I knew how to live on the cheap. Although Traci had grown up in a more financially stable family in the scenic San Juan Islands north of Seattle, she adjusted to this new age of frugality. But there was no denying that buying a house in San Francisco put an end to many of the tangible benefits of living in one of America's greatest cities. At least the spectacular views in the City by the Bay were still free.

3

Bourgeois Homeowners

I liked to believe I was immune to popular sentiment, unaffected by the predictable middle-class longing for hearth and home. I thought it was important to keep your options open, and I was drawn to journalism because it allowed me to discover a new story, a new place, and a new group of people—and then move on. I fancied myself an outsider who didn't do something just because everyone else was doing it.

So it was tough to reconcile this self-image, however delusional, with the deep satisfaction I felt as a first-time homeowner. The house was supposed to be nothing more than an investment. Just like an apartment, except it belonged to us and not some landlord getting rich off our rent. But I quickly came to love standing next to Traci in the little front yard with its overgrown vines and cracked walkway, basking in the knowledge that we actually owned a house together in San Francisco. We joked that cosigning on a home loan in this city was a far greater sign of commitment than simply getting married, which anybody could do. (At least any straight couple at that time.) It was a good feeling.

Once possessive of my free time, I now welcomed lost weekends spent botching minor home improvement projects and having long conversations with more skilled friends back in Michigan about the proper way to refinish wood floors or plane a sticky door. I hired day workers hanging out on Cesar Chavez Street to help with the more ambitious jobs. (Drywall translates into *tabla roca*, by the way.) I bought power tools. I wore a tape measure on my belt to Home Depot to look legit.

What a poser. But as much as I hated to admit it, I enjoyed acting like a regular American. I was proud of our home.

The house even altered our taste in entertainment. Who knew that *Mr. Blandings Builds His Dream House* with Cary Grant and Myrna Loy was so good? I thought Ice Cube showed real range in *Are We Done Yet?*, which was basically an updated version of the same movie, channeling the familiar couple-versus-house theme. Then there was *The Money Pit* with Tom Hanks. It sucked but we watched it anyway. Online home repair shows became porn for me. *Oh man, check out the double-pane windows on that bungalow!*

But it was a book from an unexpected source that helped me understand the psychological underpinnings of my newfound nesting tendencies. Before he became the darling of foodies and the arbiter of all things organic with *The Omnivore's Dilemma* and *In Defense of Food*, Michael Pollan wrote a book called *A Place of My Own*. It details his desire to build a "shelter for daydreams," a small wooden hut on his property in New England. It's about a writer's fastidious vanity project, a "simple" structure executed with the help of an architect, a builder, and frequent consultations with the ghosts of Thoreau, Le Corbusier, Aristotle, and Frank Lloyd Wright. But while I sometimes found the combination of philosophical musing and practical building applications a bit precious—do you really need the first century B.C. writings of Vitruvius to decide on the pitch of your roof?—there's no denying that Pollan tapped into some of the elemental forces that had a hold on me. He helped me understand the intrinsic power of houses. They aren't just investments; they define us.

"Like the clothes Adam and Eve were driven by shame to put on, the house is an indelible mark of our humanity, of our difference from both the animals and the angels," he wrote. "It is a mark of our weakness and power both, for along with the fallibility implied in the need to build a shelter, there is at the same time the audacity of it all—reaching up into the sky, altering the face of the land. After Babel, building risked giving offense to God, for it was a usurpation of His creative powers, an act of hubris. That, but this too: *Look at what our hands have made!*"

I wasn't building a house, but this was exactly the feeling that came over me after completing grandiose projects like replacing the toilet seat in our only bathroom, a seemingly simple task requiring three trips to the hardware store for expensive tools after I discovered the bolts holding the seat in place were threaded into the tank, submerged in water, totally inaccessible, and completely rusted. After puncturing my left palm with a flathead screwdriver and irreparably scratching the toilet bowl with a hacksaw, victory was mine. A new toilet seat. I, too, could exalt in the power of creation, once I disinfected my hand and stopped cursing the plumbing gods. It was glorious.

Despite the growing list of minor injuries I racked up whenever I worked with tools of any sort, the house became a refuge for us. We felt safe. Secure. For me, it was a totally unexpected development, but it wasn't the only one. Reassuring memories of the modest two-story house with faded green aluminum siding where I grew up in Flint started flooding back to me at unexpected moments. I found myself thinking about the different rooms: the upstairs bedroom with the Nerf hoop and Fran Tarkenton posters I shared with my older brother; the breezy screened-in front porch where I often sat with my mom in the summer after dinner; the tiny bathroom with a tub but no shower that all five family members somehow shared. I had odd but pleasant dreams where I was driving a convertible around the familiar streets of Flint, calling out various landmarks with a megaphone like a tour guide: "On your left is the store where Saint Mary's students used to shoplift Hostess Ho Hos after football practice. And on your right is the fence I successfully jumped in fourth grade, narrowly escaping four unknown kids intent on kicking my ass for no particular reason." It was as if the love of my new home reignited all the warm feelings I had for my old one. There was just one problem. I was pretty sure I'd never had exceptionally fond memories of Flint before. Something weird was going on here.

By the time I graduated from high school in 1984, I couldn't wait to escape Flint. A pretentious teenager with a new-wave haircut—a mullet in reverse—who made a big show of reading *Harper's* magazine and *The Catcher in the Rye,* I viewed Flint as a cultural backwater, nothing more than a dying factory town.

I thought Ben Hamper, a Flint autoworker turned best-selling author, pretty much summed up the place in his hilarious book *Rivethead: Tales from the Assembly Line:*

> Flint, Michigan. The Vehicle City. Greaseball Mecca. The birthplace of thud-rockers Grand Funk Railroad, game show geek Bob Eubanks and a hobby shop called General Motors. A town where every infant twirls a set of channel locks in place of a rattle. A town whose collective bowling average is four times higher than the IQ of its inhabitants. A town that genuflects in front of used-car lots and scratches its butt with the jagged peaks of the automotive sales chart. A town where having a car up on blocks anywhere on your property bestows upon you a privileged sense of royalty. Beer Belly Valhalla. Cog Butcher of the world. Gravy on your french fries.

There were so many residents scrambling to escape in the eighties that renting a U-Haul was almost as tough as finding gainful employment. Moving trucks beelined to places with better weather and more jobs. Florida. Georgia. Texas. California. Assembly lines had never encouraged creative thinking, and there seemed to be a bunker mentality among those lucky enough to have a job in Flint. They were hunkering down, hoping to avoid the layoffs as long as possible, maybe even make it all the way to retirement. Life in Flint was risky, but it was no longer a place for risk takers. The future was somewhere else.

My family joined the flood of Flint refugees. I headed off to college in Washington, D.C. My brother found a full-time job teaching and coaching at a small Catholic grade school in Jacksonville, Florida. My two sisters, happy to escape the Michigan winters, followed him there and soon landed work. They all lived in the same apartment complex. Jacksonville was not an unfamiliar locale. The family had briefly lived there before I was born. It was the navy town where my parents had met and fallen in love. So when McLaren Hospital offered my mom a buyout with lifetime healthcare and a small pension in 1986, she took it and moved to Jacksonville. She wasn't eager to leave Flint, but she missed her kids and didn't like living in our old house all alone. Everyone except my grandmother had said their goodbyes to the Vehicle City.

As an undergraduate studying political science, I wasn't exactly proud of my Flint heritage. I would sometimes lie and say I was from Ann Arbor to avoid the disdain that often followed if I told the truth. After all, even people from Detroit looked down on Flint. I was attempting to pass myself off as some sort of sophisticated anglophile, fond of Romantic poetry and obscure British bands, and I didn't think the Vehicle City fit the image I was trying to construct. The Smiths, my favorite band at the time, regularly sang about postindustrial Manchester, a rough English equivalent of Flint minus the gun violence and the muscle cars, but I failed to make the connection at the time. Abstract English deindustrialization was so much cooler to me than the homegrown variety. I had no regrets about being the last make and model of my family to roll off the assembly line in Flint.

After college, I became an active member of the Flint diaspora, finding work as a reporter in Little Rock, Arkansas. Compared to my hometown, it was strange and exotic. I marveled at how few bars there were, only to discover that many counties in Arkansas had none at all. They were against the law! Unions were equally scarce, although technically still legal. I regularly got to interview the state's charismatic governor, some guy I had never heard of before named Bill Clinton. It was such an insular city that I interviewed Bill and Hillary once when they were in line behind me at a Little Rock movie theater. We were waiting to see *The Doors*. Bill did all the talking. Hillary looked distracted. I was also in the crowd, notebook in hand, when Clinton announced in 1991 on the steps of the historic Old State House near downtown that he was running for president.

Just when the novelty of living in the South was wearing off, I managed to land a cushy fellowship in Great Britain. I had few responsibilities other than studying Victorian literature at the University of Nottingham and delivering speeches to drunken British businessmen about life in America. It never crossed my mind to include Flint in my presentations.

When my funding ran out, I conducted a frantic transatlantic job search and landed as an editor and writer at a mediocre alternative newsweekly in San Jose. A few years later, I migrated north to a much better paper in San Francisco. In contrast to Flint, there was an irrational sense of optimism floating around in the dry Northern California air. The weather was so mild that people whined about a little fog just so they'd have something to complain about once in a while. Everyone came off as friendly and happy and physically fit. They were brimming with big ideas. Even after the dot-com bubble burst, it was a hopeful place compared to Flint.

So why, after more than a decade in this paradise of positive thinking, did I suddenly miss the Vehicle City so much? Why was I getting teary-eyed just thinking about the city I couldn't wait to leave? Therapy was clearly in order, but getting in touch with your emotions is expensive in San Francisco, like everything else. So I did what any logical Californian would do when confronted with a profound psychological quandary that required extensive rumination. I started a blog.

4

Virtual Vehicle City

I launched Flint Expatriates in the fall of 2007. It lacked just about every attribute that guarantees a large audience in the blogosphere. It wasn't devoted to strident political views, tawdry celebrity gossip, the latest life-changing technology, or hardcore porn, unless you are turned on by graphic photos of abandoned houses, stripped bare of their aluminum siding and totally exposed to the elements. Aside from demolition crews, pawn shops, and moving companies, it had no obvious advertising tie-ins.

I wasn't expecting a blog about a troubled Rust Belt city to be wildly popular. I was hoping it would help me come to terms with my conflicted feelings about Flint without being mean spirited, depressing, or sappy. I wanted it to be funny without making too much fun of Flint. Improbably, I hoped to cover the past, present, and future of the city from my remote publishing headquarters in the cramped living room of my house in San Francisco. If I failed, it was no big deal. I figured no one would read it anyway.

The result was a jumbled collection of posts based on my mood and what I could dig up after classes at the university or during downtime between freelance assignments. A story theorizing that Flint might rebound when water shortages forced residents of the southwest United States to move north might be followed by an item about a pair of AC spark plugs, once proudly manufactured in Flint, that had been fashioned into earrings for sale on eBay. A YouTube video that used satellite imagery to compare Flint, with its acres of demolished factories, to Ground Zero after 9/11 ran the same day as a piece on urban gardens springing up on vacant lots in some of the city's worst neighborhoods. It was an odd mixture of hope and despair, wonky urban-planning material and kitschy cultural ephemera. Memories of the old days mingling with semi-informed conjecture about what might lie ahead. The blog was my way of thinking out loud about Flint.

As expected, the public response was underwhelming. A few comments trickled in, but I sensed that many of the three dozen hits the blog generated each day were mistakes—collectors tracking down info on flintlock rifles or cartoon fans searching for trivia on Fred and Wilma Flintstone. Then I realized that I had neglected to address a topic that would surely resonate with my elusive target audience. I didn't have any posts about the ultimate leisure activity in Flint—getting drunk. I remedied the situation by asking Flintoids, as we sometimes called ourselves, to name every local bar, smoke-filled tavern, and dimly lit lounge they could remember. This was apparently the supreme challenge for the current and former residents of a factory town that once felt like it had a drinking establishment on every corner. The post generated more than a hundred comments, and the list of booze emporiums climbed to well over three hundred. There was everything from strip clubs like the infamous Titty City near the Chevy plant to posh joints like the University Club in the penthouse of the now-abandoned Genesee Towers, Flint's tallest building. The names alone made you want a drink: the Argonaut, the Ad-Lib, the Beaver Trap, Thrift City, Aloha Lounge, Auggie's Garden Glo, the Treasure Chest, the Rusty Nail, the Torch, the Teddy Bear, the White Horse, the Whisper. The sheer number was impressive, although most were now closed. A clever economist could surely track Flint's decline by charting the year-over-year drop in bars open for business.

One of the dearly departed to make the list was the Copa, an improbably named oddity that stood out in a city where bars tended to have rustic names like the Wooden Keg, and references to Barry Manilow songs were frowned upon. Bill Kain opened the Copa in 1980 in the heart of downtown on Saginaw Street. Though Flint lived and died with the auto industry, Kain embraced diversification and catered to just about everyone, including high school kids with bad fake IDs. The Copa was primarily a gay bar, but Thursday was officially straight night, and the crowd was mixed on many evenings. In a largely segregated town, it was racially mixed, playing funk and hip-hop in a market that made Foreigner, Styx, and Billy Joel rich. There were house music nights, live rap acts, and male strip shows—attended primarily by straight women. New Wave music was a staple, and it was the only bar in town where dancing to the Tom Tom Club or New Order wouldn't warrant an ass-kicking. (The Copa still had its share of shoot-outs and brawls, but none appeared to be caused by musical or sexual preference.)

Kain was an outspoken critic of the harebrained schemes to revitalize Flint with auto-themed amusement parks and high-end shopping projects, but the fact that he had a thriving business didn't give him much pull at city hall. When Kain died in 1991, he was dismissed with a tiny, four-paragraph obit in the *Flint Journal*. The paper managed to spell his name wrong.

By writing about bars, I found my people. The number of hits jumped, and readers began sharing their thoughts on Flint. Only a few dozen had to be edited for excessive profanity. Some were heartfelt odes to venerable local institutions like Halo Burger, home of the deluxe with olives and the Vernor's cream ale. Others celebrated local characters like Gypsy Jack, an East Sider who turned his house into a Wild West museum, complete with a jail and saloon in the basement. He sometimes dressed like a cowboy, strolling the cluttered grounds of his small corner house in chaps, boots, and cowboy hat. Sometimes, when he'd had a few, he'd dispense with clothing altogether and ride naked through the darkened streets on his motorcycle.

But amid the drinking stories and reminiscences, I posted constant reminders of present-day Flint's condition. In Flint, autoworkers are often referred to as shop rats—sometimes affectionately, sometimes not—so it's fitting that a chain restaurant symbolized by a big, buck-toothed animatronic rat named Chuck E. Cheese served as one of the most high-profile examples of Flint's decline.

On a cold Saturday night in January 2008, a grandmother named Margie was attending a birthday party for her five-year-old granddaughter at the pizza joint/video arcade where "a kid can be a kid" and adults can struggle to maintain their sanity amid the sensory overload. It's located just outside the city limits in Flint Township on a road filled with big box stores, strip malls, and fast-food joints leading to the mall that helped kill downtown Flint in the seventies. Margie noticed more than a dozen teenage girls roaming the restaurant, probably bored with playing skeeball and crab grab and looking for trouble. A friend of Margie's took offense when one of the girls bumped into her. Words were exchanged, followed by punches. Margie's friend was quickly outnumbered. "There had to be twelve to fifteen girls on one girl," she told the local press.

The family fun was just getting started. As many as eighty people were brawling when officers from seven different police departments converged on the restaurant. "The biggest thing we did was just try to control the crowd," one cop said. "Once pepper has been sprayed, it's floating in the air so we called in for medical help in clearing it. If people aren't used to pepper spray, they get pretty scared and angry." Those just might be the two most common emotions in Flint these days, but it's not exactly what a grandmother has in mind when she plans a birthday party. "It was almost like a nightmare," Margie said. "Kids were screaming. It was almost like we were in a stampede." Police finally cleared the restaurant and shut it down for the night.

The next day, a local news crew arrived to film a segment about the brawl when another fight broke out in the parking lot. This one was minor by comparison—just ten people, all from the same family.

After initially downplaying the incident as a simple argument among friends, the Chuck E. Cheese corporate office responded by banning alcohol sales at the restaurant, along with profanity and gang colors. Less than a year later, the new policies appeared to be working, at least by local standards. The *Flint Journal* ran a feel-good story proclaiming that the restaurant was clearly a "more peaceful place" because cops had responded to *only* a dozen calls since the brawl, mainly for purse snatching and parking lot vandalism. "Nothing major," the Flint Township police chief said. "No fights."

I suppose the brawl was hardly the worst thing that ever happened in Flint. Nobody died, after all. Friends with kids have jokingly told me that visits to Chuck E. Cheese often propel them toward violence. But for me, it was a reminder that there were really no safe zones left in the Flint area. Weird shit could happen just about anywhere.

These depressing posts often prompted heartfelt laments from readers. "I moved from Flint five years ago to Seattle, Washington," read one comment, echoing the theme of many others. "I did that because I saw my beloved hometown dying. At Christmas time I visited family and friends. I took what you might call the 'Grand Tour' of Flint. What I saw just made me want to cry. I can't believe that Flint has gotten that bad. My family told me it was bad, but, wow, I didn't think it could degenerate to the point it has. I truly am sickened by what has happened to Flint. Needless to say I felt like I was escaping when I got on my flight at Bishop Airport. I hope it turns around soon. I hope that city someday returns to its former glory."

Many comments were deeply personal, and they often came from unexpected sources. Howard Bragman is a public relations guru in Los Angeles who has advised everyone from Stevie Wonder to Paula Abdul, as well as making appearances on *The Oprah Winfrey Show, Larry King Live*, and *Good Morning America*. He emailed me an excerpt for the blog from a book he had written describing his less than ideal years growing up in Flint. "I know what it's like to be an outsider—I grew up a fat, Jewish, gay guy in Flint," he wrote. "In Hollywood, those are the first three rungs up the ladder of success, but in a town like Flint, it's three strikes and you're out. It's a little like that *Twilight Zone* episode with a whole planet full of deformed people and they make fun of the normal guy."

My mom, pushing eighty and living in Florida, became a frequent contributor. Born in Flint in 1930, she grew up on Illinois Avenue, just around the corner from the house that would later become Gypsy Jack's cowboy corral. She had the same love-hate relationship with the city that I detected in many other readers. She clearly related to the working-class mentality of the place and didn't deny that she was a hell-raiser growing up, causing her parents no end of grief as she took full advantage of the bar culture Flint had to offer. She had no shortage of affectionate stories about her early life in the Vehicle City. Yet she didn't hesitate to leave when she got the chance, heading to Wayne State University in Detroit before dropping out and moving to New York City to become a department store model in the fifties. She hung out with the jazz crowd at Birdland and Minton's Playhouse. She drove with Charlie Parker to a gig in Philadelphia once. She fell in love with a saxophonist from Detroit. Then it was on to Miami, where she became a stewardess—she's still opposed to the term "flight attendant"—for National Airlines, flying regularly to Havana and New Orleans. It was the scattered trajectory of a beautiful young woman searching for something in life that she couldn't quite identify. After a short-lived marriage to a navy pilot—make that two short-lived marriages to two navy pilots—she returned to Flint, a divorced single mother with four kids. She threw herself into more mundane work in the admitting office at McLaren Hospital, supporting her family, paying for Catholic schools and expensive private colleges. Despite returning under tough circumstances, she never turned on Flint, even while acknowledging her ever-present desire to escape.

"I grew up on the East Side and recall the unexplained pride I felt when the 3:30 Buick factory whistle blew and the roughly dressed workers poured out of the General Motors labyrinth swinging their lunch pails. Some were headed for home and some for the corner bar, but all with the determined step of an army after a battle won. I somehow felt as if I were a part of this giant assembly line and the city it fed," she wrote in one post. "Nostalgia, I'm sure, is the opiate of old age. Memories over ten years old automatically become the 'good ol' days.' We remember only the happy things and leave the shaded areas behind. And yet, faintly sifting through the sands of time, I seem to recall saying, 'The day I'm eighteen, I'm leaving this town.'"

As a newspaper and magazine writer wary of online journalism, I had to admit that the blog had succeeded in ways I never could have imagined. Before long, it racked up two hundred thousand unique visitors and six hundred thousand page views. Tiny numbers compared to big blogs, but who would have imagined that many people cared about Flint? More importantly, I felt more in tune with the city than I had in years, despite going back only a handful of times over the past three decades. I reconnected with old friends and made new ones. Flint was a part of my life again. When the *Flint Journal* called to write a story about Flint Expatriates, even though I frequently mocked the local rag, I blurted out "I love Flint" in the interview, which of course became the headline for the piece. Where had that come from?

Ben Hamper, my literary hero and author of *Rivethead,* wrote to tell me he enjoyed the blog and inadvertently gave me the answer. He lives in northern Michigan now but made frequent visits back to Flint. He managed to capture my simultaneous repulsion and affection for our hometown in a single line near the end of his email: "It's a dismal cascade of drek, but it's still home."

Like a lot of people who hit midlife in an adopted city, I began to think of my hometown as a center of authenticity—my authenticity. It took a couple of years of blogging for me to realize it was a place where I knew every street, building, and landmark. A place where I still had a deep-rooted connection to people, even after all these years. No matter how long I live in San Francisco, I sense I'll never know it like I know Flint.

My family had no direct connection to the auto industry. My mom logged one day at AC Spark Plug and called it quits. My distant father was a navy carrier pilot who had degrees from Annapolis and the Naval Postgraduate School. He drove a Mercedes he couldn't afford, not a

Buick. I've never changed the oil in my car by myself. But there's no denying I'm a product of Flint culture, both high and low. There are things I still hate about it, but my identity is wrapped up in the place that Hamper called "the callus on the palm of the state shaped like a welder's mitt."

Even the smells that trigger my strongest emotional response snap me instantly back to Flint. One is the dry, papery odor of books, which reminds me of the long summer days I spent reading in the air-conditioned splendor of Flint's well-stocked public libraries. The other is that pleasantly repulsive mixture of spilled beer and stale cigarette smoke, spiced with a delicate hint of Pine Sol and urinal cake, that you find in a certain kind of bar. It conjures memories of eating fish dinners as a kid in places like Jack Gilbert's Wayside Inn, and the mysterious darkened interiors of taverns you could peer inside on hot days when the door was propped open, not to mention the various Flint bars my friends and I frequented in high school and college. It didn't matter that I had lived in California longer than I lived in Flint. Flint was part of me, and I was part of Flint.

5

Bad Reputation

Thanks to a spellbinding high school European history teacher who looked like a taller, dark-haired version of Albert Einstein and delivered his lectures engulfed in a cloud of pipe smoke, I knew more about the Austro-Hungarian Empire than I did about Flint when I left for college. He threw parties at his house, where teenagers from across the city drank wine coolers, smoked pot, and had break-dancing competitions in his low-ceilinged basement, proving that odd things passed for normal in Flint in the eighties and that a Catholic education wasn't just choir practice and all-school Masses.

Now, as the publisher of what was apparently the only blog dedicated to the glories of Flint, I felt compelled to augment my meager knowledge of the city's history, which, if it were a pithy advertising slogan, might be condensed to "Flint: A lot of bars and even more cars." I soon discovered that Flint's bad reputation wasn't exactly a new development. It has recently been labeled "Murdertown, U.S.A." and "the toughest city in America" while charting on a list of the most depressing places in the country, but the area that would become Flint had image problems from the start, at least among potential white settlers. It was seen as a swampy, dangerous backwater with brutal winters, impenetrable forests, and swarms of bloodthirsty mosquitoes, long considered the unofficial state bird. In some ways, Flint's recent decline was a return to its roots in terms of public perception.

The first batch of bad PR came shortly after Congress reserved two million acres in the Michigan Territory for veterans' land grants in 1812. Government officials then penned such awful reviews of the peninsula surrounded by the Great Lakes that the land was set aside in the Missouri and Illinois Territories instead. The surveyor general of the United States land office, in a "labored and depressing" report, declared that not one out of a hundred acres was farmable, maybe not even one out of a thousand. The commander of Fort Saginaw, located north of present-day Flint, penned a distressing official report to the War Department just before the outpost was evacuated. "Nothing but Indians, muskrats and bullfrogs could exist here," he wrote. Thanks a lot, buddy.

These bad write-ups didn't bother the local fur traders, who were happy to burnish the region's reputation as an inhospitable place unsuitable for newcomers. They could be considered the area's first NIMBYs for their not-in-my-backyard approach. "Many tall tales came out of the woods—tales of ferocious animals and treacherous Indians and strange diseases," read one history of the city. "The men who lived by trapping and trading in furs did not want the country settled for that meant the end of the wild life on which they existed."

With this antigentrification campaign in place, coupled with the white settlers' abject fear of the local Chippewa tribes, it's little wonder that the 1820 U.S. Census counted fewer than ten thousand settlers in the Michigan Territory, which then included the present-day states of Wisconsin and Minnesota. Nearly everyone lived in or near Detroit.

None of this deterred a crafty and ambitious Canadian with a taste for adventure named Jacob Smith. He was happy to find a place where beavers, muskrats, skunks, weasels, otters, minks, and raccoons easily outnumbered humans. Born in Quebec in 1773, Smith was a fur trader facing dim prospects in a crowded Canadian market tightly controlled by the British. He migrated to Detroit with his wife and newborn daughter in the early 1800s in search of less competition and more opportunity.

Described as powerful, agile, and resourceful, Smith was adopted into the Chippewa nation and given the name Wahbesins, which means "young swan." Not exactly the toughest name for a bad-ass fur trader, but it reflected his graceful nature and ability to get along with the local tribes that would supply him with pelts. He forged a strong relationship with Chief Neome, who led one of the largest bands of the Chippewa. Time would prove that Smith had motives far more complicated than mere friendship when he bonded with Neome.

Smith did well for himself. Though Detroit was always his home base, he traded frequently in other areas of the state. One spot was a shallow crossing on a river about seventy miles north of Michigan's largest settlement, an area that French fur traders had already named Grande Traverse and which would eventually become Flint. Native Americans making their way south to Detroit with their furs were likely to pass the spot on foot or via canoe, creating the equivalent of a backwoods Times Square. A trading post would shorten their journey and allow Smith to buy the best furs before they reached Detroit. Smith is often credited for his entrepreneurial foresight and dubbed the first white settler in the region. But setting up shop on the river was hardly an original idea; white trappers and traders had been operating in what was known as the Saginaw Valley for a century before him.

Sitting at my kitchen table in beautiful San Francisco, surrounded by Flint books purchased on eBay or secured through interlibrary loan at the university, I was happy to discover that people had been drawn to the area that would become Flint for hundreds of years. The unromantic would argue that it was simply a convenient point to cross the river and get to a more desirable place. But I wanted to believe Flint was something more than an accident of geography. Maybe it possessed some ineffable quality that pulled the Chippewa and Jacob Smith to it, the same pull I was feeling now. But as I'd learned over and over again as a reporter, the more you know about something, the less magical it becomes. Flint was no different.

Jacob Smith built a small outpost on the riverbank sometime around 1810—it's impossible to know for sure—but war with the British soon interrupted his plans. He fought in the War of 1812 and did a little networking in the process by ingratiating himself with white power brokers like Lewis Cass, who became the territorial governor after hostilities ended. Smith's close ties with Chief Neome and Cass led to an active role at an 1819 treaty negotiation between the territorial government and various Native American tribes. Smith often gets credit for safeguarding Chippewa interests—think Kevin Costner in *Dances with Wolves*—but he didn't exactly secure a good deal for the local tribes. The Treaty of Saginaw transferred more than four million acres of Chippewa lands to the U.S. government for white settlement. The Chippewa received yearly payments in return. In fact, Smith was on the Cass payroll, receiving the equivalent of more than $10,000 in today's currency to help further the interests of the U.S. government.

Smith also carved out his own personal reward in the treaty, pulling off a real-estate sleight of hand that makes all the disreputable land speculators in present-day Flint look like amateurs. In a "concession" to the Chippewa, Cass set aside eleven sections of land totaling some seven thousand acres in and around present-day Flint. The parcels were reserved for "mixed blood" individuals, harshly known as "half-breeds." By using their Chippewa names, Smith managed to reserve parcels for five of his own white children. Cass caught on to the con, so Smith had to round up five full-blooded Indians to act as stand-ins for his own kids to pass muster with the governor. After a protracted legal and political battle that lasted for years, Smith's children eventually gained control of the parcels. My hometown, I discovered, was founded on a shady, under-the-table land deal. A ruse, a feint, a dodge. A swindle, to put it another way.

Despite its advantageous location, Smith's riverbank trading post was not a success. A man of many talents, Smith proved to be a poor businessman. He extended thousands of dollars' worth of goods to the Chippewa but received no furs in return. He ran up big debts and was dragged into court by his creditors. "It would seem that he was a very careless man in his business affairs," wrote one federal official who examined Smith's finances, "and somewhat extravagant."

Smith's wife had died in 1817 and his children were grown, so he was on his own. One of Chief Neome's daughters described his lonely death in 1825: "When Wahbesins sick, nobody come; him sicker and sicker; nobody come. Wahbesins die."

There's no shortage of irony in what happened next. Smith's son-in-law came and took all his possessions, leaving the trading post where he worked and lived to sit empty. It was a dubious day in local history, one unlikely to be commemorated by a plaque or a marker. What is arguably Flint's first permanent structure—built by a man who could be considered its first speculator and failed businessman—became its first abandoned property. Obviously, it wouldn't be the last.

The Flint area's reputation had hardly improved by the time Alexis de Tocqueville and Gustave de Beaumont visited the area in July of 1831 on the journey that would form the basis of *Democracy in America*, the classic outsider interpretation of religious, political, and economic life in the United States. A cranky innkeeper in nearby Pontiac tried to dissuade the two Frenchmen. "Do you know that from here to Saginaw you find hardly anything but wilds and untrod solitudes? Have you thought that the woods are full of Indians and mosquitoes?" Sound familiar? If this guy had been born about 150 years later and been a little more politically correct, he could have been dissing Flint in the pages of *Forbes*.

Undeterred, the pair pressed on, arriving late at night in utter darkness, which has never been a good time to show up in Flint. "At last we saw a clearing, two or three cabins, and what gave us greatest pleasure, a light," Tocqueville wrote. "The stream, that ran like a violet thread along the bottom of the valley, sufficed to prove that we had arrived at Flint River. Soon the barking of dogs echoed through the wood, and we found ourselves opposite a log-house and only separated from it by a fence. Just as we were getting ready to get over it, the moon revealed a great black bear on the other side, which, standing upright on its haunches and dragging its chain, made as clear as it could its intention of giving us a fraternal welcome. 'What a devil of a country this is,' I said, 'where one has bears for watch dogs?'"

Well, that would be Flint, muthafucka. (Pardon my French.)

Unsure of how to proceed but unwilling to tangle with a bear, Tocqueville and Beaumont called out until a man appeared at the cabin window. He invited them inside and gave the bear permission to turn in for the night: "Trinc, go to bed. To your kennel, I tell you. Those are not robbers."

Despite the need for such elaborate security measures—rendering the popularity of pit bulls in modern Flint almost quaint by comparison—the Flint settlement grew steadily. Before long, against all odds, it was seen as a desirable place to live. "The tide of emigration is rapidly increasing," a settler observed in a letter dated November 28, 1837, just a few months after Michigan became a state. "The village presents a fine appearance in the evening when going in from our way, the lights from so many undiscernible windows upon the heights among the trees and bushes, have the appearance of beacons to guide the weary traveler."

The local chamber of commerce couldn't have come up with a better promotional blurb. Settlers from New England and New York began arriving, often combining farming and fur trapping to make a decent living. Businesses opened to serve the growing population. Before long, Flint was a prosperous county seat known for tree-lined streets, comfortable wood-framed houses, and spacious lawns.

The City of Flint was incorporated in 1855. The name is appropriate for a tough frontier town that would grow into a hardworking industrial center. But no one is quite sure how the name came to attach itself

to the river crossing. The unpopularity of the French probably eliminated Grande Traverse as an option, although an anglicized version
lives on today as a major street. Other Michigan cities—Kalamazoo,
Muskegon, and Saginaw, for example—simply adopted the Native
American names already in place. But the Chippewa names for the Flint
area were far more challenging for white Americans. Muscatawingh,
which translated to "an open and burned-over plain," didn't catch on,
for obvious reasons. Pewonigowink, meaning "place of flints," was
equally perplexing for English speakers, but its simple translation did
the trick, even though the area wasn't particularly flinty. Perhaps the
name was simply the easiest to pronounce. "After wrestling for several
years with these Chippewa jaw breakers, the early settlers ended the
struggle by calling both river and settlement Flint, and Flint they are,"
according to Colonel E. H. Thomson, one of the city's prominent early
citizens. So much for symbolism. Forget creativity. Flint residents were
a practical lot from the beginning.

Though the city chose the moniker of least resistance, it appears it
was never meant to be an easy-going municipality. Slow and steady just
weren't part of its civic DNA. The fur trade was declining, but there was
another natural resource to be exploited. An unsullied white pine forest
stretched for miles on either side of the winding river. From 1855 to
1880, Flint emerged as a thriving lumber town, and that meant prosperity and a healthy dose of drunken buffoonery. "The bearded lumbermen
with their coonskin caps, red sashes, and hobnailed boots brawled from
tavern to tavern," explained Carl Crow in a 1945 history of the city
commissioned by General Motors and characterized by endearingly
flamboyant prose. "Lumbering was rough business and lumbermen were
rough men. They worked hard, played hard, and usually drank quanti-
ties of hard liquor. There was a story throughout the logging camps that
some of the lumberjacks would cheerfully eat pine chips or sawdust if
generously moistened with whisky." Now that sounds like the Flint I
know. The drinking part, not the lumberjack fashion statements.

The city reached its peak as a lumber town around 1870, when the
population climbed to five thousand and the city boasted eighteen lumber dealers, eleven sawmills, nine planing mills, a box-making factory,
and a dealer in pine lands. (I couldn't get a count on bars and taverns,
but I'm sure it was impressive.) At its height, the lumber industry generated more than $1 million annually for Flint.

In the midst of this abundance, the next big thing was already emerging. The lumber industry required transportation. Oxcarts were needed

to haul logs from forest to town. Farmers claiming the deforested land needed wagons. And well-off shopkeepers and other locals needed horse-drawn vehicles to get around town. By the 1880s, when there weren't enough trees left to keep the lumber industry from fading, it didn't take carriage making long to ramp up and take its place. Flint may have exhausted its supply of high-quality pine, but there were buggies to be made and plenty of people to buy them.

By the turn of the century, the city's numerous carriage firms were producing 150,000 vehicles annually. One merchant was selling 23,000 a year all over the country and maintained a permanent office on Broadway in New York City. Over half of the roughly thirteen thousand Flint residents were connected with the carriage business in what was now known as the "Vehicle City," a catchy nickname that had nothing to do with automobiles. Yet.

The transition was possible because Flint's lumber industry was run by local entrepreneurs who had a stake in the community. They weren't looking to make a quick profit and then hit the road. "In other places the timber had been cut by companies from out of state, companies which regularly remitted their profits for deposit in eastern banks," Crow wrote. "When their mills closed down, the only mementos of the former prosperity they left consisted of piles of rotting sawdust and mill buildings which had been stripped of machinery."

Alas, Flint would eventually suffer a similar fate when GM decided to skip town, but let's not get ahead of ourselves. We're coming to the really good part of Flint's history, when the growth and good times seemed limitless. The horse and buggy era didn't have many years left, and the city was poised to transform itself once again. This time into the epicenter of the automobile industry, the headquarters of the American Dream.

6

The Road to Prosperity

I made a surprising discovery as I blogged about Flint and immersed myself in its history for the first time. In the early days of the auto industry, my moribund hometown had been the gritty equivalent of Silicon Valley, a freewheeling city with go-getters eager to put their ideas on the line. A place where people sought their fortune. Billy Durant is a perfect example. The charismatic grandson of a local lumber baron, he dropped out of high school and sold cigars before he teamed up with his friend J. Dallas Dort to launch a carriage company with two thousand dollars of someone else's money. By 1900, it was the largest horse-drawn vehicle maker in the country, if not the world. Durant was initially so skeptical of automobiles that he allegedly forbade his daughter to ride in one, but that didn't stop him from investing heavily in Buick, one of the many manufacturers emerging at the turn of the century. Before long, Buicks were the most popular cars in the country.

A mesmerizing salesman, Durant believed in offering consumers variety and consolidating the gaggle of competing car companies. With that in mind, he combined Buick with an assortment of automakers and parts suppliers to form General Motors in 1908. Although based in Flint, GM was incorporated in New Jersey, a state that placed no restriction on the amount of stock a venture could issue, regardless of its actual assets. This allowed Durant to dazzle investors with his vision for the future rather than the company's current reality.

Durant was not easily satisfied. After marrying one of the prettiest girls in Flint in his younger days, he divorced her when he was in his midforties to wed his twenty-one-year-old secretary. He overextended GM in his rush to expand the company and was forced out by skittish financiers in 1910. After teaming up with Louis Chevrolet, he managed to regain control five years later, only to get bounced for good in 1920. He was replaced by Alfred P. Sloan, who lacked Durant's endearing panache and dapper style but relied on a shrewd, methodical management style that led to unprecedented growth. Undeterred, Durant moved to New York and made another fortune in the stock market, his latest obsession. After the market crashed on Black Tuesday in 1929, Durant, along with other financial giants like the Rockefellers, disregarded the advice of friends and bought heavily to show confidence in the market. He declared bankruptcy in 1936.

A crazy dreamer if there ever was one, Durant returned to Flint for one final venture. He opened an eighteen-lane bowling alley in 1940 and later combined it with one of the country's first drive-in hamburger joints, creating perhaps the quintessential Flint enterprise. He thought bowling and fast food were the next big thing, but he never got a chance to see his hunch pay off. After suffering a debilitating stroke in 1942, Durant and his wife survived on handouts from members of GM's early board of directors until his death in 1947.

I couldn't help but like Durant, despite his many faults, as I read about his triumphs and failures. For me, he came to personify that hard-to-define spirit that Flint possesses, a certain exuberant recklessness that I wanted to somehow be a part of again. Durant's approach to business may have robbed him of prosperity in the end, but he was a visionary whose ideas transformed Flint. By 1929, on the eve of the Great Depression, GM had produced ten million cars for consumers and was well on its way to becoming the world's largest corporation. In the process, Flint gained a reputation for plentiful jobs and good wages, causing the population to jump from 13,000 to more than 156,000 between 1900 and 1930. Finding a comfortable place to sleep was a real challenge for the new arrivals. "In the worst areas, like the notoriously overcrowded section known simply as 'the Jungle,' hundreds of families paid one dollar down and fifty cents a week to purchase tiny lots for their tents and tarpaper shacks," wrote historian Ronald Edsforth. "Elsewhere, homeowners took in lodgers, while many rooming houses converted to double shifts, using every square foot for extra beds."

Verne McFarlane and Leone Stevenson, my grandparents, were part of the influx. In my mind, they were always the picture of calm stability. I don't remember seeing my grandfather in anything other than a suit or the well-ironed work clothes he wore on weekends. Their home was always spotless. They expressed the same disapproval of a neighbor's uncut grass as they conveyed when someone appeared to be spending money unwisely. I didn't think of them as particularly adventuresome, but on a visit to see my mom one Christmas at her cozy house in Florida, decorated with much the same furniture and artwork that once filled our old house in Flint, I learned that they fit right in with the spirit of the Vehicle City during the boom years.

Sitting on the indestructible couch where I had lounged as a kid, my mom broke out her meticulously maintained photo albums and filled me in on the family history that I'd never really known. My grandparents both grew up on forty-acre family farms in the northeast corner of Iowa near Maple Leaf, which no longer warrants a mention on state maps. My grandfather wasn't meant to be a farmer, but he promised to help his dad for several years after graduating from eighth grade. Tall and lanky, he pitched for the local barnstorming baseball team and was known to participate in weekend wrestling matches. My mom showed me a flyer from one bout with his personal commentary written in neat cursive above his opponent's name: "He got nothing but abuse!" Given my grandfather's gentle demeanor and sense of humor, this was surely more of a joke than a boast. My grandmother was shy, smart, and good looking. She grew up with seven brothers and sisters in the house with three tiny bedrooms that her father built. After finishing high school, she taught in a one-room schoolhouse. My grandparents met at a dance called the Turkey Trot.

I had always assumed they were married in Iowa, but that was not the case. They eloped in the early 1920s and eventually made their way to Flint. They were in love, but that didn't mean they abandoned the frugality imparted by their hardscrabble Scottish parents. They lived together but pledged to save one thousand dollars each before they got married, a lofty financial goal at the time. (Actually, it would be ambitious for many Flint families even today.) The fact that my grandparents had "lived in sin" for a short time was my first big surprise.

My grandfather worked at "the Buick" for a little while, but he was as ill suited to life on the line as he was to life on the farm. He soon started a small trucking outfit with a friend, but the entire enterprise folded when their lone asset—the truck—caught fire. My grandmother was not pleased with this development. She was more pragmatic than my grandfather and always acted as the family bookkeeper. After a few tries at other businesses, he gravitated to real estate, studying up and passing the licensing exam to buy and sell property.

My mom opened the cedar chest in her bedroom and pulled out the well-preserved, amazingly detailed financial logs my grandmother kept her entire life, tracking every penny made and spent. The dark green ledgers included all the real-estate commissions my grandfather earned, but they also listed the financial breakdown on dozens of houses he personally bought and sold. My mom told me that my grandparents had regularly purchased rundown houses with their own money. Grandma, using the carpentry skills she learned from her father on the farm in Iowa, was in charge of rehabbing the properties. A long-forgotten memory of helping her lay down a linoleum floor in the kitchen of a cold, empty house flashed into my head. We were both on our hands and knees, and she was teaching me how to measure out the tiles with a yardstick. She was a stickler for getting it right. I remember pulling up linoleum squares because they didn't fit perfectly into a corner. My grandparents then resold the properties. The logs offered a blueprint of the entire process—the purchase price; the cost of lumber, nails, and other supplies; and the sale price. The profits, small but steady, were recorded with a blue-leaded pencil. I suppose my grandparents were early house flippers. Another revelation.

My mother was born in 1930, an event recorded in the financial journals with an entry in the debit column: "Cigars: $3.25." The family soon moved from a downtown rental to a modest two-story house with a cherry tree in the backyard, just a few blocks from Kearsley Park and Homedale School in the working-class East Side. They would never move again, despite my grandfather's success as a real-estate agent. My grandparents generously exported a lot of the money they made in Flint back to Iowa, helping numerous relatives stay afloat with "loans" that they knew would never be repaid. When my grandmother's brother couldn't come up with enough cash to purchase a farm of his own, my grandparents bought one for him. Several Iowa relatives journeyed to Flint in search of work, staying in my grandparents' spare bedroom for long stretches. A few moved in to attend high school in Flint, which was considered a better option than their rural schools back home. This reminded me of immigrants in San Francisco who sent money back home and helped others make the journey to a better life. It was a reminder that Flint wasn't always a place people longed to escape.

My mother showed me black-and-white photos of my grandparents from their early years in Flint. I remembered my grandma wearing modest house dresses she had sewn herself, accented with blue canvas Keds when she worked around the house. But here she was with her hair in a stylish bob and dressed in full flapper mode. My grandpa was decked out in a tailored suit with wide, peaked lapels and a fedora set at a rakish angle. They were both smiling, their arms around each other, gazing straight at the camera. They looked like Bonnie and Clyde, not the low-key couple I remembered. America was making the transition from an agricultural to an industrial economy, and my grandparents seemed happy to be a part of it all, eager for what might happen next. Flint and my family had a far different history than I had imagined.

Without any facts to back it up, I'd always assumed that Flint experienced ever-increasing economic success once the auto industry got up and running. A little research revealed that this wasn't the case. Flint was harder hit during the Great Depression than many other cities around the country. Plummeting nationwide demand led to unemployment rates in the city that hovered around 50 percent in the early 1930s. By the time my mother was a third-grader at Homedale Elementary in 1938, more than half of all Flint families were on some type of relief. And although the population dipped as the jobless returned to their original homes in other cities and states, Flint continued to face a chronic housing shortage and abysmal public health standards. There were high rates of infant and maternal death, typhoid fever and diphtheria. It was hardly a workers' paradise.

In this atmosphere, union organizing culminated with the Flint Sit-Down Strike during the bitterly cold winter of 1936–37. It was still a legendary event when I was growing up, and I knew of it despite having scant knowledge of Flint's history. For many it was the city's greatest achievement, and it was spoken of with pride, if not reverence. For forty-four days, workers aligned with the recently created United Auto Workers occupied the massive Fisher Body No. 1 plant on the South Side, the smaller Fisher Body No. 2, and the Chevrolet No. 4, located at the sprawling Chevrolet manufacturing complex along the Flint River, which came to be known as Chevy in the Hole. (The charitable might attribute the nickname to geography—the factory was situated in a valley—but it's more likely that it stemmed from the less than ideal working conditions inside.)

Typical of a populace apparently incapable of half measures, this was no ordinary labor action with picketers chanting defiant slogans on the sidewalk and management complaining in the press. This was war. In what the strikers dubbed the Battle of the Running Bulls, local police attempted to reclaim Fisher Body No. 2 on the night of January 11, 1937. The strikers were in no mood to leave. "The tide of battle ebbed and flowed outside the plant," wrote Sidney Fine in *Sitdown: The General Motors Strike of 1936–1937*. "Hurling cans, frozen snow, milk bottles, door hinges, pieces of pavement, and assorted other weapons of this type, the pickets pressed at the heels of the retreating police. Undoubtedly enraged at the humiliation of defeat at the hands of so motley and amateur an army, the police drew pistols and riot guns and fired into the ranks of their pursuers."

Gunshots and tear gas weren't enough to deter the workers or their family members, who often supplied the strikers with food passed through the factory windows. The strike ended when GM agreed to recognize the UAW and engage in a limited form of collective bargaining, leading to better wages and working conditions in Flint and, ultimately, the rest of the country as the union launched a national organizing effort. It also set the pattern of contentious negotiations between labor and management that were as much a part of life in Flint as drinking Stroh's beer and rooting for the Detroit Tigers.

A few years after the strike ended, production at the auto factories shifted to M-18 Hellcat tank destroyers and other armaments during World War II, but it was just like the good old days in Flint when the fighting ended and a postwar economic expansion swept the nation. In 1955, Flint held its centennial parade and two hundred thousand boisterous spectators showed up to take in the marching bands, admire the colorful floats, and perhaps catch a glimpse of GM spokesmodel Dinah Shore or Vice President Richard Nixon. (It's hard to imagine a whiter, more unhip couple than Dinah and Tricky Dick.) There was good reason to be festive. "An industrial marvel," wrote one historian, "Flint was home to more GM workers than any other city in the world." There were close to thirty thousand at Buick; Chevy in the Hole and AC Spark Plug employed nearly twenty thousand each; and another eight thousand punched the clock at Fisher Body. A report by the Federal Reserve Bank of Chicago succinctly captured the essence of the place when Ike Eisenhower was in the White House: "The Flint economy, probably to a greater extent than that of any other city of comparable size, can be described in a single word. That word is automobiles."

Flint's population was near its peak of nearly 200,000, and confident local leaders envisioned 350,000 prosperous citizens residing in what was being called "Fabulous Flint" and the "Happiest Town in Michigan." Flint's per capita income was one of the highest in the world, and it had perhaps the broadest middle class on the planet. The American dream was alive and well in Flint. You could even argue that it was born there.

And what would a thriving industrial city be without a strong-willed, wealthy industrialist to animate it? More than any other citizen, Charles Stewart Mott shaped the character and feel of Flint as it became an American success story. Known as Mr. Flint, or, more informally, Charlie Sugar for the gifts he bestowed on the Vehicle City, Mott had moved a family wheel and axle business to Flint from Utica, New York, in 1906 after being courted by Billy Durant, who needed a local parts supplier. Mott sold his company to GM in 1913 in exchange for stock, making him the company's largest individual shareholder. Talk about getting in on the ground floor of a company with growth potential. Mott went on to serve on GM's board of directors for sixty years. Showing a personal knack for economic diversification, which never caught on in Flint, he created the United States Sugar Corporation in 1931.

Mott became one of the richest men in America, and he certainly looked the part. Balding with a thick white mustache and bushy eyebrows, the three-time mayor was a familiar figure in Flint with his dark suits and ramrod-straight posture. He had a reputation for thrift, sleeping on a cot-like bed with no headboard and tooling around town in a modest Chevy Corvair. Despite a kindly smile, he could be a distant, imposing figure. He signed notes to one of his sons "Very truly yours, C. S. Mott" and employed a coach to teach the kid how to ride a bike.

Mott was an enthusiastic Republican "who believed deeply in the virtues of self help, privatized charity, and laissez faire approaches to social welfare." This often put him at odds with many of Flint's left-leaning citizens. Reflecting on the Sit-Down Strike, he told journalist Studs Terkel that the workers deserved to be shot for illegally occupying the auto factories.

He created the Charles Stewart Mott Foundation in 1926 to help ameliorate the problems that accompanied Flint's rapid growth. It was also an excellent tax write-off that might help blunt the appeal of unions and government programs, but it's obvious that Mott sought to improve Flint through his philanthropy. The foundation funded free medical and dental clinics for children. It launched a community education program in the Flint schools that became a national model, providing students with an array of after-hours recreational activities and offering adults low-cost enrichment courses in everything from gift wrapping to sheet metal drawing to creative writing.

Mott was also a driving force behind the Flint College and Cultural Center built in the 1950s and 1960s, kicking in millions of dollars via the foundation and donating thirty-six acres of land from his sprawling estate, known as Applewood. Along with a community college, the collection of public institutions included the Flint Institute of Arts, Sloan Museum, Bower Theater, Dort Music Center, and the Robert T. Longway Planetarium.

The best example of what it meant to grow up in a place with GM money coursing through its civic veins and wealthy elites driven by a sense of noblesse oblige along with a desire to keep the masses happy came from a guy named Mark, who emailed me after reading the Flint Expatriates blog. Now a professional harpist living in the Chicago area, he had learned to play in Flint in the late sixties and early seventies. There were five "public harps" available to residents who had an interest, along with complimentary lessons. He played in the Flint Youth Symphony Orchestra, sharing the stage with a fellow musician who went on to become the principal percussionist for the New York Philharmonic. "Somehow I thought it was normal for a town the size of Flint to have a dozen harp students," Mark told me.

That's right. The Vehicle City once provided free harp lessons to its residents. I felt like I needed to apologize to my much-maligned hometown. I'd been way too hard on it. I began to realize that the multitude of cultural and recreational activities available to me as a kid had been a little unusual, especially in a town now considered one of the worst places to live in the nation. I took tennis lessons at public courts in the summer, ran track at city-sponsored meets, participated in a local sports extravaganza modestly called the Flint Olympian Games, and learned to swim at a neighborhood community center. I joined baseball, soccer, and floor hockey teams. I took driver's ed before I was ten at a place called Safetyville, a miniature town in Kearsley Park with tiny cars and classroom sessions on how to make a left turn and parallel park. I still have my license and a few tickets for moving violations. My friends performed in children's theater productions and took painting classes at the art museum. All of it was free or close to it.

I had lived in the city during a transitional phase when things were just starting to go downhill. The tipping point may have been 1973, when I was a seven-year-old student at Saint Michael's on the edge of downtown. That's the year C. S. Mott died at the ripe old age of ninety-seven.

His foundation would live on, continuing to generously fund local initiatives and projects around the world, but it was hard to imagine Flint without the paternalistic guidance of Charlie Sugar. It was also the year when the OPEC oil embargo caused a spike in gas prices, followed by fuel shortages and lines at service stations. GM was near peak employment in the Flint area, with roughly eighty thousand workers at the time, but the crisis triggered a round of layoffs, a trend that would plague the city for decades as "Generous Motors" abandoned its birthplace in search of cheaper labor in right-to-work states and foreign countries.

By accident of birth, I came of age in Flint when it still had a remnant of the old prosperity. I caught the end of an era when shop rats could drive new Buicks, buy a vacation cabin up north, and send their kids to college. The utter despair that would grip the city in the nineties was looming, but there was still hope that things could be put right. How else would a crackpot scheme like transforming the city into a tourist destination with the doomed AutoWorld amusement park seem feasible, at least to Flint's delusional civic leaders? By the time I was in high school, the rising crime rate meant that cops couldn't be bothered with trivialities like underage boozing, trespassing, or petty vandalism. That translated into a lot of freedom. There were abandoned buildings to explore, fake IDs to perfect, and bars to discover. I had to admit there were certainly worse places to grow up than Flint, Michigan. I just didn't realize it at the time.

Over three generations, my family had experienced the extremes of capitalism in a city that was a bellwether for the nation. We stuck with Flint from boom to bust, from the emergence of a thriving manufacturing economy to deindustrialization and the advent of the information age. We were there as the middle class emerged, prospered, and began to wither. We were part of history.

I came to realize all this by blogging, taking full advantage of the technological innovations that had left places like Flint behind. But while a virtual Flint was a lot safer and had better weather than the real thing, the blog didn't soothe my nagging feelings about my hometown. Even as Traci and I tended to the little house we owned together, I was filled with nostalgia—and something more. Despite the vital role Flint played in my life and the life of the nation, it was slipping away, becoming nothing more than a catchall for urban decay, a handy joke when references to Detroit were too obvious. It was losing more of its identity with every passing year. I thought it deserved better and I wanted to help. The question was how.

7

Bar Logic

It's fitting that the notion of buying a house in Flint began to take shape in a bar, like so many other ill-formed and potentially disastrous ideas. I played basketball every Saturday morning at the Mission Playground in San Francisco. A collection of players would retire after the game to the grimy gravel patio of Zeitgeist, a dumpy bar that has the trappings of a tough dive without the credentials to back it up. Yes, people who ride motorcycles hang out there, but so do aging punk rockers, bike messengers, assorted hipsters, uninhibited pot smokers, and the occasional yuppie types slumming from the more upscale Marina District, all united in the desire to start drinking at 1 P.M. on a Saturday or as soon as the morning fog burns off. The Zeitgeist motto showed that it didn't take itself too seriously: "Warm Beer/Cold Women."

Although our gang of mediocre basketball players was a mixture of native Californians, Midwest transplants, and a few Texans, we were all conditioned by the exorbitant cost of local real estate, even in the midst of the Great Recession. In 2008, a few players were unsuccessfully trying to buy houses, and they were frustrated by the fact that a down market meant a two-bedroom house in a decent San Francisco neighborhood was now going for $775,000 instead of $800,000. The minor drop in price was offset by stiffer mortgage requirements that demanded 20 percent down. "Can you imagine writing a check for $160,000?" one of my friends asked. It was a big shift from the easy-to-find, no-money-down, interest-only loans that were prevalent just a short time earlier. The kind of loans that enabled Traci and me to buy our house and pushed the planet to the brink of economic collapse.

After a few beers, I inevitably began regaling the Zeitgeist crew with tales of Flint gleaned from my blog, both depressing and uplifting. There was the one about the family who posted a "No Ho Zone" sign in their yard to ward off the neighborhood prostitutes. Or the retired blues musician who was nurturing a huge garden on the vacant lot near his home. And of course there were stories about all the Flint houses going for pocket change on eBay with the option of buying them by the dozen, like the jelly rolls I used to love at Dawn Donuts. With a little cocktail napkin math, we determined that I could own a Flint house for the cost of our bar tab. Wild speculation ensued. I could snap up a house in Flint, quit my job, and survive on the free-lance income Traci and I could generate once we were freed from San Francisco's crushing cost of living. I would be embarking on a grand adventure and helping Flint at the same time. Or I could buy a few Flint houses, rehab them, then rent them out—stabilizing the local housing market and making a modest profit at the same time. Or I could improve the city by transforming a junker into a summer house, allowing me to reconnect with Flint without abandoning San Francisco. Or instead of giving money to charity, why not buy a house, make it livable, and give it away to a needy family? The ideas came fast and furious, and the possibilities were intoxicating, perhaps because we were often intoxicated.

My friend M.G. understood the appeal of a Flint house. He grew up in a small town in the suburbs of Los Angeles, the kind of close-knit place where you could return books to the police station if the library was closed. He had no desire to ever live there again, but he liked the idea of it enduring more or less as he remembered it. Being a homeowner meant something to M.G. His father had immigrated from Iran, where property symbolized wealth and success. His mother was on her own at an early age, paying rent in San Francisco when she was only sixteen, so a house equaled stability and security. While I was still parsing my feelings about Flint, my motivation was fairly obvious to M.G., regardless of how many pitchers we'd finished off. "I think you're selling yourself on something," he told me one Saturday after he'd bummed a cigarette off three women at a nearby table. "You're selling yourself this ideal of small-town America being feasible in a world that's constantly changing. It's a real possibility that the kind of towns we grew up in are going to disappear. They aren't going to exist anymore. A house in Flint is your way of trying to hang on to something from your past that's important to you."

Leave it to a tipsy Persian-Irish guy from LA who had never been to the Midwest to sum up my feelings about Flint. As I unsteadily rode my old Schwinn home that day, I started to believe a house would be the best way to forge a connection with Flint and do my part to preserve the city I remembered, or what was left of it. I could make this happen. I could go home again.

The wondrous World Wide Web aided and abetted this half-baked bar logic. No sooner had the Zeitgeist sessions picked up steam than I read a story online about a guy who bought three houses in Detroit for a dollar each. He planned to fix them up and donate them to needy families. Apparently, someone had already adopted our brilliant idea.

I scoured the Internet for more examples and discovered John Law, a colorful San Francisco character who was an early member of the Suicide Club, a group that had illegally climbed the towers of the Golden Gate Bridge more than a hundred times. He was also one of the creators of Burning Man, a weeklong experiment in radical self-expression that takes place every year in the Black Rock Desert of Nevada. Think drugs, art installations, naked people, and sand. Law had a distinctive mustache reminiscent of Greg Norton of the band Hüsker Dü. And according to his website, he had recently purchased a summer home in Detroit. "It's a small but comfortable three-bedroom house in good condition that sits on a shorefront plot of land along the banks of an actual river," he wrote. "The location is serene, and the price was right—the whole thing cost less than a new Cadillac Escalade."

I posted an item about John on Flint Expatriates, and he responded with a concise rationale for his purchase. "Phoenix, Vegas, El Paso, LA, and most of the rest of the cities of the Southwest will be ghost towns in twenty years if the hydrologists are right and the water tables sink to nothing and the drought-ridden countryside ceases to provide water for reservoirs," he wrote. "If the hippies are right and global warming is real, where do you think those displaced by rising sea levels and unlivable climates will go? It's not rocket science to figure it out. They'll go where there is water and land. If you're thinking long term, now is the best time ever to buy in Detroit (or Flint)."

This was the kind of quasi-scientific underpinning that the Zeitgeist sessions never achieved, mainly because the conversations often veered wildly to other weighty topics: Was Magic Johnson better than Larry Bird? If we trained hard, could we dunk? Do we want to order another pitcher? John Law was showing me the way, making it all sound simple and logical.

Then I got an email in early 2009 from a San Francisco real-estate agent named Rich who had grown up in Flint. He had seen the blog and wanted to meet for drinks. It turned out that Rich was only a grade ahead of me, and we'd attended the same schools without ever managing to meet. He had clearly kept a low profile in the Catholic school system, somehow managing to make it through Saint Mary's without ever getting paddled by Sister Ellen, which I didn't think was possible. Sitting in another bar, this time the Latin American Club in the Mission, I told Rich about my crazy idea of buying a house in Flint.

"That's not crazy," he said, taking a sip of his beer and looking at me over the top of his small, wire-rimmed glasses. "I already own three houses in Flint."

Rich is decidedly mild mannered, often speaking in such a soft voice that it's difficult to hear him. So he hardly fits the stereotype of the aggressive real estate agent. But he definitely has the trait of people who sell things, especially things as wrapped in emotion as houses: he never says anything negative. He calmly rattled off all the good things happening in a city typically defined by bad news. Development in the urban core of Flint was taking off, he said. There was talk of a tapas restaurant. The new loft apartments downtown on Saginaw Street were rented out. Flint was on the cusp of becoming a full-fledged college town, and an increasing number of students would need places to live near the downtown campus of the University of Michigan–Flint. Prices were so low that there was nowhere to go but up.

I countered that I'd been away from Flint so long I wasn't even sure what neighborhoods would be best for me. "No problem," he said. "I can tell you anything you need to know. I'll put you in touch with a few homeowners who know the neighborhoods. I can even let you stay in one of my houses when you go back to visit."

He was already planning a trip to Flint for me. And given our shared background, he knew when to play the ultimate trump card—Catholic guilt. "You know Flint's not going to save itself," he said, raising his eyebrows. "A big corporation like GM isn't going to rescue it. It's going to take people like us to help turn it around. People who grew up there. People who remember what a great place it was. We owe something to Flint." He paused, put his beer on the bar, and pointed at me. "You owe something to Flint."

Unfortunately, I also owed something to Wells Fargo Bank, $551,000 to be exact. The relief that came with refinancing our mortgage in 2006 had quickly worn off, and the reality of our monthly payments was weighing heavily on us. Despite our scrimping, it was nearly impossible to save any money or make payments each month that covered even a tiny portion of the principal. If I allowed myself to think about it, I knew Traci and I could easily find ourselves ten years older with the same mortgage, no equity, no retirement savings, and payments well over $4,000 a month.

The situation got worse when Traci lost her job as an editor at the magazine where she worked in San Jose. We had talked about the possibility of this happening—the publication was of dubious quality thanks to the aging frat boys who ran the place—but it was still a shock. She threw herself into freelancing but wasn't making close to her old salary, and the feast or famine nature of being an independent writer made budgeting impossible. I called a mortgage broker about the possibility of another refinancing, but we didn't have enough equity or cash to meet the down payment requirements. Just when I had come to fully embrace the joys of home ownership, there was a looming possibility that we might lose our house.

I became obsessed with reading anything I could find about real estate, somehow thinking that being more informed would improve our financial situation. That's how I discovered a way out, a logical proposition that would rescue us from the ongoing worry and stress of owning a home we couldn't afford. Two words: loan modification. Traci and I would simply ask Wells Fargo, our loan servicer, to change the terms of our mortgage to make it less burdensome for us. We envisioned a reduction in the principal and a lower interest rate. It seemed like a reasonable request given the utter collapse of the housing market. How could the bankers refuse? We were doing them a favor by helping them avoid another foreclosure.

Based on home sales in our neighborhood and casual conversations with real-estate agents, I knew we were not underwater on our mortgage. We'd lost a lot of value from the stratospheric prices at the height of the bubble, but the house was still worth more than we'd paid for it. After the house-hunting process and the refinancing odyssey, I felt prepared for the long, frustrating modification journey that articles and web forums warned me about. I also knew our chances of success were slim. The mortgage industry was in disarray. It was often difficult to determine who held a mortgage, especially if it had been sliced and diced into the toxic securities the media was trying to explain to the public. But, aside from the lottery, we didn't have a lot of other options.

It appeared the best chance for a modification was being in a little trouble but not a lot. If you were too broke, the lender wouldn't bother because you'd probably default on the modification anyway. And if your financial situation was too rosy, you could probably make your current payment. You needed to find the sweet spot between skid row and easy street. But even if you did, there were endless tales online of homeowners who were refused a modification for no apparent reason. It was all a leap into the unknown.

With this nebulous background information, we composed a letter explaining our situation to Wells Fargo. We were not in danger of missing a payment, we wrote; we were thinking ahead to the day when our interest-only payments would balloon into principal plus interest. We were being responsible by recognizing trouble down the line and trying to correct it early. At the same time, we explained that Traci had lost her job and my freelance income was dwindling as a result of the bad economy and the death of journalism as we knew it. An unexpected financial setback—a leaky roof or a major car repair—might cause a missed payment.

"Kafkaesque" is a pretentious and overused term, but I feel justified in relying on it to describe the loan modification process with Wells Fargo. The bank's symbol is a stagecoach, and I wondered if the corporate monolith relied on a team of horses to slowly transport our financial documents between far-flung outposts. I imagined our modification application and income tax forms bouncing off the top of the stagecoach on a bumpy road in Utah. Why else would they request them three times? And each request came with an urgent warning that we needed to fulfill it within twenty-four hours. Frantically faxing 170 pages of documents before work—a two-hour ordeal complete with multiple misfeeds, numerous disconnections, and several paper cuts—was enough to make me question the point of home ownership, if not life itself.

I spoke to a bevy of polite but clueless representatives in Des Moines, Saint Paul, and Milwaukee. I chatted with Larry, Kary, Tanisha, Danielle, Nathan, and others. I got conflicting information from each of them. It really wasn't their fault. One representative confided to me that he had been thrown into the job with little training. He was just happy to have work in the crumbling economy. I took notes on all the conversations, filling a fat notebook that I kept next to the phone for easy access. Some days, just for fun, I'd hang up with one representative, then immediately call back just to see if the next one would tell me the same thing. They rarely did.

One day, after about five months, I called and was told that Wells Fargo had no record of our modification request. "Oh," I said, deciding it was best to simply hang up rather than let loose on the phone. I stood in the living room, working my way through the list of profanities in my repertoire, most of them old standards introduced to me in Flint. Then I forced myself to try out some breathing techniques I had learned at the San Francisco Zen Center. I threw in a Hail Mary just in case. I invoked Saint Jude, the patron saint of lost causes. Apparently, there are no atheists in foxholes or the San Francisco real-estate market. Then I called Wells Fargo back and got a different representative. No problem. They had my request. They simply hadn't made a determination yet. At that point, a visit to Zeitgeist seemed the logical next step.

Finally, a letter arrived saying we'd been approved for a three-month trial period with reduced payments. Apparently, it was like a tryout for a final modification, a chance for the bank to see if we could even handle a smaller payment. We were halfway home. Or, more accurately, halfway to staying in our home. We made the three payments and were rewarded with a letter from Wells Fargo indicating that because we were not paying the full amount on the mortgage, they might "have no choice but to pursue other options, up to and including foreclosure." I called and was told to just ignore the letters. "Those generic letters go out automatically," Brian in Des Moines told me. "You're in the trial modification period, but you're viewed as someone who's four months behind on his mortgage." Very reassuring. I ran a credit check and sure enough we were getting dinged for missing mortgage payments, even though we were paying the amount Wells Fargo told us to pay. I called again to see if they could fix our credit. No dice, Janet told me. That was the price of going through the process. If we didn't want our credit damaged, we could have simply paid the mortgage and not asked for a modification. She had a point. It was a reminder that banks aren't in the business of helping you stay in your home. We'd get a modification if it made sense for them, not us.

But what was I complaining about? A mere eight months, 406 phone calls, and $378 in fax and FedEx fees later, Wells Fargo modified the loan. The principal stayed the same, but the interest rate plummeted to 2.75 percent before returning to 6.625 percent after six years. At that point, we'd be required to make the full principal and interest payments for the last twenty years of the loan. We'd save more than $100,000 on interest payments. And with payments down to around $1,200 a month, we could start whittling away at the principal right away.

I greeted this news with a huge sigh of relief, but at the same time I felt guilty and ashamed that it had come to this. I took no real satisfaction in beating the system when I read about other families who were denied modifications and lost their homes. But maybe the modification wasn't just a lifeline for me and Traci. I saw it as a way to help Flint. I now had some extra money to buy a house in the Vehicle City, even if it would have been more wisely spent paying down my San Francisco mortgage.

I'd joked with Traci for months about the two of us getting a house in Flint, but a few weeks after the modification I presented a serious proposal. She has a skillful technique for dealing with my latest Big Idea, like the plan to rip out the ceilings of the entire house to expose the attic space above, an idea that was also hatched at Zeitgeist. She had feigned mild enthusiasm before pointing out a few minor sticking points: *The attic is framed with ancient, discolored two-by-fours. Do we want to look at that? I'd have to remove all the rat-turd-infested insulation even though I'd been too squeamish to crawl up there to investigate a possible leak a few months back. I'd be dumping five hundred square feet of old drywall onto the floors, so we might have to relocate for a few days. I'd have to rewire the ceiling lights, and I didn't know anything about electrical work.* Yeah, yeah, whatever. I toyed with her trivial concerns for a few weeks before announcing that the time probably wasn't right for the ceiling project. I managed to do it in a way that made it seem like it was *her* idea all along, and I was reluctantly saying no.

To my surprise, Traci didn't reject the idea of a Flint house in its broadest form. After losing her job, she was suffering through the indignities of freelance journalism in the Internet age—low pay, intense competition, and the necessity of taking lame assignments because we needed the money. It was hard for her to get inspired writing about "Twenty-Five Fun Things to Do with Your Kids" when she didn't happen to have children. "I feel sort of like an autoworker," Traci said. "The job I've done my whole life is disappearing."

The stock image I have of a shop rat—the sobriquet for autoworkers in Michigan—is Ben Hamper on the cover of his book *Rivethead*. He's a solidly built guy with a mustache, a trucker's hat, and an expression that asks, "What the fuck are you looking at, asswipe?" Traci is five feet three and weights about 110. She has thick dark hair and beautiful eyes with impossibly long eyelashes. She's very calm, able to talk me down when I start ranting about double-parkers or the guy who keeps letting his dog poop in front of our house. It's hard to equate her with an autoworker in any way, but I knew what she meant. She was open to new possibilities. We were both ready for a change.

I hatched a plan. I'd travel to Flint in June of 2009 as soon as classes ended at the university to rediscover the city and look at houses. Given that any money I spent on the trip would cut into my house-buying budget, I thought I should try and scare up some freelance writing work to finance the excursion. I didn't have high hopes when I started calling various Flintoids in search of story ideas. I came up with about a dozen and spent the spring pitching to various newspapers and magazines. I was a little stunned when *Slate*, an online magazine published by the Washington Post Company, wanted a feature on my search for a house and a story on the special election for mayor of Flint in August. Then, shockingly, the *New York Times* approved a piece on the uneven and unexpected revival of Carriage Town. Apparently, the fickle world of journalism—so averse to my brilliant ideas in the past and experiencing an economic collapse of its own—found a downtrodden city like Flint as compelling as I did.

8

Downward Mobility

I spent a rainy morning driving around Flint with two real-estate agents in the cramped confines of a lime-colored Jeep Rubicon. Jennifer, a forty-seven-year-old who had grown up in the city but now lived in the suburb of Fenton, was at the wheel. Ryan, who had purchased his first Flint home ten years earlier, when he was just seventeen, was folded into the backseat. It was a queasy mix of nostalgia, tanking property values, and mild motion sickness.

I had determined that my budget for buying and fixing up my dream house in Flint was three thousand dollars. But I was purposely vague about my price range with Jennifer and Ryan, happy to let them assume someone who owns in San Francisco must have some real buying power, in order to get a close look at the range of Flint real estate. I wanted to understand the entire market before I made any decisions. As we rolled out of Carriage Town, I asked about the infamous eBay houses going for pocket change online, curious about their reaction to a city effectively being auctioned off in cyberspace.

"You probably wouldn't want to live in those houses or those neighborhoods," Ryan said without hesitation. "Most of those places are scrapped out or burned out." Jennifer joked that I would probably want a house that still had plumbing, wiring, and windows, preferably one located in an area where you could venture outside after dusk without a sidearm. The day had just begun and I was already a little worried. If the eBay houses were that bad, maybe my budget wasn't realistic.

Stop worrying, I told myself. They were probably just doing a little upselling. They were real-estate agents, after all.

We arrived at a 1,524-square-foot house on Cartier Street in the Mott Park neighborhood near Mott Golf Course along the Flint River. (It's nearly impossible to escape the legacy of Charlie Sugar in Flint. There are reminders everywhere.) My friends and I had regularly played at the public course in grade school. We spent most of our time goofing off in the woods in search of errant drives. My first high school party took place a few blocks away, and I still picture the house on Nolan Drive where it transpired whenever I hear songs off the album *Q: Are We Not Men? A: We Are Devo!*, which played endlessly on the living room stereo all night long. This was a solid Flint neighborhood then, a mixture of modest homes and a few larger Tudors. Now the houses looked a little worse for wear, and some of the yards were shaggy and overgrown—signs of trouble but not imminent collapse.

The light yellow house with three bedrooms and two bathrooms was immaculate. New siding, carpet, windows, kitchen, and roof. A family had lost it to foreclosure, and a group of guys who worked for Chrysler in Detroit picked it up for $17,000 as an investment. They put more than $50,000 into it and hoped to flip it for $79,000. After more than a hundred showings, Ryan still didn't have any offers. The price was down to $57,900, as low as the investors could go and still repay their mortgage. Ryan said if it didn't sell soon, the only options would be turning it into rental property, unloading it with a short sale, or just walking away from it.

To illustrate just how unlikely it was for this house, however shiny and refurbished, to sell for anything near $57,000, Ryan and Jennifer drove me to a similarly sized house on Cadillac Street. It was only a few blocks away, but I was learning that small distances make a big difference in Flint real estate. This neighborhood was more run down, with a sprinkling of abandoned houses. It was near Kettering University, an engineering school that used to be known as General Motors Institute. Kettering was still a pipeline for the automotive industry, but its presence did not seem to be a stabilizing force for an area less than a mile southwest of downtown. The house itself was livable, but not as pristine as the one on Cartier. It had the depressing feel of numerous cheap apartments I've called home, with a cracking linoleum floor in the kitchen, cheap appliances, and worn beige carpeting. It was hard to imagine basking in childhood memories or reconvening the Zeitgeist gang for a Midwest vacation in this place. Ryan said it went for $70,000 a few years ago. Now it was listed at $7,000.

"There are so many short sales that there's a glut of low-cost houses," Ryan said. "The danger is that speculators will snap up a house like this, rent it for $500 a month, and just slum it out. There could be ten students living in a place like this. That means too many cars, too much foot traffic, and too much partying. But I'd rather have twelve kids in a house instead of six gangbangers or drug dealers."

Ryan was lamenting how low property values had fallen, but I was worried that they hadn't fallen enough for my budget. If dumpy houses suitable for drug cribs were going for $7,000 in one of the country's most depressed real-estate markets, my $3,000 budget was looking highly suspect, the very definition of fuzzy math. A familiar dread was washing over me, one I had experienced regularly during my San Francisco house hunt. I was wondering if I had enough money to make this happen.

Back in the jeep, we headed east past the massive vacant lot along the river that used to be Chevy in the Hole, the setting for some of the Flint Sit-Down Strike's most memorable scenes. It was the first time I'd been to this spot since the automotive complex was largely demolished over a decade beginning in 1995. I mentioned how geographically disorienting it was without the factories. I knew this area, but I couldn't figure out where we'd turn to head back downtown without the familiar industrial landmark. Ryan said the same thing happened to him after AC Spark Plug, where his grandfather and uncles worked for decades, was torn down. He used to pass the plant every morning, but he started taking a different route. "Human tragedy is not a great way to start your day," he said.

Next, we drove to the upscale College Cultural District, although locals often refer to the handsome residential area near Mott Community College and the city's cultural attractions as "off East Court Street," a utilitarian designation that used to imply money and sophistication. When my mom was growing up on the East Side, this was where many of "the four hundred" lived, meaning the sons and daughters of Flint's elite. The rich kids. It still retained some of its lofty status, but like everything else in Flint, it was slipping. The mansions and impressive homes in an array of architectural styles were still a sight to behold, but there were also foreclosures in the area. And renters. And residents with rusted-out cars that indicated they weren't bankers or professors at UM-Flint. One Flint resident, trying to impart the depths of Flint's decline, whispered conspiratorially to me over lunch a few days later that even black people were living off East Court. (One of the profound drawbacks of being of Scottish and Dutch descent, with blond hair and blue eyes, is that other white people often feel free to share their unsolicited racist thoughts with me.)

We passed the house where one of my high school girlfriends used to live. I lost my virginity and smoked pot for the first time there—two momentous rites of passage—although they didn't occur on the same night. Or did they? It was hard to remember. Around the corner we pulled into the driveway of a tasteful two-bedroom, two-bath house that Jennifer was trying to sell. The interior was a little dated, but in a good way. There was a basement rumpus room complete with a full bar and a fireplace—a good place to relax after spending some time in the dry sauna on the second floor. It felt a little like the Brady Bunch house, if Mike and Carol were a little more stylish and liked to drink. I envisioned myself writing for hours in my private study, perhaps smoking a pipe, before descending to the bar in my smoking jacket for a batch of Manhattans. Preferably this would happen in the early evening rather than the morning.

Every house has a story, and this one was a reminder that not every Flint resident saddled with a depreciating property was completely destitute. The couple who owned this place happened to be vacationing in Italy at the time. The house was completely paid off when they decided to retire and leave Flint. To pay for a new home in Florida, they took out a $175,000 mortgage with an interest-only teaser rate in 2005 because they planned to pay it off quickly when they sold the house. It was a great plan until the bottom fell out of the market. "Now they're stuck maintaining two homes, flying back and forth to Florida, and slowly bleeding their retirement account dry," Jennifer said.

The solution? A short sale. Although the house was officially listed at $180,000, the bank would settle for $80,000. "Someone is going to get a beautiful house, the kind of house you'd be happy to retire in, for the price of a starter home," Jennifer said.

Obviously, this was way too much house for Traci and me, but I was enjoying the voyeuristic thrill of touring such a desirable residence. During my unfortunate Great Gatsby phase in high school—when I wore saddle shoes and patchwork pants—I longed to live in one of these places instead of our humble home on Bassett Place. But even if I could afford it, this house would be all wrong. I'd almost be taking advantage of Flint rather than helping it. The only sweat equity I'd earn here would be in the sauna.

All that remained now was Flint's finest neighborhood, Woodcroft Estates, an enclave of mansions and high-end trophy homes built with GM lucre when life was good in the Vehicle City. It didn't take long to get there after we cut through downtown and drove south on Miller Road. We turned onto a secluded, winding street, and I spotted the sprawling house of a childhood friend, complete with an in-ground pool. I asked Jennifer if the family still lived there.

"Nope, we sold that to a stripper last year for a buck ninety," she said.

"You mean like an exotic dancer?" I asked. "For $190,000?"

"Oh yeah, she got a good deal. I tell you, if you have a decent job, do what you're supposed to do with your money, save your pennies and pay off your bills, you can have the world by the tail in Flint."

The specs on the house were staggering given the low price: 3,870 square feet, 5 bedrooms, 4.5 baths, 3 fireplaces, 1.6 landscaped acres.

A few minutes later I was standing in the marble foyer of a nearby house owned by the former editor of the *Flint Journal*, which had recently cut publishing to three days a week, laid off more than a third of its staff, and slashed the pay and benefits of those who remained. He had left for an online newspaper startup in Ann Arbor, but his 3,159-square-foot house on an acre of land, with a new kitchen, a chandelier in the dining room, and inlaid mahogany floors, sat unsold. The basement was bigger than my entire house. Jennifer told me the publisher bought it for $320,000 three years ago. It was now listed at $236,000. Using the stripper's house as a benchmark, the newspaper industry would post record profits before he got that price.

"People ask me why I live in Flint," Ryan said as he took in the beamed ceiling and fireplace in the large den. "Besides the fact that I love it here, it's so cheap! I mean you can afford to go to Florida on vacation or Chicago on the weekend."

In other words, the low-cost housing means you can escape to more appealing places when you need a break from Flint. I was planning to do the exact opposite of what many people in Flint hoped to achieve. I was juggling my finances and ready to turn my life upside down to spend more time in Flint and less in San Francisco. Counterintuitive thinking at its best. Or worst.

We were getting hungry, so Jennifer canceled an appointment with her personal trainer, and we headed downtown for lunch. Our options were somewhat limited, but the fact that there were actual choices could be seen as progress compared to a few years earlier, when almost nothing was open. There was Halo Burger, the trusty Masonic Temple, and a cool little sandwich shop called the Lunch Box. But we chose the latest addition to downtown's sparse gastronomical offerings— Blackstone's, an Irish-themed pub that had generated a buzz after opening a couple of months earlier. It was one of several projects backed by Uptown Developments, a group of local investors who had recently renovated two downtown buildings and rehabbed several loft apartments and retail spaces.

There was a crowd inside and out front at the sidewalk café tables. Yes, *plein air* dining in Flint. The sun was finally out, and it was good to be in a bustling place just across the street from the Copa nightclub, even if my old haunt was boarded up and had a tree growing out of the roof. We ordered lunch and a round of drinks. It all felt reassuringly familiar after a morning spent touring empty houses, and it helped temper some of my uneasiness. I thought I would easily find dozens of cool old houses that triggered warm, nostalgic feelings. The kind of places that would be easy to rehab in neighborhoods where I could help make a difference. And as I've mentioned, they would be ridiculously cheap. I hadn't seen any houses like that today.

On his second Bacardi and Coke, Ryan told me that he and Michael Moore were both graduates of Davison High School, located in a small town near Flint. Ryan had led an unsuccessful campaign to get Moore into their alma mater's hall of fame. "People think I'm friends with Michael, but we're really just acquaintances," he said. "There were all these rumors that I was dating his daughter, but they're not true. I don't even know her."

This confirmed my theory that every extended conversation with a Flintoid ultimately touched on Michael Moore. Like many locals who go on to bigger and better things, Moore is a touchy subject in his hometown. In fact, many refuse to even let him claim Flint as his own, pointing out that he was born in the city but grew up in the suburbs. And Ryan's failure to secure a hall of fame nomination for the filmmaker indicated that the movers and shakers of Davison didn't want to bond with him either. Everything about Moore I posted on the blog was met with a barrage of negative comments. It was hard for me to understand. I always felt that *Roger & Me* captured the real Flint, the cinematic equivalent of what Ben Hamper did in the pages of *Rivethead*. Raw and unvarnished, funny and sad, but accurate nonetheless. And many people in Flint have never forgiven Moore for doing it. Why would you hate a guy who became famous by standing up for your city?

I ordered another beer, and the conversation turned to politics. Flint was electing a new mayor in August. I'd noticed campaign signs dotting yards and vacant lots for the two candidates fighting to replace Don Williamson, a convicted felon turned millionaire who had abruptly resigned in February rather than face a recall vote. I was covering the special election for *Slate*, so I did some preliminary reporting by getting Jennifer and Ryan's take on the race. "Williamson was rough and tough, but he got a lot of things cleaned up, sometimes with his own money," Ryan said. "Some people call it buying votes; some people call it helping the community."

Jennifer pointed out that for all his faults Williamson, who is white, knew how to win a Flint election. "He spent a lot of time in black churches," she said.

When it came to replacing Williamson, they both supported Dayne Walling, a white, thirty-five-year-old Rhodes Scholar with an urban-planning background. He was running against Brenda Clack, a sixty-four-year-old African American grandmother, former state representative, and current county commissioner. Not exactly the type of candidates I expected to see fighting it out for a chance to run Flint. They both seemed so, well, competent.

Just as some of my friends couldn't figure out why I would ever want to spend more time in Flint, I found myself wondering why two smart, successful people would be so eager to take on what just might be the toughest job in politics: mayor of Flint. You'd be expected to solve problems caused by complex global economic forces that you were powerless to control. At the same time, you'd have to tackle all the mundane tasks that come with running a devastated city short on jobs and revenue. *Hey, I got a pothole on my block, and the garbage truck missed my house yesterday. And while you're at it, you should really do something to stop that deindustrialization thing.* It didn't sound fun.

We finished lunch, and I thanked Jennifer and Ryan for showing me so many houses. In five hours, they'd given me a crash course in the realities of a shrinking city caught up in a post-bubble economy. I decided to walk back to Carriage Town and enjoy the Michigan summer weather, absent the fog and wind of San Francisco. On the way, I tried to relax and appreciate being back in Flint on what had turned into a beautiful day. But I couldn't help worrying that I needed to seriously reevaluate what sort of house three thousand dollars would buy me in the city that Dayne Walling and Brenda Clack wanted to lead.

Black and White

I've been obsessed with politics since grade school. I collected campaign buttons in Flint, tacked an electoral college map on my bedroom wall, and lamented that more Americans didn't vote for Jerry Brown—who stood alongside Evel Knievel in my pantheon of childhood heroes—when he ran for president in 1976. I'd had a brief and regrettable fascination with Ronald Reagan and neoconservatism in high school, but I had since dismissed that as a youthful indiscretion. Even though I'd written about bigger, more important elections, I was excited to be covering the Flint mayor's race for *Slate*. There was a certain thrill in gaining access to a process that had been so mysterious and far removed from me as a kid, when I read the *Flint Journal* for news about local politics. Access was easy in a downwardly mobile city like Flint. All you had to do was show up at campaign events and talk to the candidates. No handlers. No PR flacks running interference. It was a great way to get an insider's perspective on the city where I hoped to buy a house.

Although elections in the city are nonpartisan, Flint is a Democratic stronghold. In 2006, a nationwide study determined it was the tenth most liberal city in the United States, just behind San Francisco in the rankings, proving that the two cities where I'd spent most of my life had something in common besides me.

It didn't take a political junkie to know that Flint needed stable if not stellar political leadership if it was ever going to reverse the economic and social problems that had come to define it. Numerous conversations over beers with patrons at Blackstone's and the Torch, which I considered research and an excellent way to pump money into the local economy, indicated that this had not been the case in recent years. A day spent talking to local politicos off the record confirmed it. Flint's highest office had not attracted the best and the brightest lately.

In 2002, voters had recalled three-term mayor Woodrow Stanley with the city facing a $30 million deficit. The state placed the city in receivership that same year, appointing an emergency financial manager to run things, effectively declaring that Flint's leaders couldn't be trusted to dig themselves out of a very deep financial hole. (A powerless interim mayor and a temporary mayor were thrown into the mix, but let's not confuse things.) A bond measure and a series of brutal cuts ensued before the city was returned to local control with a balanced budget. After the humiliation of a state takeover, I figured voters would have embraced a reliable, fiscally responsible leader, someone who could make the tough decisions in an age of decline. Again, this was not the case.

Don Williamson was elected mayor in 2003. As if to prove Flint's inextricable link with the auto industry, he had been convicted in 1962 for a scam involving the purchase of cars with bad checks, served his time, and made his postprison fortune manufacturing bumpers. Williamson and his wife, Patsy Lou, run several highly successful local GM dealerships, and her smiling face appears on billboards throughout the area. Once in office, "The Don" proved he was anything but a bland technocrat. He bragged about being a high school dropout. He was accused of bribing voters by handing out money from his own pocket during weekly open office hours with citizens. He once remarked that the city council was "about as valuable as puke on a brand new carpet." A nice line, I must admit, but not indicative of a mayor working with the council to solve problems. He sought to reverse Flint's economic misfortune by installing a drag strip on a city street, only to drop the idea when liability issues proved overwhelming. But that ill-advised venture probably cost the city less than the lawsuit that resulted after the mayor had a paper carrier arrested for delivering the *Flint Journal* and its unflattering editorials to city hall.

Although he was reelected in 2007, defeating neophyte Dayne Walling in a close race, Flint residents turned on Williamson a year later, when they signed enough petitions to force a recall election scheduled for early 2009. He resigned before voters could make good on their threat to remove him from office. With the city confronted with yet another budget shortfall—this time more than $8 million—yet another interim mayor filled in until a new one could be elected. Flint-style democracy, with its recalls and special elections, was costing the city a lot of money it clearly did not have.

Walling, in his second campaign for mayor, had cruised to victory in the May primary with 45 percent of the vote. Brenda Clack barely escaped, finishing a distant second with 16 percent and beating the third-place finisher by just fifteen votes for the right to compete against Walling in the August special election. It didn't seem like she had a chance, but I changed my opinion after running into the father of a childhood friend one day on a downtown street. He had been active in local and state politics, so I asked for his take on the election. He pointed out that Walling had been the only white candidate in a field of six. If Clack could pull in most of the black voters who had supported other black candidates in the primary, she could pull off an upset.

I had my doubts. Flint didn't seem like a place where race determined elections. African Americans had achieved a plurality in the nineties and now accounted for 53 percent of the population, while whites accounted for 42 percent. Yet Williamson was white and he'd won the last two elections. Another white mayor, a graduate of my high school, had been elected to a single stormy term in the late eighties before being defeated by Woodrow Stanley, who was African American. "Is race really that big of a factor?" I asked. Despite my Flint roots, I was playing to perfection the role of the ignorant out-of-town journalist parachuting in to cover a local story.

"Are you kidding me?" he answered. "This is Flint. Williamson won because he was able to peel off enough black votes. Besides, he beat Walling the last time. It was easier for him to beat a white opponent."

It was another reminder that I had been away a long time.

"You need to brush up on your Flint history, kiddo," he said, giving me a friendly pat on the shoulder. "Race still matters here."

I didn't mind being called kiddo, even though I was in my forties. It was the same term of endearment my mom still used on me. Besides, he was right. I was probably trying to make Flint conform to some naive vision I had of the place when I used to live here. It was the same uninformed mindset I had taken with me to Little Rock as a reporter. Like any good Northerner, I had felt more than a little superior on matters of race. Flint may have had its share of racial tension, but I thought it was enlightened compared to the South. After all, black and white students attended the same Flint schools long before the U.S. Army had to escort black students into Little Rock's Central High in 1957. I had thought of the Vehicle City as a place where good paying factory jobs had been the great equalizer, fostering a black middle class and eliminating much of the economic disparity that often divided blacks and whites. The notion that a rising tide lifts all boats seemed to apply in Flint, and I believed money had a way of smoothing over even the most deep-seated conflicts. Once again, a little research proved that I didn't know shit about my hometown.

I settled with my laptop into a well-worn desk in the reference section of the Flint Public Library, taking in the comforting smell of old books. It was same spot where in high school I had studied Frederick the Great, made token efforts to finish my geometry homework, and labored over term papers about Jimmy Carter's foreign policy. Now I was there to tackle a subject I'd never given much thought—Flint's racial history.

I ran across a 1927 photo of Kearsley Park taken just a few years before my grandparents moved to their house a couple of blocks away after my mother was born. The steep hillside where I used to go sledding in the winter was dotted with white-hooded Ku Klux Klan members holding a rally. The crowd was nearly as big as the gatherings for the Fourth of July fireworks I happily attended for many years in the park, and I discovered that the Klan had "substantial political popularity" in Flint in the 1920s and 1930s and a lingering presence decades later.

One of the clichés of journalism that I often repeated to my students is that you can never assume anything, and that photo revealed that I had made a lot of assumptions about Flint. Then I began reading "Demolition Means Progress: Race, Class, and the Deconstruction of the American Dream in Flint, Michigan," a dissertation by a PhD candidate at the University of Michigan named Andrew Highsmith. It revealed that nearly every aspect of life in the Vehicle City had been influenced by race. Highsmith wrote that houses built by GM before World War II to accommodate workers flooding the city banned what were considered unsavory practices like raising pigs, making moonshine, installing cesspools, and letting anyone live there who was "not wholly of the white or Caucasian race." Well into the 1960s, redlining, restrictive loan policies, and housing covenants specifically blocked African Americans from buying or building in white neighborhoods.

Instead, black residents were forced into tightly controlled neighborhoods in the North End near the Buick factory and areas southeast of downtown like Floral Park and Elm Park, featuring some of the worst

housing stock in the city. As the black population grew, these neighborhoods became increasingly crowded. One housing inspector discovered
twenty-two people living in a five-room house in the North End in the
midfifties, and that was not particularly unusual.

Though I had been clueless about it, Flint's racial divide wasn't a big
secret. A national housing survey published in 1951 ranked Flint the
third most segregated city in the nation, worse than any of its counter-
parts in the Deep South, including Little Rock, the city I had written off
as a racist backwater. Highsmith pointed out that segregation extended
even to the grave. It wasn't until 1964 that a court order forced all pri-
vately owned cemeteries in Flint to allow the burial of blacks alongside
whites.

An incident described in an NAACP newsletter illustrated that the
public school system wasn't immune to the racism that permeated Flint.
In 1959, a black second-grader at Homedale Elementary, the same
school my mother had attended, was forced to move his desk "inside a
cramped and dark coat closet" after white parents complained about an
integrated classroom. There were only eleven black kids out of 831
total students at Homedale at the time, typical of a system that acro-
batically rejiggered district boundaries to ensure that elementary and
junior high schools were predominantly one race or the other.

By this point, I knew that my half-baked economic theories about GM
jobs leading to racial harmony probably wouldn't hold up. All it took was
a little more reading to learn that while there were plenty of black workers
at the auto factories in the boom years after World War II, they tended to
fill out the custodial ranks or hold tough, low-paying jobs in the foundry
pouring molten steel into molds. There were so many complaints about
working conditions that in 1964 the NAACP protested in front of the
Buick factory, chanting "Jim Crow must go, GM Crow must go."

GM wasn't alone, of course. In the late fifties, the more than two
dozen stores downtown hired only eleven black sales clerks during the
bustling holiday season. Smith-Bridgman's, the preeminent department
store owned by the Mott Foundation, didn't have a single African
American clerk. My mom had sold records in the music department at
Smith-B's for a few years after high school, around the time Johnny Ray
was topping the charts with hits like "The Little White Cloud That
Cried," and she had shopped there for decades. She couldn't remember
ever seeing any black workers on the sales floor. Well into the 1960s,
the *Flint Journal* allowed race-based classified advertisements, which
made it clear that only whites need apply.

Local activists had fought against discrimination much earlier, according to Highsmith, but it wasn't until the civil rights movement reached full force that things began to change in Flint, albeit slowly and grudgingly. Simple demographics made it nearly impossible to maintain the status quo. The city's African American population tripled to roughly eighteen thousand between 1940 and 1955, and by the close of the sixties it had climbed to almost thirty-five thousand. The traditional black neighborhoods were too small to handle so many people.

In the midsixties, the push for an open housing ordinance that would allow African American residents to live anywhere they wanted began to build momentum in Flint. Up to that point, only a small number of all-white neighborhoods had opened up via what was known as "block-busting." A single black family would manage to move into a previously off-limits neighborhood, then real-estate agents would call white residents and ask if they wished to move, aware that they were likely to engage in panic selling. The homes would be sold to other black families or turned into rentals for black tenants.

In the midst of this long-simmering tension, Floyd McCree was appointed mayor in 1966 by the Flint City Commission, becoming the first African American mayor of a large U.S. city. The event was not as momentous as it sounds. Flint had a council-manager form of government at the time, and voters did not directly elect the mayor, so it was "essentially a symbolic position." McCree was a smart, capable politician, but there's no denying that his appointment was partly a calculated move by the white establishment to calm the black populace and garner some good press for the city.

McCree may not have had much formal power, but Highsmith described how he bravely used his new forum to call for an open housing ordinance. The city commission dragged its heels, avoiding a formal vote on the proposal. When the Detroit riots broke out in the summer of 1967, unrest also spread to Flint's North End, though on a much smaller scale. Activists—both black and white—pushed hard for a vote on the open housing ordinance in the aftermath of the disturbances. The commission finally relented, but the measure was defeated by a 5–3 vote. In response, McCree resigned. "I'm not going to sit up here any longer and live an equal opportunity lie," he said.

Demonstrations followed, including a ten-day sleep-in on the city hall lawn. The national media showed up, shining an uncomfortable spotlight on the city. "The summer 1967 protests forced the editorial board of the *Flint Journal*, several key downtown retailers, the presidents of the Mott Foundation and the board of education, and other civic leaders to throw their support behind municipal fair housing legislation," Highsmith wrote. McCree soon reconsidered his resignation. He cobbled together a majority on the commission, made some concessions, and got a measure passed by a 5–4 vote.

There wasn't much time for celebration. Backed by commissioners opposed to the measure, a local member of the John Birch Society united a broad coalition of white homeowners, developers, and real-estate agents to place a referendum overturning the ordinance on the ballot. Fifty members of the local Ku Klux Klan paraded through downtown to support it.

In the end, the referendum was defeated by forty-three votes out of more than 40,000 cast. Flint was officially the first city in America to implement an open housing ordinance by will of the people.

"It's just wonderful," a triumphant McCree declared. "The people won."

I was relieved to know that my hometown had the capacity to break with its past in such dramatic fashion, but I was careful not to misread the impact of the fair housing law. Though it was a great victory for civil rights, finally opening Flint housing to all residents, it did not foster integrated neighborhoods. Many white residents responded by fleeing the city, exacerbating a trend that had begun in the fifties. Majority white neighborhoods often became majority black neighborhoods. Reflecting back forty years after the historic vote, one black resident who had camped out at city hall during the sleep-in for open housing admitted that the ordinance may have changed the laws that discriminated against African Americans, but it hadn't necessarily changed the "hearts and minds" of whites. "I wonder if it's all for naught," he said.

Floyd McCree stayed active in local politics, but he continued to be reminded of Flint's racial divide. In 1975, after Flint had switched to a strong mayor system with direct elections, he campaigned for the city's top job. He lost by 206 votes to James W. Rutherford, the city's white former police chief. He lost to Rutherford again in the 1979 mayor's race.

I couldn't help feeling ashamed as I sat in an air-conditioned library built largely with Charles Stewart Mott's money, discovering another part of Flint's history that I had never known. Like many seemingly enlightened white people, I'd let my friendly personal interactions with African Americans blind me to Flint's embedded institutional racism. I had the urge to go up to the first black person I saw and apologize. Not for being a racist, but for being so woefully uninformed. I'm sure the unlucky person I approached would have been thrilled to encounter some earnest white dude, awash with guilt, searching for absolution.

Since I'd arrived in Flint, I'd been looking forward to visiting Adrienne, who is African American and one of my mom's oldest friends from high school. I figured now was the time to do it. I needed to process what I'd learned with a real person. She had grown up in a black neighborhood on the South Side called Elm Park, adjacent to Floral Park. Now in her late seventies, she lived off Lapeer Road in Evergreen Valley, a housing development that had figured prominently in Flint's desegregation battles. When I arrived, she was preparing for a family party later that afternoon. She offered me a beer from a big cooler she had set up near the in-ground pool in her tidy backyard. "Your mom and I sure had a lot of fun," she said as I cracked open an ice-cold Budweiser. "She was my sister."

Adrienne described the confusing dynamics of race in Flint. She remembered Central High as being about 85 percent white when she and my mom went there. They had both graduated in 1948. It was not uncommon for her to be the only black student in a class. But she said she never encountered any racism on a personal, face-to-face level growing up in Flint. "I never ran into any prejudice," she said. "No one ever called me a nigger or anything like that."

It was fine for my mom to accompany Adrienne to places typically off limits to whites, like the Golden Leaf, a private black club that's still open across from the abandoned Clark Elementary School on Harrison Street. "She was my friend and she was with me, so it was fine," Adrienne explained.

But despite her friendships with white classmates like my mom, Adrienne noted that Flint's institutional racism was ever-present. The IMA Auditorium on the edge of downtown regularly held dances, drawing big names like Count Basie and Duke Ellington, but they always performed two acts: one for whites in the evening, and one for blacks in the early morning. "Now that hurt," Adrienne said. "These were black performers. They were *our* performers, but we had to wait our turn to see them."

Although my mother was always welcome at Adrienne's house, it would have been highly unusual for a black girl to visit a white friend in the working-class East Side at the time. There were clear limits to interactions between blacks and whites. To illustrate the point, Adrienne told me a story about her father, who was a landscaper in addition to working at the Buick factory. One day he was driving through downtown Flint in his truck and he passed my mom, who was waiting to catch a bus over to Adrienne's house. My mom figured it would be faster to ride with Adrienne's dad than to wait for public transportation, so she called out to him, waving from the crowded sidewalk. He ignored her and sped up. Assuming he hadn't heard her, she chased after him, waving and calling out, "Mr. Wilson, can I have a ride?" He floored it and finally pulled far enough away for my mom to give up.

Later, when my mom arrived at the house, he wasn't pleased. "Girl, don't ever flag me down on Saginaw Street," he said. "What would happen if all those people saw you getting into my truck?"

Adrienne was laughing about it now. "Pat and I thought that was so funny, but my dad sure didn't."

Adrienne, her husband, and her children had moved into their current house in 1964 when only one other African American, a professor at UM-Flint, lived in the all-white neighborhood. They were what whites would consider blockbusters, but Adrienne never saw it that way. Her previous home had been seized by eminent domain when a large section of the black South Side was leveled for a highway project, one of the urban-renewal efforts that eliminated black neighborhoods across the country. She and her husband took the payout, worked with a black real-estate agent, and happily settled into a nicer home in Evergreen Valley two years before the open housing ordinance went into effect. "My white neighbors were very friendly," she said. "But they couldn't move fast enough. They were smiling as they packed their bags."

One day, Adrienne's son walked home from school with the daughter of a white neighbor. The girl's father stormed out of the house, angrily yelling at the girl and ordering her to get inside. He put his house up for sale a month later. The neighbor was none other than James Rutherford, the cop who would later defeat Floyd McCree to become mayor of Flint.

Before I left Adrienne's house, she lobbied me not only to move back to Flint but to bring my mom with me. "Tell your mother I've got a spare bedroom she can have," Adrienne said as she hugged me good-bye. "Flint isn't what it used to be, but I know we'd have fun together just like we always did."

On the drive back to my pink house in Carriage Town, I tried to reconcile what Adrienne had told me with what I had discovered in the library about Flint's racist past. It was confusing. Although she clearly recognized the rigid institutional racism that dominated the city, she had nothing but fond memories of the bulk of her personal interactions over the years. When I called my mom in Florida later that day, she said more or less the same thing. Racism was built into Flint, but that didn't mean it infiltrated every personal relationship between blacks and whites. Of course, my mom had dated and been in love with a black musician from Detroit when she was in her twenties, so I knew she probably didn't represent a typical Flint resident when it came to racial tolerance. But I trusted her opinion. Like Adrienne, she had lived in Flint as a child and as an adult. They had a much broader understanding of the place than I did.

I thought about what it was like to grow up in Flint during the seventies, when neighborhoods weren't so much integrating as transitioning from white to black. I had black friends at the Catholic schools I attended, but the majority of students were white. I knew there were black neighborhoods and white neighborhoods, and it was not advisable to cross those boundaries. I rarely ventured east of Dupont Street or north of Pasadena Avenue on my own, and when I did I took elaborate, out-of-the-way bike routes that would keep me in the "safe" neighborhoods. Likewise, black kids knew to avoid all-white neighborhoods like the East Side.

When my mom drove me on weekends to my friend Markie's all-black neighborhood near the Buick factory, I felt a certain uneasiness. I knew it was strange for me to be there, sitting in a black friend's bedroom listening to his dad's old Redd Foxx records. I remember an elderly white couple driving down one of the main thoroughfares and doing a double take when they saw Markie and me walking to the corner store to load up on candy, no doubt saying, "What the hell is that white kid doing in the North End?" I was too little to label this de facto segregation or institutional racism. It was just reality. It never occurred to me that things might be different somewhere else.

I knew that if I happened to encounter a group of unknown black kids in one of the emerging transitional zones between historically white and black neighborhoods, it was time to haul ass, or "book it," as we used to say. At the same time, I'd do the same thing if I saw a group of tough-looking, unfamiliar white kids. I was a lousy fighter, but I was a fast runner. Perhaps my speed came from being on those summer track teams, paid for by the city. Flint was a place where you could easily get your ass kicked if you weren't careful. Sometimes the kids who beat you up were black, sometimes white. Maybe that's what passed for diversity in Flint in the seventies.

The street I grew up on had one black family. John and Christine moved into a house very much like ours in the spring of 1978. They were starting a family. They had young kids to take care of, but they both went out of their way to befriend me. I was a latchkey kid without a dad in the house. John invited me on bike rides around town. He always had time to talk to me, even when he was trying to get yard work done and I was pestering him with the annoying questions of a twelve-year-old.

After my visit with Adrienne, I was roaming around the city one day with no particular destination in mind and happened to drive down my old street. The neighborhood was almost exclusively African American. I saw a car in John and Christine's driveway. I knew they still lived there, because I had looked up every house on my block of Bassett Place in the City of Flint's property tax records, trying to figure out what home values were in the area. I hadn't talked to either one of them in more than two decades, but I decided to stop.

"Who's there?" I heard John yell through the door after I knocked, remembering once again that unannounced visitors are cause for alarm in Flint.

"My name's Gordon Young. I used to live . . . "

"Gordie Young!" John shouted before I could finish. I heard the locks click, and he ushered me into the living room, putting his arm around my shoulder and shaking my hand.

"I didn't think you'd know who I was," I said as Christine came downstairs and gave me a hug.

He offered me a perplexed look. "Of course I know who you are," he said. "I recognized your voice."

This was the first house they'd ever owned, and they'd lived in it for more than thirty years. They liked the neighborhood so much that John's father had bought the house next door. John remembered hearing about the days when black residents could "get financing for a Cadillac but not a house," regardless of their good credit score. His father had told him about sellers who would arbitrarily raise the price on a house to keep African Americans from buying it.

But John and Christine had a very different experience. They had no trouble financing their house, and the rest of the street didn't put their houses up for sale when they arrived. "We were welcomed by our neighbors," John said. "People brought us housewarming gifts, including your mother." The conversation reminded me that the open housing ordinance did a lot more than just prompt whites to leave the city. It made it possible for people like John and Christine to live where they wanted, in a neighborhood that John remembered fondly from playing baseball games as a kid in Bassett Park.

I told him I'd been blindsided by Flint's racial history, that it caused me to question the attachment I had to the city. But John didn't have any doubts about the place where he had lived his entire life. "There will always be racism, but that doesn't mean everyone is racist," he said. "I've always loved Flint. Living here has been a beautiful experience for me. That's why I'm staying right here."

Just to prove how difficult it is to draw any grand conclusions about race and politics in Flint, I told John and Christine I was covering the mayor's race and asked who they supported. They gave me the same emphatic, unequivocal answer that Adrienne had provided when I asked her the same question: Dayne Walling, the white candidate.

10

The Forest Primeval

I was driving through downtown after another haphazard house-hunting expedition. My real-estate quest had already become highly unfocused. I'd spent the morning wandering aimlessly in search of neighborhoods that appeared both inviting and inexpensive. The more I looked, the farther I seemed to drift from making a decision.

I fiddled with the needlessly complicated car radio, hoping to find some cheery, superficial pop songs to propel me into a good mood. It wasn't easy. A Jay-Z hip-hop number was far too realistic. A corporate rock "classic" like "Dust in the Wind" was just depressing. I finally resorted to AM radio and was startled by a famous voice discussing Flint. None other than Rush Limbaugh was offering advice for my hometown on WWCK. He had apparently gotten hold of a comment made at a Rotary Club luncheon in March by interim mayor Michael Brown—filling in until either Walling or Clack was elected—about the possibility of "shutting down quadrants of the city" in response to blight and population loss.

"All right, folks, I have thought about it; I've given this considerable thought," Limbaugh declared with typical self-assurance. "I've given this more thought in the last ten minutes than most people think about anything in their life. And I am ready to change my mind on bulldozing Flint. I say go for it. Let's just bulldoze it."

I was clearly not Limbaugh's target demographic. I lived in San Francisco. My representative was Nancy Pelosi. I grew up in one of

America's most militant union towns. My unfiltered initial reaction was that an overweight right-wing millionaire with a history of drug abuse didn't have the right to say shit about Flint, Michigan. But while Limbaugh's uninformed opinions didn't resonate with me, it was exciting to know that a large segment of the nation was focused on Flint at that very moment, even if the discussion concerned wiping the city off the map.

Limbaugh was all riled up about a man named Dan Kildee, the county treasurer and president of the Genesee County Land Bank, who was getting international publicity for refining and vigorously promoting what had come to be known as the shrinking-city concept. Kildee's urban-planning theory called for essentially abandoning irrational hope and moving on. He believed that cities like Flint should accept that they're not going to regain their lost population anytime soon. Derelict houses and buildings should be leveled and replaced with parks, urban gardens, and green space. Eventually, incentives could be used to lure residents into higher-density neighborhoods that had been reinvigorated with infill housing and rehab projects. Although there were no hard numbers, the city could theoretically save money by reducing infrastructure costs. There would be fewer sparsely populated neighborhoods in need of city services like garbage collection and police protection. Some sewer and electrical lines might be eliminated, reducing maintenance costs. The housing market would stabilize, if not improve. Think of it as manifest destiny in reverse for urban areas, a radical urban-planning concept that rejected growth as the fundamental goal of cities.

For a small-town politician with a résumé heavy on obscure county government jobs, Kildee sure had a knack for attracting attention. He talked to everyone from National Public Radio to unknown wonks at obscure policy journals. He had shown up on Al Jazeera and in the pages of the *New York Times*. When a Dutch film crew wearing hoodies and complicated sneakers found its way to the Vehicle City, he piled them into his Jeep Grand Cherokee and gave them a tour of Flint's troubled neighborhoods. He was big in Japan, where numerous cities and towns were losing population. Despite never earning a college degree, Kildee had lectured at Harvard's Kennedy School of Government. He had huddled with Barack Obama on the campaign trail and helped draft a transition memo for Housing and Urban Development secretary Shaun Donovan after the presidential election. There were rumors that he was considering a job at HUD.

With his well-honed promotional skills, Kildee wasted little time using Limbaugh's tirade as yet another opportunity to advertise his ideas. He sent a letter to the conservative icon that later surfaced on Facebook, inviting him to broadcast his show from Flint, take a tour, and enjoy Flint's signature heart-attack-friendly culinary delight—the Coney Island. It's a locally made Koegel Vienna hot dog covered with a spicy, finely ground beef topping, onions, and mustard—not to be confused with a chili dog, which is what passes for a Coney in Detroit and other parts of the country. (Fail to recognize this distinction and you're likely to catch hell from Flintoids. There may be lack of consensus on how to turn the city around, but residents are unified on one thing—Detroit-style Coneys suck.) Kildee even offered to personally pay for Limbaugh's flight and hotel. "The people of Flint deserve to live in clean and safe neighborhoods, free of blight," Kildee wrote in the letter. "We don't want to 'bulldoze' Flint as you say, just bulldoze the empty and abandoned houses left behind by the economic dislocation resulting from the loss of 70,000 GM jobs." Limbaugh declined the invitation, passing up the chance for a free lunch.

The controversy was a reminder that Flint's descent into economic chaos had the unintended consequence of turning it into an urban-planning proving ground, a living laboratory of civic and economic experimentation. A city on its knees was apparently willing to entertain almost any plan to get back on its feet. Flint's new motto might be "What the hell, let's give it a try."

Kildee's plan was the most comprehensive and high profile, but there were others. Take the ongoing study by sociologists and grass experts to determine if lush, well-groomed yards and parks can help turn a city around. "At one of the areas we're looking at, there's basically a park but no one is playing in it," explained the Michigan State University turf grass specialist who was leading the study. "We want to come back in a year and see people throwing a Frisbee around."

Setting aside the possibility that the park might be empty because the surrounding neighborhood is a ghost town, this testament to good intentions and the esoteric nature of academic grants may be surprisingly difficult to complete. The desperation of many Flint residents meant almost anything was a target for theft—copper plumbing, gas meters, manhole covers . . . even landscaping. Sod and freshly planted saplings were sometimes stolen from city parks. In 2008, a suspect was charged with two counts of "tree larceny" for walking off with valuable black walnut trees from the parkway of a busy city street. (Imagine the awkward jailhouse conversation between cellmates: Whataya in for, homes? Grand theft tree, two counts.) Increased demand in Asia had driven up the price of the trees, which were popular with furniture makers. They were worth three thousand dollars each.

But there was a brutal practicality driving other ventures, and they held more promise. One involved a commodity that seemed immune from criminal intent, even in Flint: shit.

In the fall of 2008 King Carl XVI Gustaf of Sweden visited Flint's Kettering University to mark a joint venture between the university, the city, and Swedish Biogas International to build a plant that will convert human waste into biogas for use as vehicle fuel, heat, and electricity. A Flint native then serving as U.S. ambassador to Sweden had been instrumental in brokering the deal.

The Flint plant was a test to determine if the idea is feasible nationwide. Flint and Swedish Biogas signed a twenty-one-year contract and would split revenues from the project. Construction on a $10 million conversion facility at Flint's sewage plant was scheduled to begin soon.

It wasn't quite the same as churning out shiny, chrome-laden Buick Electras with three-speed Super Turbine 400 automatic transmissions for car-crazy Americans. Or producing battle-ready tanks for the American war effort in World War II. But biogas had its advantages; it was made from an endlessly renewable resource that was rarely subject to a product recall.

But transforming poop into prosperity was hardly a radical notion compared to Kildee's plan, which seemed at odds with America's can-do spirit, its reputation for boundless optimism. Kildee was declaring that we can't have it all, that Flint can't be a booming metropolis where thousands of well-paid workers owned snowmobiles and looked forward to cushy pensions when they retired. Americans, myself included, aren't exactly big on accepting reality, as indicated by my mission to own a second home when I could barely afford my first one. Americans don't give up. We fight. Even when it doesn't make a lot of sense. So of course Rush Limbaugh hated Kildee's plan, as did many Flint residents. Even a largely positive profile in the *New York Times* described it in almost apocalyptic terms: "A city built to manufacture cars would be returned in large measure to the forest primeval."

I was familiar with Dan Kildee. I had grown up next door to his younger brother. In college, I served as a profoundly incompetent congressional intern for his uncle, U.S. representative Dale Kildee, the long-serving Democrat from Flint. Dan was an obvious person to get to know, especially if I wanted to figure out which neighborhoods he was likely to "shrink" before I bought a house.

I met with Kildee early one morning in an empty conference room at the downtown offices of the Genesee County Land Bank. We sat across from each other at a long table, but Kildee couldn't stay put. An energy-saving device kept automatically turning off the lights, plunging us into gloom, so Kildee would occasionally jump up and wave his arms above his head in midsentence to reactivate the buzzing fluorescents above us. Once he was on his feet, he would pace the room, eager to spell out the shrinking-city concept. "It really comes down to getting people to stop assuming that expansion is always desirable," Kildee told me. "The important thing is how people feel about their city when they stand on their front porch in the morning, not how many people actually live in the city. It's just irrational to simply pursue growth."

For someone who is often accused of trying to undermine the very fundaments of America's capitalist society with his unorthodox approach, Kildee doesn't exactly look the part. He's a big guy with sleepy eyes and a sympathetic, hangdog look. At fifty-one, his once dark hair is receding and going a little gray. The only thing even mildly counter-culture about him is the well-trimmed beard, a much more sub-dued version of the Grizzly Adams look he had going when he played hockey at Flint Northern High School. (Hey, it was the seventies.) He is partial to conservative dark suits similar in style to those favored by his more diminutive uncle, Dale the congressman.

Kildee mixed the fervor of a true believer with a big dose of shame-less self-promotion. He undercut every statement that might be consid-ered tooting his own horn with a self-deprecating declaration. He casually mentioned that his pal Michael Moore put him in *Capitalism: A Love Story*, before he shrugged and added that his segment didn't make the theatrical release and was only included as a DVD extra. It didn't take long to discover that Kildee possessed the gift of all skilled politicians; he made you feel like he was listening to you, *really* listen-ing, even though he was doing most of the talking. Although I viewed it as the most overrated quality in an elected official, he was very likable. Spend a few minutes with him and you felt like you were both on the same page, fighting to save Flint in the only way possible, even if you were not really sure you agreed with his approach.

These traits had paid off for Kildee at the ballot box. He won a school board seat when he was only eighteen, right before he got married and had his first child. He went on to serve twelve years as a Genesee County commissioner before being elected county treasurer in 1997, a job he had held ever since.

Despite his obvious ability to get his message across, Kildee admitted that there were numerous misconceptions swirling around his shrinking-city plan. He dispelled them in rapid-fire fashion. He did not advocate eliminating entire sections of the city. Instead, he favored a block-by-block approach. He explained that though cities tend to grow in a fairly orderly pattern of expanding concentric circles, they decline haphazardly. Although there are areas of more intense abandonment, the blight is scattered throughout the city. There's no obvious section to eliminate, even if he wanted to. He would never use eminent domain to force residents to leave their homes. In fact, Kildee wrote a prohibition of the use of eminent domain by land banks into state law. He didn't endorse punitive measures, such as reduced city services, to achieve the same goal. Instead, he advocated offering reluctant residents incentives to move, including tax breaks, cash payments, or even swapping their house for a newly restored home in a different part of town. "We created sprawlville with incentives in the United States," Kildee said. "We can use incentives to create more sustainable neighborhoods in cities."

Finally, Kildee made it clear he had not invented a new economic model. There was nothing in his plan that would create a large number of new jobs. It was simply a way to stabilize Flint, the first step in a long process of regeneration. "We are forced to use this emergency room strategy now because we don't have any other choice," he said.

While we were on the topic of misconceptions, Kildee was quick to point out that he didn't even invent the shrinking-city concept. The approach emerged in Germany, where the central government was forced to deal with rapidly depopulating cities when two million residents abandoned the former Communist East for the more prosperous West after the fall of the Berlin Wall and reunification in 1990.

As much as I liked to think of Flint as a unique locale, a place with a special status in history, Kildee explained that its transformation from thriving metropolis to troubled town wasn't exactly a new story. Communities have always operated in a state of flux, their size and prosperity subject to change. War, disease, famine, immigration, economic shifts, environmental disasters, and political upheavals are just a few of the factors that can lead to decline. Rome was the most vibrant city in Europe for a thousand years with a population that surpassed one million at the end of the first century B.C. Several decades of internal decay and a few barbarian invasions later, it was reduced to less than twenty thousand inhabitants living among the ruins during the early Middle Ages.

If ancient Rome seems too far removed from present-day Flint, there are plenty of more recent examples closer to home. Gary, Indiana, was a thriving municipality known as the Steel City with more than 175,000 residents in 1960. Then the layoffs at the steel mills started, and Gary lost half its population, including the city's most famous residents—the Jackson Five—when they relocated to California. Gary hasn't bounced back like Rome, but at least it still exists. The ghost towns of the American West and the Mayan ruins in Central America are a reminder that not all towns, cities, or even civilizations last forever.

While the world population increased at a steady, if not alarming rate, more cities in the developed world shrank than grew in the past thirty years. In the United States, fifty-nine cities with more than one hundred thousand people lost at least a tenth of their population over the last fifty years. Flint may seem like an extreme example because the number of residents was cut in half, but the same thing happened in Buffalo, Cleveland, Detroit, Pittsburgh, and Saint Louis. But this is hardly just a Rust Belt phenomenon. The housing collapse ensured that even parts of the South and the Sunbelt, where Flint residents once flocked on their vacations and later in desperate search of jobs, are part of the trend.

The collapse of the housing bubble and the ensuing economic catastrophe have given cities as unlikely as Flint and Las Vegas something in common: high unemployment, a declining population, abandoned housing, and all the problems that go with them. After being the fastest growing city in America for nearly two decades, a net of roughly thirty thousand people left Las Vegas between 2007 and 2009, prompting one Sin City journalist to admit, "We can no longer be sure that we are the city of the future. Like it or not, we've got a little bit of Detroit and Cleveland in us."

Even the residents of Flint, who had every right to be self-absorbed as they battled the forces of decline or simply tried to make it through the day, recognized that other cities faced similar problems, or would face them in the future. A line I heard more than once around town was "Flint: Coming to a city near you."

This blizzard of statistical affirmation and historical precedent from Kildee had the surprising effect of making me feel a little better about my hometown. It was like realizing you're not the only one with a family that's a little weird and dysfunctional. The Vehicle City was not alone. And Kildee was standing before me, eager to explain how to turn Flint and cities like it into better, more livable places, but he kept getting interrupted. Land bank planners stuck their heads in to ask questions, assistants reminded him of upcoming meetings, and the lights kept turning off, periodically forcing him wave his hands like a conductor guiding an orchestra. But Kildee is tough to derail.

The fine-grained details of the shrinking-city model he advocates can sound complicated. With a willing audience, he can wax poetic about "scattered site cross collateralized tax increment financing" the way a Flint car buff might lyrically describe the angle on a 1958 Chevy Impala's chrome-edged tail fin. But the key component for making all this happen can be boiled down to a very simple concept—keep distressed property away from real-estate speculators. Don't let that abandoned house on Flint's East Side, where a Buick worker once raised a family, fall into the hands of some guy in Nevada looking to make a quick buck. Cities facing economic decline and a dwindling population must have a way to control their own real estate outside of so-called market forces. They must have a way to control their own territorial destiny.

That was certainly not the case when Kildee first became county treasurer. He was in charge of collecting property taxes, but if homeowners fell behind on their payments, the county eventually sold off to speculators the right to collect the back taxes, plus stiff interest penalties for late payment, for pennies on the dollar at a public tax-lien auction. In effect, the county privatized tax collection. If the homeowner didn't pay, the speculator holding the lien could foreclose on the property. Again, Flint wasn't unique; municipalities across the country did more or less the same thing.

Kildee jumped out of his seat and attacked a large white board with a red marker to illustrate everything that was wrong with the system he inherited. From a purely fiscal standpoint, auctioning off the right to collect delinquent property taxes cost the county money because many homeowners eventually paid what they owed, along with the interest penalties. The county got a short-term cash infusion at the auction, but lost out on a bigger payday down the line if the treasurer worked on collecting the debt. "Selling tax liens is like eating potato chips for breakfast," Kildee said, opting for one of the tortured metaphors he breaks out when he's warming to a topic. "It tastes good at first, but it's extremely unhealthy in the long run."

But lost revenue wasn't the real problem. It was rare for someone to acquire a lien on a house at auction and end up moving into the property. Instead, the system had put thousands of houses into the hands of speculators who had no real interest in the future of Flint. Their goal was a quick profit. Many were from out of state and had never been to the city, let alone laid eyes on the property they now controlled. They might flip an empty house to another speculator, who in turn would try to flip it again. That explained the scores of ramshackle houses in Flint's worst neighborhoods that were for sale on eBay. Or speculators might sit on a property in the foolish hope that it would somehow rise in value. Sometimes they had so many houses that a few simply got lost in the shuffle, all but forgotten by their absentee owners.

The system Kildee inherited was also tailor-made for abusive landlords. It was not uncommon for speculators to acquire property through the tax-lien auctions, rent it out at rock-bottom prices, depreciate the property on their income taxes, and make minimal, if any, repairs. When the property decayed to the point that even desperate renters wouldn't touch it, the landlord simply stopped paying taxes, happy to let the county take it back.

In each case, a Flint house sat empty and decaying, a target for squatters, vandals, drug addicts, and arsonists. It dragged down property values, destabilized the real-estate market, and gave more conscientious neighbors one more reason to give up and move out. "Speculators treat houses like left-handed golf clubs," Kildee said. "They're a disposable oddity instead of the linchpin of a neighborhood."

It was a vicious cycle, and it was a slow one. Once a speculator stopped paying property taxes, it could take nearly eight years before someone else could acquire a lien and foreclose. And that often just started the process all over again. The county treasurer had no power to control or condemn property. The state or the City of Flint handled all demolitions, and that process could take more than a decade thanks to laws that emphasized property rights over all else.

Some argue that vigorous code enforcement might have prevented some of these practices. But this was Flint. It wasn't a high priority in a cash-strapped city with few housing inspectors and so much violence that cops sometimes referred to it as Beirut. (Besides, code violations might provide added incentive for an owner to walk away from a property. Kildee cautioned that more housing inspectors wouldn't necessarily lead to fewer abandoned houses.) In this atmosphere, large-scale real-estate fraud was being perpetrated on a regular basis. I mentioned to Kildee that one of my high school classmates had recently been sentenced to six to twenty years in prison on a racketeering charge for "adopting" abandoned houses, posing as the owner, and selling them to unsuspecting victims. Yes, he was renting and selling houses he didn't own. A lot of them. One woman handed him fifteen thousand dollars that had taken her a decade to save in exchange for a worthless quit-claim deed.

My classmate had shown an early flair for gaming the system back at our Catholic high school, which had a dress code requiring all boys to wear a collared shirt. He'd arrived one day with a glorified T-shirt featuring something that was relatively rare at the time—a mock turtleneck. "They can't say shit about this shirt," he announced to a group of kids after gym class. His plan worked, and he single-handedly started a minor fashion trend. He was now in a prison in the Upper Peninsula of Michigan.

Kildee had realized he was an elected middleman for speculators, an unwilling participant in Flint's decline. Every ounce of value was being drained out of the city's abandoned houses as they crumbled into the ground, but none of the profit was going back into the community. Wall Street was accused of privatizing gains and socializing losses as the mortgage meltdown unfolded, but the same thing had been happening on a smaller scale for years in cities like Flint. "The speculators weren't really investing in anything," Kildee said. "They were liquidating an asset."

Kildee started going on long runs after work in his hilly neighborhood near McLaren Hospital, where my mom used to work, and thinking about how to change things. He looked at other cities and connected with urban planners, land-use experts, and economists. Kildee wasn't one to tinker around the edges. He not only came up with a dramatically different model, but he managed to shepherd a series of bills through the Michigan legislature between 1999 and 2004 that made his dream a reality. It also made Kildee one of the most divisive figures in Flint.

Under the new legislation, Kildee became president of the newly empowered Genesee County Land Bank in addition to fulfilling his duties as treasurer. The land bank is a public entity charged with acquiring, developing, and selling vacant and abandoned properties. Land banks had existed before, but they typically dealt with only the worst property in an area, the odd-shaped lots and toxic sites that even speculators wouldn't touch. This was different. Kildee could now control almost any property that went through the tax foreclosure process. He could keep property away from speculators, eliminate blight, and, he hoped, help reshape the look, feel, and density of Flint. He even figured out a way to pay for it. Well, some of it, anyway.

The county began actively collecting delinquent taxes and penalties instead of auctioning off liens on the property. Kildee hired a full-time foreclosure prevention specialist to assist troubled homeowners. "Private investors would do the bare minimum, so they could tiptoe past the courthouse and end up with ownership of the property," Kildee said, his excitement growing as he described the changes he had brought about. "We did just the opposite. We didn't want the property unless the owner really had walked away." As Kildee predicted, it wasn't that tough to work with taxpayers to ensure payment, resulting in a county surplus of between two million and four million dollars a year. Those surpluses were split between the county's general fund and the land bank. More importantly, many Flint residents were able to stay in their homes by working out payment arrangements with the county.

When the county did foreclose, the newly streamlined process typically took about two years to complete before the property ended up in the land bank. It could be targeted for rehabilitation or demolition. More than 1,100 structures had already been torn down, but that was just the start. There were still more than 6,000 abandoned homes in the city. Demolition cost about $9,000 a pop, so there wasn't nearly enough money to finish the job.

But though razing houses had garnered Kildee the most publicity—and criticism—he insisted that it was just part of the plan. The real "genius" of his approach is that it implements a regional land-use strategy that redistributes real-estate wealth. Kildee was able to talk Genesee County's more prosperous suburbs and municipalities into giving up a share of their tax revenue to help Flint. The land bank often gains control of valuable suburban property that can be sold or rented on the open market. A single such sale had recently netted $323,000. That money can then be used to fund rehab or demolition projects in Flint. Kildee also convinced reluctant county commissioners to back bonds to pay for risky downtown Flint redevelopment projects. This sort of regionalism has never been widely embraced in America.

Getting the suburbs to buy into this regional approach may have been Kildee's greatest political triumph. After all, these were some of the very places that grew at the expense of Flint, the beneficiaries of the white flight that helped speed the Vehicle City's race to the bottom. It's not uncommon to encounter county residents who brag that they *never* go to Flint. There's a sense among many Flint residents that the suburbanites look down their noses at them.

The city-versus-suburbs mentality was ingrained in me growing up. My mom certainly understood the need for locals to leave Flint in search of work and adventure in faraway places. After all, she'd done it herself. But abandoning the city to move ten or twenty miles away to areas that were nothing but farmland when she was a kid just seemed wrong to her. She frequently implied that suburbanites were cowardly snobs who just weren't tough enough for Flint.

In our household, Flushing was viewed as a small town bloated with Flint refugees who had fled the city's growing African American population. Grand Blanc was the ritzier version of suburban escape. Western Hills was a well-off housing development in Flint Township near Carman High School, a local soccer powerhouse, which tells you all you need to know. I now realize that these characterizations were vast oversimplifications, unfair in many ways, but they were held by many Flint residents, and the animosities frequently rose to the surface.

My high school was technically not in Flint. The low-slung, prison-like building was located just across the northern city limit on West Carpenter Road. Walk across the street to the 7/11 and you were in Flint; walk back to school—or run back, depending on the level of violence you encountered while buying a cherry Slurpee and a Snickers—and you were in Mount Morris Township. Yet the school referred to itself as Flint Powers Catholic, perhaps the only local entity that willingly aligned itself with Flint when it wasn't necessary. Maybe I'm rationalizing, but it felt like Flint to me, given the number of city kids from the various Catholic grade schools that filled the ranks, along with a dose of suburbanites whose parents saw fit to forgo one of the chief advantages of leaving Flint—decent public schools—to pay for a Catholic education.

My older brother and sisters went to Powers, so I learned at an early age that the suburban schools were our biggest rivals in sports. I remember walking to our car after an away football game against Flushing one Friday night when I was about ten. We had lost the game. I randomly stopped and picked up a nut from under a tree at the edge of the parking lot and held it up for my mom. "Look, an acorn," I said. Before she could respond, an older man behind us decked out in a satin Flushing High jacket, dress slacks, and one of those dumb tam-o'-shanter hats in the school colors announced, "Actually, that would be a black walnut."

How can I put this? My mom is a person you might describe as outspoken, to put it mildly. She is also a devout Catholic who views football as an official extension of the faith. She worked bingo to pay for our Catholic schooling. She put a statue of the Virgin Mary on top of the TV set before every Notre Dame game. Losing to a suburban public school, let alone Flushing, had put her in a no-nonsense mood. She stopped and turned around. A familiar look came over her face as she took in the guy's clothing. My mom has an eye for fashion, and she seemed particularly displeased by his funny hat. A sense of excitement and dread came over me. I'd seen that look before.

"Oh, really?" she said, a fake smile on her face. "I didn't realize you allowed anything black in Flushing."

The guy frowned and veered quickly away from us. I wasn't exactly sure what had just transpired, but I sensed that he had insulted us, and mom had put him in his place. I mean the guy had no comeback at all, a sure sign of defeat in the verbal showdowns that transpired daily at Flint playgrounds. He could have at least thrown out a "yo mama" in desperation. I briefly considered chucking the acorn, or black walnut, or whatever it was, at the back of the guy's head. With good aim I might dislodge his tam-o'-shanter. That would have been the Flint thing to do, giving me the satisfaction of defending my mom—even though I still wasn't sure what I would be defending her from—and confirming to the good people of Flushing that Flint residents were violent, confrontational, and kind of crazy.

Although this anecdote reveals as much about my family as the relationship between Flint and the surrounding area, it provides a sense of what Kildee had been up against when he set out to talk these municipalities into helping the city. Yet seventeen agreed, including Flushing and Grand Blanc. But even Kildee wasn't able to get everyone on board. Burton, a small town separated from Flint by Center Road, took a pass. Burton was looked down on by many Flintoids, who sometimes refer to it as Burtucky, a reference to the large number of Southerners who came north for auto jobs and settled there. "The city of Burton says no every time, and there's no rational justification for it," Kildee said, rolling his eyes. "It's this belief that they're somehow separate from Flint, as if Center Road is that moat across which no bad things can travel. Burton's not exactly Sausalito."

Kildee made it clear that he thought places like Burton and the other local hamlets owed something to Flint. "The model I've created is basically a regional tax-base redistribution system when you get right down to it," he said. "Flint helped these outlying areas for decades. Now it's their turn to give something back to the city. In the end, everyone will benefit."

This is just the sort of talk that rankles critics like Limbaugh. It sounds a lot like socialism, a term that had been thrown around derisively in the 2008 presidential campaign. But Kildee didn't care. "Rush went crazy for a few days, but it was the best thing to ever happen to me because a couple million people heard it," said Kildee, who nonetheless admitted he was weary of the mocking calls to his home and office from Limbaugh's "dittoheads."

Kildee was equally blunt when critics argued that market forces, not government intervention, would solve Flint's problems. "That's bullshit," he said. "The old system was a perfect example of letting so-called market forces deal with the situation. We saw how well that worked over the last thirty years."

It's worth noting that Kildee does not live in Flint. He has a Flushing mailing address, although he clarified that he technically resides in Flint Township. He made the decision to leave the city proper when his children were old enough for middle school. He just didn't trust the Flint school system anymore. His kids went to Flushing High. I was trying not to hold this against him, because I sensed that Kildee and I shared the same intense loyalty to Flint. For all his evangelizing on behalf of right-size cities and the undeniable exuberance he exhibited when discussing urban-planning arcana, Kildee never wanted it to come to this. "I wish that thirty-five years ago some American city had gone through what Flint is going through, and they could have given us some advice to produce a different outcome," he told me.

We had been talking for two hours. Kildee acted like he was just warming up, but he was late for another appointment. When the energy-saving lights flicked off once again, it was a sure sign to wrap it up. I still wasn't completely sold on Kildee's ambitious plan, but it was a relief to know that someone was still out there trying to save Flint. I wanted to believe I was doing the same thing, in my own unlikely way.

The Naked Truth

As June stretched into July, I'm sure I came across as an increasingly unreliable narrator in my conversations with Traci. I often called her on my cheap pay-as-you-go cell phone while I sat in the shady backyard of my house in Carriage Town. A familiar pattern began to emerge. I would talk about how much I liked being in Flint before I launched into another mildly disturbing story about the city. There was the time I noticed the beautiful light cutting through the mist as I picked up the empty booze bottles left in the front yard one morning. I decided to grab my camera and take some pictures for the blog. I wandered a few blocks away and was standing between two abandoned houses, photographing a battered old garage and feeling like Walker Evans, when someone pulled open the tattered curtains in a broken ground floor window a few feet to my right.

"What are you doing, muthafucka?" yelled a man standing in the window.

He was angry. And naked. (Please note that this was not the same man who called me a muthafucka the day I arrived in Flint.)

I froze, realizing how ridiculous the truth would sound: through the magic of digital photography, I was trying to capture the unexpected splendor of Flint for a blog that I published from San Francisco. Before I could speak, Naked Man reached for something behind him in the darkened room. The last thing I saw before the curtains fluttered shut was his bare ass. Was he grabbing his pants or a gun? It didn't matter.

I sprinted home as fast as I could, just like when I was a kid in Flint and needed to escape a threatening situation. Who says you can't relive your childhood?

As I finished telling Traci about this odd encounter, I was pacing around the backyard and gesturing for emphasis, a habit I may have picked up from Dan Kildee. She managed a nervous laugh. "It's good that you're making new friends," she said. "If we buy a house, we'll have a built-in social network."

I tried to play it off like it was no big deal, but Flint was certainly confusing. Part of me wanted it to be a place where naked guys shouted obscenities from abandoned houses, an otherworldly arena that made me seem adventurous simply by being there. At the same time, I was constantly in search of reassuring signs of normalcy, indications that the city could be dull, safe, and predictable. I had come to accept that being in Flint forced me to constantly deal with mixed emotions.

The shrinking-city concept was a good example. I kept thinking about it as I traversed Flint, becoming increasingly familiar with its altered, emptied-out landscape. In the abstract, Kildee's plan made perfect sense. Flint was getting smaller all by itself, so it was only logical to manage the transition instead of letting it unfold in a random, unchecked manner. Though it was an ambitious undertaking, it was less daunting than figuring out a way to somehow rebuild Flint's economy in the midst of the Great Recession and repopulate the city.

So why was it so difficult to find local proponents of the plan? It was easier to scare up an Ohio State football fan in Flint than somebody who enthusiastically supported Kildee's vision for the city. Maybe the plan worked *too* well. The land bank controlled more than 10 percent of all parcels in the thirty-four-square-mile city, including 3,000 abandoned houses and more than 3,500 vacant lots. (The total number of abandoned parcels in Flint controlled by the city, private owners, and the land bank was close to 20,000.) The land bank often failed to board up and secure all of its far-flung holdings, let alone keep the yards mowed and the debris cleared. As a result, many land-bank houses looked very much like those owned by the speculators the agency was trying to combat. I repeatedly heard residents call Kildee "the biggest slumlord in Flint," even as he was being lauded by urban planners around the country.

Though the shrinking-city plan could be criticized for taking away the hopes and aspirations of Flint residents, it did give them a place to focus their anger about how this all came to pass. They couldn't exactly give an abstraction like "deindustrialization" or "globalization" a piece of their mind. Two other popular targets—GM and the UAW—were esoteric entities that had more of a historic than an actual presence in the city now. The much-maligned speculators were shadowy figures in LA or Chicago or who knows where. I spent weeks trying to track down the owner of a crumbling brick house near my temporary residence, eventually coming up with nothing more than a useless PO box in Atlanta and a disconnected phone. Then there were the well-meaning locals who let property slide because they were out of work and struggling to survive. There was little satisfaction in confronting someone who felt worse about the condition of a particular house than you did.

Enter the land bank—an easily accessible public entity with a high-profile leader who wasn't interested in bobbing and weaving to avoid criticism. Kildee took ownership of a vexing, seemingly unsolvable problem. He gave a frustrated, disillusioned populace a way to channel their rage over what had happened to their city. "I'm prouder of the work I've done around the land bank than anything else I've ever done," Kildee told me. "I've also made more people angry at me, disappointed in me, than ever before. I don't blame the residents for complaining, but popularity doesn't equal good policy."

Unsurprisingly, Kildee's approach was not warmly endorsed by the candidates for mayor. After all, admitting that some voters probably wouldn't get everything they wanted is hardly a popular strategy for winning elections. Brenda Clack took a generalist approach by maintaining that she would represent and support all Flint neighborhoods. No one would be left behind. Walling, with his extensive urban-planning background, took more precise aim, saying he wasn't even convinced Kildee's plan would save the city any money in the long run. "There are no hard numbers on estimated costs or estimated savings," he told me at a campaign stop. "It sounds more like a book-club discussion than a serious policy debate."

Over time, I discovered a deeper, more emotional element to the opposition. Even though Kildee's plan was a blueprint for Flint that sounded like it had a realistic chance of improving the city, it appealed more to the head than the heart. It might make economic sense to swap a worthless house on a decaying street for a nicer one in a better neighborhood, but it was not easy to walk away from all the memories built up over the years. Many residents loved their homes, no matter how undesirable they might appear to outsiders. The thought of walking away seemed wrong, like turning your back on an old friend. These houses were a lot more than mere financial investments. I was reminded of this one day as I wandered around the Saint Vincent de Paul thrift store, not far from my grandparents' old house. It was the same place that I bought my bat when I first arrived in Flint, and I was hoping to find a used lawn chair for the porch. I spotted a cheaply framed square of light blue cloth embroidered with a needlepoint saying: "A house is made of walls and beams. A home is built with love and dreams." Extremely corny, but true.

I remembered when the family tried to convince my grandmother, then in her late seventies and living alone after my grandfather's death, to move to Florida and live with my mom. My grandma came down to Jacksonville to stay for a few weeks, and it became clear that she had no intention of leaving 1515 Illinois Avenue, where she had lived for more than fifty years, for the balmy climate of the Sunshine State. We worried about her living on her own in the rapidly deteriorating East Side, but the alternative—somehow forcing her to leave the home she loved— seemed far worse. I imagined my grandma, in her homemade dresses and *Gilligan's Island*–style slip-on sneakers, when I thought about Dan Kildee trying to coax longtime residents into picking up and moving. She would have chased him out of her yard, with its lush green lawn and flowerbeds filled with tulips, with a broom—the same treatment door-to-door salesmen often got.

Kildee's approach was an equally tough sell with the city's African American residents. They tended to associate it with a series of failed urban-renewal projects in Flint during the fifties, sixties, and seventies that destroyed black neighborhoods, displaced residents, and provoked a racial mistrust that still lingers. Similar projects were launched in cities across the country with predictable results. I had written about one in Little Rock that wiped out the traditional black business district and replaced it with a highway. The Fillmore District in San Francisco has yet to fully recover from attempts to "save" it in the fifties and sixties. This pattern led critics to redub the programs "negro removal."

A large section of the black South Side, the area where my mom's friend Adrienne grew up, was all but obliterated by a massive highway interchange. When you look at a satellite map of the city, the huge clo- verleaf is one of the most distinctive geographic features of Flint, sur- passed only by the gray scar that was once the Buick factory complex.

But the worst example of Flint's urban-renewal failures was an ill-fated project in the Saint John neighborhood, described in depressing detail by historian Andrew Highsmith in "Demolition Means Progress."

It was once an integrated working-class neighborhood with a white majority. Between 1940 and 1950, the number of black households nearly tripled. This was around the time when my mother, then a teenager who played sax in the Central High band and palled around with a crowd of musicians, regularly hung out in Saint John, shopping at Cal's Record Mart and no doubt causing a lot of headaches for her parents, whom she suspects had never seen a black person while growing up in Iowa. She remembered going to an unlicensed bar, known as a "blind pig," in the early fifties to catch a performance by an obscure trumpet player by the name of Miles Davis.

By 1960, Saint John was 95 percent African American, the epicenter of black life and one of the poorest sections of the city. The sprawling Buick factory complex cast a gloomy shadow over the neighborhood's collection of ramshackle houses. "When sunlight did arrive over the towering multi-story plants, it had to pierce through dense clouds of soot and ash that emanated from Buick's smoke-belching foundry," Highsmith wrote. Saint John was also home to the city's largest rat population. It was a prime example of Flint's segregated housing policies and a flashpoint for growing racial conflict in the city.

In the sixties, the city proposed razing the entire neighborhood to create room for GM expansion, a section of the new Interstate 475 that would slice through Flint, and an industrial park that promised jobs and growth. Despite their skepticism, local chapters of the Urban League and the NAACP, along with numerous block clubs and many local residents, initially supported the plan, viewing it as an opportunity to obtain better housing, promote desegregation, and escape the grit and pollution of Saint John.

As the project progressed, it became clear that black residents wouldn't get much out of the deal. Highsmith revealed that most ended up in segregated public housing or rentals in predominantly black neighborhoods. Only a small number of the five hundred homeowners in Saint John could afford to buy elsewhere in Flint. The city realized few jobs and little long-term economic growth from the $130 million project. Highsmith blamed Interstate 475 and the destruction of Saint John for helping make "metropolitan Flint one of the most racially segregated, economically polarized, and spatially divided regions in the United States."

Today, the entire Buick complex has been torn down, creating one of the country's largest brownfields. Despite its location in the geographic heart of Flint, wild deer have been spotted on the land once claimed by the auto plant and the Saint John neighborhood.

Though Highsmith's work helped fill the gaps in my knowledge of Flint's racial history, it didn't touch on the shrinking-city plan. I decided to call Highsmith, who had gone on to become an assistant professor at the University of Texas at San Antonio, to talk about how race played into Kildee's approach.

Like any good historian, Highsmith was a skilled storyteller. He described traveling to Flint to give a series of lectures based on his research. One was at the Urban League office on a stormy, miserable day. He was expecting a sparse turnout, but fifty people showed up, many of them older African Americans who had lived in Saint John. "I gave this sort of wonkish talk about urban renewal, but the entire discussion afterwards was about the land bank," he said. "A lot of people view the shrinking-city plan as round 2 of urban renewal."

No wonder black residents were suspicious of a plan touted by a white elected official promising to relocate them to better, more vibrant neighborhoods. They'd heard that one before.

Near the end of the conversation, I mentioned my plan to buy a house in Flint. Highsmith laughed and said he'd beaten me to it. His wife had been in medical school at Michigan State, and she was assigned a rotation in Flint at the same time that he was working on his dissertation. Prices were amazingly low compared to Ann Arbor, where they had been living, so they bought a "great old house" in Mott Park for eighty thousand dollars in 2003. "It was so cheap," he said. "It seemed like a no-brainer."

When the couple finished school and got ready to relocate to Texas, they couldn't sell the house. It sat empty for two years. There were break-ins. The pipes were stolen, along with the air-conditioning unit. Highsmith and his wife made the necessary repairs and were finally able to rent it to a nice family that loves the place. They're considering just giving the house to them. "It's been kind of a saga," Highsmith said. "We never had these humanitarian goals when we bought the house, but now we just don't want it anymore. We're tired of worrying about it."

It was hard not to view the conversation as a personal warning. I was talking to a college professor who wrote extensively about Flint and owned a house in the city, a house that caused him no small amount of stress and regularly burdened his bank account. If I was looking for a real-world example of the flaws in my house-hunting plan, I had found it.

12

The Toughest Job in Politics

Dayne Walling, the leading candidate to become the next mayor of Flint, was a rarity: someone who grew up in the city, left for college and a career, then came back. I saw him as a person who was following through on a much more inspired variation of the hazy plan I was trying to put into place.

Like my mom, he attended Central High School. But while the beautiful brick building had been an educational showcase when she attended, Flint police and security guards with metal-detecting wands roamed the halls by the time Walling graduated in 1992. Central had closed for good shortly before I arrived in Flint that summer, a victim of budget cuts and falling enrollment.

Walling went on to Michigan State University, where he became the first Rhodes Scholar from Flint. He studied at Oxford and earned a master's degree in urban affairs from the University of London. He eventually made his way to Washington, joining the staff of Mayor Anthony Williams to be part of a large team that reprioritized citywide services after gathering input from residents on how to improve the nation's capital. Any process that changes how government money is spent is bound to be stressful, but Walling liked the idea of laying out a new blueprint for a city. "I wanted the toughest job in D.C. for a young white guy from the Midwest," he told me the first time I met him.

Walling moved on to Minneapolis when his wife began a PhD program there. He worked as a community organizer and completed the coursework for a doctorate of his own, studying community and economic development in midsize cities. But instead of writing his dissertation, he returned to Flint to take on the incumbent, Don Williamson, in 2007.

It was not the ideal race for a rookie candidate with wonkish tendencies who was coming home after a long absence. Walling, who has a lot of nervous energy and can come off as earnest but awkward on the campaign trail, went up against an outspoken politician fully at ease with himself. The controversial mayor used his own money to outspend Walling, unapologetically portraying him as a carpetbagger and drawing solid support from the city's majority African American population. Williamson won by 581 votes. "I couldn't keep pace with his attacks, and I wasn't well known enough," Walling said. "I may have the lead in this race, but after what happened against Williamson I wake up and run scared every day."

Walling had a predictable threefold plan to revitalize Flint's moribund economy. He wanted to build growth around the city's existing colleges and universities, especially the downtown University of Michigan campus; promote neighborhood businesses; and draw some manufacturing jobs back to the 1,500 empty acres once home to factories. Of course, these goals have been attached to every mayoral candidate in Flint for the past thirty years. They're easier said than done. But Walling described them with an exuberance that made it seem like he actually believed it was all possible.

There were moments, though, when Walling dropped the sunny optimism that is clearly his default mode. Like many Flintoids, myself included, there's an anger lurking somewhere in him—anger over what has happened to Flint. "It's my hometown, and no matter where I've lived I have a special place in my heart for this city," he said. "It's terrible to see this kind of suffering inflicted on a community. It's wrong. It shouldn't happen anywhere in this country."

Walling had opened a strategically placed satellite campaign office on Welch Boulevard in a strip of worn storefronts, just up the street from Lovely Nails and Assetou African Hair Braiding, in a space once occupied by a drugstore where I used to buy candy. It's not far from my childhood home, meaning it's an ideal location to court black voters.

With a newly installed "Working for Change" sign out front, Walling held an open house on a Saturday afternoon, complete with veggies, onion dip, and fried chicken. It was a chance for him to meet voters and showcase three high-profile endorsements from African Americans, including an opponent who pulled in 11 percent of the primary vote and a former deputy sheriff. But Vera Rison—a local politician who served as a county commissioner and state legislator—was clearly the guest of honor. "Auntie Vera," nearly blind at seventy and wearing a sharp blue blazer and stylish pink shoes, snacked on a plate of peanuts while holding court at a table near the front of the room. "I do feel in my heart that Dayne Walling will commit himself to the city," Rison told me near the end of the event. "I want a new direction for Flint. That's what it's about, sweetheart. Thank you."

Our chat apparently over, a friend took Rison's hand and guided her slowly outside to a pearl-colored Cadillac parked in front. Walling tagged along, giving Auntie Vera a tentative hug and kiss on the cheek before she settled into the passenger seat for the ride home. He stood on the sidewalk as the Caddy pulled away, exhaled loudly as he briefly surveyed the street, then headed back inside for more campaigning.

When I caught up with Brenda Clack, she was not impressed by Walling's endorsements and brushed off the lopsided primary results. "My record shows I've endeavored to help all the people of this community—not just some of them—and they'll remember that," she said, clearly getting annoyed with the notion that she couldn't win this race. "They'll be there for me."

But just twenty supporters showed up at a banquet room on North Saginaw Street when Clack sponsored a Juneteenth celebration commemorating the end of slavery in America. Her husband, Floyd, a former state legislator who lost the mayor's race to Williamson in 2003, was working the room along with his wife. I was the only white attendee and the only member of the press. With my newfound knowledge of race in Flint, I felt especially out of place, and I probably smiled too much in an attempt to convey that I was a friendly, good-natured guy. A former student of Clack's who was now a reverend at a church south of Detroit delivered the invocation. "Although we are small in number, we are big in spirit," he proclaimed, drawing amens from the audience.

After a poetry reading and a performance by Dance Ministry—three teenage girls from the Grace Emmanuel Baptist Church wearing matching black skirts and purple shirts—everyone lined up at a buffet table for hamburgers and fruit salad. Over lunch, the reverend sat next to me and did a little campaigning. "Miss Clack understands financing and budgets," he told me. "She can motivate people. She got me to work in high school, so you know she's good. She'll be able to bring the city council and the mayor's office together."

He paused before adding, "You know it's going to take Dayne Walling the entire term to figure out how government really works."

A local singer who performs under the stage name DeVynne and had once opened for the Emotions wrapped up the entertainment with an impressive rendition of "That's What Friends Are For." It included a heartfelt spoken-word interlude: "Be sure to vote for Brenda Clack because she'll always be there for you." It was probably the first time Burt Bacharach and Dionne Warwick, albeit unknowingly, were enlisted in a Flint mayoral campaign. The small crowd clapped loudly and Clack teared up, dabbing her eyes with a napkin. "The Lord has something in mind for me," she told the audience, hugging her six-year-old granddaughter as she spoke. "This race will be won by people who believe, so I know I'm going to win this race."

My first chance to see both candidates together came on a gloomy afternoon at the Landmark Food Center, the kind of grocery store in the North End where a security guard patrols the fluorescent-lit aisles and customers are required to check their bags at the counter. Flanked by stacks of Star Trek–themed Apple Jacks, Fruit Loops, and Frosted Flakes—a "Trek-Takular" value at just $4.99—Walling and Clack were judging a Kool-Aid-making contest sponsored by three local churches.

The mixologists tried mightily to influence their decision. "Taste number 4 and taste no more!" one contestant yelled out, prompting a round of cheering from two dozen spectators gathered around a pair of tables covered with neon-green tablecloths and littered with plastic pitchers, spent Kool-Aid packs, and sacks of sugar. "Number 5 tells no lies!" countered another contestant. Momentarily joining forces, Walling and Clack sipped from Styrofoam cups and huddled over a score sheet.

A fifty-one-year-old former GM worker named Terese, wearing a tidy skirt and flower-patterned top, was the exuberant winner of one hundred dollars and a trophy, which she proudly held aloft. I was standing next to the only person in a jacket and tie during the victory celebration. It turned out to be the store owner. "This is a great event," he said. "I've been here in the community thirty-four years."

I asked if he lived nearby, trying to get a gauge on Flint's rapidly changing demographics. "Well, I actually live in Grand Blanc," he said with a tight smile, referring to the unfortunately named suburban enclave that has been a popular destination for the white residents who have left Flint in droves over the years.

A few feet away, Clack put her arm around a contestant who didn't finish in the money. A hundred bucks went a long way in Flint, so this wasn't just fun and games. After more than three decades as a teacher, Clack knew how to read a crowd and how to console. "You did a nice job, young man," she said to a guy who could have been in his midtwenties, maybe older. "You can be proud of yourself." Nearby, surrounded by his wife and two young sons outfitted in black campaign T-shirts, Walling was invigorated by the contest. Looking tall and a little gangly, he surveyed the crowd. "That was fun!" he said to no one in particular, perhaps a bit too enthusiastically.

I worried that Walling, a model UN geek who once lost a race for student government president at Central High, might face a steep learning curve if he won, enduring a crash course in reality far removed from the graduate seminars where he studied urban planning. And I fretted that Clack, with her deep connection to Flint politics, might find it difficult to make the tough decisions, to say no to her various constituencies for the good of the city. But the air-conditioned camaraderie on a muggy summer day made me feel optimistic about Flint. Walling and Clack were two competent candidates for a job that most people wouldn't want. Either one would be an improvement over recent years. And either one could help nudge Flint toward a better future.

Or maybe I just drank too much of the Kool-Aid.

On election night in early August, Dayne Walling walked into UAW Local 599 to the schmaltzy strains of "Nothing's Gonna Stop Us Now" by Jefferson Airplane and declared victory well before midnight. "Tonight we celebrate; tomorrow we go to work," the newly elected mayor told a throng of supporters in a raspy voice. "We won because we decided to turn to each other and not against each other."

A few miles away, standing next to her husband and surrounded by blue and white balloons, a vanquished Brenda Clack wasn't quite so magnanimous at her election-night party. "The only difference between my campaign and my opponent's is that one was telling the truth and one was not," she told her supporters, sounding more strident in her concession speech than she had on the campaign trail. She eventually conceded and wished Walling well, but in an interview with a local reporter she chided Flint's black residents. "I think we, as African Americans, sometimes don't support our own, and you have to do that," she said. "Even though as the mayor you work for all the people, which is so very important, there are instances where, because African Americans have been denied access to political positions, many political positions for so long, that we're still afraid to actually venture out and support another black [person]."

Clack was accurate in pointing out that Walling had cut into what she considered her natural constituency. In winning 64 percent of the vote, he managed to take five predominantly black precincts, even though the Genesee County Democratic Black Caucus and several influential black pastors endorsed Clack. Though the numbers showed that race was not the dominant factor in the election, Clack's comments implying that black voters should vote for black candidates showed that there was still a strong racial subtext to Flint politics, regardless of how many other things had changed in the city.

Walling wouldn't get to celebrate his landslide victory for long. He inherited a city budget that was already in place, but it was based on overly optimistic revenue projections. Worse, the state of Michigan, reeling from the Great Recession, had recently announced cuts in the money it shared with local municipalities. As a result, the city was facing an estimated $18 million deficit. Flint was not alone. The total budget deficit of American cities adds up to more than $14 billion a year, but having company didn't make Walling's task any easier. He would have to slash Flint's already meager budget, and that meant gaining concessions from the police, fire, and public employee unions, whose contracts had recently expired. He was about to discover that getting elected mayor was a lot easier than *being* mayor. There would be no honeymoon while he settled into his first elected office.

13

Urban Homesteaders

I was becoming more and more at home in Carriage Town. It was where I was staying, after all, the place where I was bridging past and present. I soon realized that my initial fears, prompting the desire to carry my bat at all times, were based more on the neighborhood's circumstances in 1989 than 2009. Rich, my friend from San Francisco, had been singing its praises from the start with the fervor of a real-estate agent who genuinely loved Flint but also had a financial incentive in the form of three Carriage Town houses he was trying to rehab and rent. I saw various neighbors on a daily basis, working in their yards or going for runs around the neighborhood. (News flash: people jog in Flint without a sidearm!) I began each morning at the Good Beans Cafe, a coffeehouse that had been the primary gathering spot for locals since a middle-aged guy who owned two houses nearby opened it in 2000. I liked the sound of the semipro football announcers on the PA system from nearby Atwood Stadium, where I used to play soccer, echoing throughout the tree-lined streets on weekends. (Who needs the Forty-Niners when you can watch the Flint Fury?) It was also one of the neighborhoods that would be growing, not shrinking, under Dan Kildee's plan. There were several land-bank rehab projects already in the works. It was the epicenter of the shrinking-city movement.

For all my talk about escaping the pretensions of San Francisco, Carriage Town offered a little of the look and feel of my West Coast home. I emailed Traci photos of restored Victorians that she said reminded her of the Haight-Ashbury neighborhood. Good Beans had the do-it-yourself feel of our favorite neighborhood coffee shop. And the sense that Carriage Town could actually improve, that the residents were making progress, was rare in Flint but commonplace in San Francisco.

It was also reassuring to know that the true urban homesteaders had already done some of the heavy lifting before I arrived. Carriage Town was just gritty enough to make you feel like you were being edgy without taking your life in your hands every time you left the house. This was reinforced when I talked to a neighbor named Erin, a blonde thirty-one-year-old horticulturalist who leased a blue two-story house with pink and purple trim that I could see from my porch. It was owned by a guy who worked at the land bank. Erin shared the place with three housemates, and her rent and utilities worked out to just three hundred dollars a month. They had a back deck and a yard with an apricot tree, raspberries growing along the fence, and a vegetable garden. "I've got a little urban homestead going on," she told me.

Erin had grown up in Burton, graduated from Michigan State University, and was working as an outreach program coordinator for the Ruth Mott Foundation, promoting urban gardening and local beautification efforts. (It seemed like everyone I met in Carriage Town, aside from the owner of Good Beans, worked for a nonprofit, some type of government entity, or a college.) A lot of her work centered on the downtown area, and she thought it was important to be fully immersed in the community. That's one of the primary reasons she was hoping to buy a house nearby. She didn't want to spent more than fifty thousand dollars, including renovation expenses. "I love old houses," she explained one day. "I want the character and the history you can't get from a new, cookie-cutter house."

Friends and relatives from the suburbs had expressed concern about a single woman living in Flint, but she had curtly dismissed their worries. "Downtown Flint is safer than Grand Blanc," she said emphatically. But she had one reservation that surprised me, one I had never heard from anyone else in Flint, given its dizzying array of urban ailments. She worried that Carriage Town would become too gentrified. "I don't want to live in an area that's like a suburb," she said. "I don't want Carriage Town to become the hip neighborhood. I like it the way it is now. It still has a few crazy people left in it."

Coming from San Francisco, where gentrification swept through neighborhoods faster than hipster trends like fixies, tattoos, and retro eighties wardrobes, I didn't think Erin had anything to worry about. It was not uncommon in my Bernal Heights neighborhood for buyers to shell out $700,000 for a decent 1,200-square-foot house, then immediately gut the interior and build an addition before moving in. The sound of nail guns and table saws was ever-present, and contractors clogged the coffee shops every morning. With money like that flowing through a neighborhood, the wine bars, Audis, and art galleries soon followed. That was real gentrification, complete with rising rents and a tide of bland white middle-class culture. The tenuous renewal of Carriage Town was glacial by comparison. But the fact that Erin even considered this a legitimate concern was strangely heartening; it meant Carriage Town was building some sort of momentum. And her confident plans to buy a house reassured me that I wasn't alone. (Let's set aside the obvious fact that Erin lived in Flint, already had a job, and enjoyed a much bigger budget to work with, while I wasn't even exactly sure what I'd do with my Flint house. No need to complicate my thinking and challenge my resolve with petty details.)

I got more inspiration when I interviewed David White, an archivist at Kettering University who possessed the calm, seen-it-all demeanor and quiet resolve of a true urban homesteader who was in it for the long haul. He and his former partner, Nick Hoffman, were considered the founding fathers of the Carriage Town revival. Although David had since moved to the nearby Grand Traverse neighborhood on the other side of downtown, he still owned a house in Carriage Town and had an endless arsenal of stories, including a highly personal tale about the Nash House, where I was sleeping on the floor. It was the first house he and Nick had bought back in 1983. He quickly established, with a roll of his eyes, that they had not painted the house pink. That was the work of the couple who later bought the house. By the early eighties, the neighborhood had fully devolved from the thriving carriage manufacturing hub it was at the turn of the century into a decaying collection of historic homes chopped up into apartments and rooming houses, along with a handful of ramshackle abandoned buildings. It had the highest crime rate in a city consistently ranked among the most dangerous in the United States. Statistically speaking, it was a great place to get robbed, beaten, or murdered. Perhaps the best place in the country to suffer such a fate.

David and Nick got a bird's-eye view of their new environment when yelling woke them up in the middle of the night shortly after they moved into the battered Queen Anne–style home they planned to restore. They peered out the upstairs bedroom window and watched several men hustle the manager of a nearby apartment building through the darkened street. "They were literally dragging him along by his necktie," David told me. "They stuffed him into the trunk of a car and roared off around the corner. We had no idea what to do. We didn't even have phone service yet. I remember thinking, 'What have we gotten ourselves into?'"

As he told me the story, I realized that this happened when I was a junior in high school and regularly going to the Copa, the bar just a few blocks away in downtown. I very well could have been dancing to the Thompson Twins, drinking whiskey sours, and fretting about my curfew, blissfully unaware of the drama that was unfolding nearby. Of course, I was unaware of most things happening around me at that point in my life. I was a teenager.

When the manager reappeared in the neighborhood the next day, freed from the trunk but with his arm in a sling, David drew on the ample reserve of optimism demanded of anyone trying to improve Flint at the time: "Well, at least he didn't die," he thought. The couple later learned that the manager had been stealing welfare checks from his tenants, which led to the late-night vigilante justice. The incident made David and Nick realize they needed to save more than just their house. "All of a sudden we became community activists," David said. "We had a lot to fight—the prostitutes, the drug dealers, the petty thieves, and the slumlords." The couple helped create a neighborhood association, organized massive yearly cleanups, and eventually rehabbed several homes.

With David and Nick leading the charge before they broke up, Carriage Town continued to improve in fits and starts over the years. Dozens of Victorian-era houses and buildings were restored, and home ownership had increased in the past decade, a miracle in Flint. I learned that in the midst of a worldwide recession, development projects brokered by Dan Kildee and the land bank worth more than $47 million in public and private financing were in progress or recently completed. There were even plans for a neighborhood grocery store.

But Carriage Town was still a work in progress, and anyone who called it home had to deal with numerous hassles, including absentee landlords, abandoned houses, and lack of code enforcement by the city. Residents had lobbied unsuccessfully for years to have the city shut down the drug house that was in full swing across the street from Good Beans and the house where my neighbors Nathan and Rebecca lived. (Nathan told me one day that if you looked up the house on Google street view, you could see an alleged deal in progress.) Though Carriage

Town was racially and economically diverse, nearly all the homeowners were white, with African Americans occupying the rental units. Many structures had been lost to demolition or fire, and empty houses with wild, overgrown yards still sat beside pristinely restored homes. There was certainly no guarantee that Carriage Town would continue on its upward trajectory. Despite the optimism of the residents, there was also an undercurrent of uncertainty that emerged in conversations. "I'm excited about all the new projects, but I'm also a little wary," the owner of Good Beans admitted one morning as the café filled with customers. "I can't help wondering if it will all last. In the same breath, I want Carriage Town to succeed more than anybody."

The urban pioneers of Carriage Town had good reason to be cautious. Flint's past redevelopment projects, all spectacular failures, are the stuff of legend. Yet they have also proved that even colossally bad ideas can have an unexpected silver lining. Take AutoWorld—famously skewered by Michael Moore in *Roger & Me*—which closed soon after it opened in 1984. This multimillion-dollar dud, an unsatisfying hybrid that was neither amusement park nor auto museum, was the linchpin of Flint's desperate plan to replace auto manufacturing with tourism. It has since been demolished, but it played an unexpected role in spurring Carriage Town's revival. Anticipating that the neighborhood could become a quaint tourist attraction, the city helped restore Water Street, which had some dilapidated carriage factories and the crumbling brick building where GM was born, the place where Billy Durant worked much of his chaotic magic. It was now the handsome, well-preserved U.S. National Historic Landmark across the street from my house. There were obviously cheaper and less roundabout ways to achieve this modest accomplishment, but for a city that often felt cursed, this bit of inadvertent foresight was certainly welcome.

The old Hyatt Regency Hotel, located nearby on the banks of the Flint River, was constructed to provide upscale lodging and fine dining for all the tourists who never arrived. It was eventually sold off to a quasi-religious self-help outfit called the Institute in Basic Life Principles and rechristened the Character Inn. Inexplicably, a pair of huge, taxidermied brown bears were installed in the lobby, two lonely, misplaced sentries in a sea of red pile carpeting, who were nonetheless more intriguing than AutoWorld had ever been. But now the building was being transformed into housing aimed at local college students. (Alas, I couldn't come up with any information on the fate of the bears.)

Then there was the failed restaurant and retail emporium across the street from the Hyatt, confusingly named Water Street Pavilion, even though it was located on Saginaw Street. It was now University Pavilion, home to various UM offices, a food court where hungry people actually ate, and a bookstore where customers often bought things with real money, which were not small accomplishments in downtown Flint.

The focus on students was no accident. While Dan Kildee's shrinking-city model was moving forward despite vocal criticism from some residents and elected officials, there was stronger support for rebranding Flint as a college town.

It was a tough sell. It naturally invited comparisons with nearby Ann Arbor—the quintessential college town—and the city's amateurish attempts at promoting the idea via Facebook and YouTube probably left some potential students laughing. Though the marketing needed improvement, local community and career colleges did have more than 25,000 students. The downtown University of Michigan–Flint campus had seen record growth, with enrollment climbing to more than 7,000 with a goal of 10,000 students. The first dorm on campus had opened the previous fall. The city was pumping money into what was now called University Avenue—formerly Third Avenue—which connected UM-Flint with nearby Kettering University and its 2,600 students. Carriage Town was situated in the midst of all this activity, just across the river from downtown and the UM campus, about a mile from Mott Community College with its 12,000 commuter students, and ten blocks from Kettering.

But the biggest boon to Carriage Town in recent years had been the restoration of the Berridge Hotel in 2008, another reminder that Kildee's plans involved more than simply tearing down abandoned buildings. When its ninety-nine rooms were renting for nineteen dollars a night, the Berridge was well known as a haven for people plying the drug and sex trades, as well as providing housing of last resort for some of Flint's poorest citizens, including recent parolees, who were often dumped at the hotel's entrance. "The residents basically had the private-sector equivalent of a jail cell," Kildee told me one afternoon during a brief tour of the building. "They didn't have a bathroom, they didn't have a sink, and they didn't have a kitchen. It was a living situation that forced them out onto the street and into the neighborhood on a daily basis. It wasn't good for the residents, and it wasn't good for Carriage Town."

Kildee had managed to cobble together $6.2 million from eighteen financing sources—including county bonds—to transform the Berridge into seventeen apartments, almost all now rented, and to renovate the Tinlin House, an American Foursquare–style four-unit apartment building next door. He believed this success had encouraged other development projects, such as the nearby Durant Hotel, a majestic building shuttered since the seventies that was being converted to housing aimed at students and young professionals by the land bank and a collection of public and private investors. It also encouraged Nick to open Hoffman's Deco Deli and Café, a hopping lunch spot located across the street from the Berridge in the same refurbished warehouse as the antique store he had run for several years. "The new Berridge is a monumental change," Nick told me while I waited in line at the deli to buy a sandwich and a smoothie one day. The place was filled with college kids, office workers, and a few cops.

But the notion that Carriage Town could transform itself into a vibrant, fully functioning neighborhood really took hold when I was standing in the music room of a house Michael Freeman and Perry Compton were restoring just a couple of blocks from my place. Eva, their Doberman, who is slightly less menacing because her floppy ears haven't been clipped, was also with us, eyeing me suspiciously. One wall was dominated by a fireplace mantel from the 1790s, originally salvaged from a London hotel and repainted white after Perry painstakingly removed years of accumulated paint using dental tools. Stacks of vintage vinyl records took up space on the polished hardwood floors near an antique gramophone in a corner. A compact square grand piano, which Michael admitted looks better than it sounds, was situated beneath an ornately framed stained-glass window. The room was painted the imperial yellow of the Habsburgs' Schönbrunn Palace, a tribute to the year Michael spent as an exchange student in Vienna. "It's probably a little too garish for the Victorian era, but it reminds me of Europe," he said. "I loved it there."

Of all the unexpected things I encountered in Flint, this room just might be the most surprising. I knew that houses were being brought back to life in Carriage Town, but I didn't anticipate decorating schemes with links to European royalty. Everyone I'd talked to in the neighborhood had told me I should meet Michael and Perry and check out their house. Now I understood why. I thought of the nails popping out of the drywall and the dark stains accenting the creaky wood floors of the house Traci and I shared in San Francisco. I tried to take consolation in reminding myself that our lot alone was probably worth ten times what Michael and Perry could get for their place, but it didn't help.

Of course, it hadn't been easy getting the house to its present state. Michael was a twenty-four-year-old AmeriCorps volunteer, and Perry had a degree from the Fashion Institute of Design and Merchandising in Los Angeles when they bought the battle-scarred, 3,850-square-foot Italianate home with some Carpenter Gothic flourishes in 1994. They had both grown up in the Flint area, loved the architecture, and appreciated the fact that the house was just a block from the site of an old dairy once run by Michael's family. Aggressive lobbying from the pied pipers of Carriage Town also helped. "David and Nick were very persuasive in convincing new people to buy in the neighborhood," Michael said. "They laid the groundwork for everything that's happening now."

Oh, and then there was the price: $25,000.

"We signed a purchase agreement two weeks after we spotted it," Michael told me as we walked through the house. "Fortunately, I was young and stupid. There's been some agony, but that's what wine is for, right?"

The original twelve-room house—built by a transplanted New York businessman in 1872—had been chopped up into five apartments. Michael and Perry had lived in one unit and rented out the rest to cover the mortgage, restoring parts of the home as tenants moved out. A studio unit on the first floor had been home to a prostitute named Marjorie; customers continued to stop by in search of her services for months after she left. The burned-out remnants of Third Avenue Fish and Chips, a popular restaurant where my family frequently ate on Fridays during Lent, was next door. The alley between the two properties continued to be popular with hookers and junkies until the building was demolished and the couple was able to purchase the land to create a side yard. They salvaged twelve Pyrex place settings from the old restaurant, which they ate off of daily.

Slowly but surely, they went to work on the house. They stripped damaged walls down to the lathe, ripped out multiple layers of linoleum and old carpet, removed cheap drop ceilings to reveal the eleven-foot ceilings throughout the house, discovered beautiful wood pocket doors hidden behind walls, and removed an aftermarket enclosed front porch that "looked like someone had parked a mobile home next to the house," according to Michael. Armed with bleach and rubber goggles, they spent nearly five hours cleaning a single bathroom so they could use it. They filled dumpster after dumpster with debris. "The house was basically one big piece of nasty," Perry said.

They connected with an aging third-generation plasterer who taught Perry the trade while he worked on the house with an oxygen tank by his side, a necessity after decades of inhaling plaster dust. "My father died on the scaffolding and that's where I'll die, too," he told them. Perry, who also attended culinary school, discovered that applying plaster was a lot like putting frosting on a cake. Michael and Perry became experts in everything from faux finishes to boiler repair.

After $100,000 worth of restoration, the house features a sweeping staircase, elaborate plaster work, and personal touches like a wooden pulpit bought on the side of the road in Flint for fifty dollars. (It's great for parties, when guests can get up and preach after a couple of drinks.) The large yard is so lush that Michael returned home one evening to find a deer nibbling at his lilac bushes. They figured it would take another $100,000 to get the place where they wanted it, including the solarium they hoped to build off the back of the house. So there was still a lot of work to be done, but the worst was over.

The house was appraised at $144,000 in 2007, which is great for getting home-improvement loans but doesn't mean much in the actual Flint market. Who, after all, would pay that much for a house in Carriage Town? But it didn't matter. Michael and Perry weren't going anywhere. Michael was a senior program officer at the local office of a national nonprofit that helps residents transform distressed neighborhoods and had financed various Carriage Town projects. Perry worked at a care facility for schizophrenic men. They were happy to finally enjoy Carriage Town's upward trajectory after years of effort. "The neighborhood is so radically different now," Michael said. "I have to laugh when I hear the things some of the newcomers complain about. They don't realize what it used to be like."

Standing with Michael and Perry in their music room, surrounded by the results of all their hard work, I began to feel like my housing search was finally getting somewhere.

After weeks of touring the city, I had a good sense of the local real-estate market, which wasn't a functioning market in any normal sense, given that it was almost all supply and little demand. Lavish homes that would cost millions in San Francisco could be had for $100,000 in the Vehicle City. I had experienced the guilty pleasure of wandering through the empty bedrooms and cleared-out kitchens of houses I had longed to live in while growing up. The homes my mom couldn't afford and my grandparents would have considered ostentatious and impractical. Rich people's houses.

But even at their dramatically reduced Rust Belt prices, Traci and I weren't in the market for those enormous homes. And I'd already determined that the cheap eBay houses that popped up in national media stories were often nothing more than shells in the most dangerous, depopulated neighborhoods, disposable entities owned by speculators. My three-thousand-dollar budget might get me a generic but livable house on the periphery of the better Flint neighborhoods, those lonely transition zones that were still in the process of tilting from bad to worse, but what would be the point? I didn't think our presence would do anything to help those places. Besides, they held no emotional appeal for me. It would be hard enough bonding with my hometown after all these years, but starting over in a neighborhood that held no memories, no tangible link to the old Flint, seemed like a lonely and pointless endeavor. Over the past few weeks, I had begun to feel the anxiety that had been a regular feature of my San Francisco house hunt—the fear of dwindling options.

Now I was thinking that Carriage Town might be the most logical place to put my illogical plan into action. A house like Michael and Perry's was too big and too pricey, but I'd passed numerous modest wood homes in various states of decay on my neighborhood walks, many of them clearly abandoned for years. How much could they possibly cost? And it had to be cheaper to rehab a house in Flint, a city with massive unemployment, than in San Francisco, where it would cost six thousand to ten thousand dollars just to replace our tiny roof. Plus, Traci and I would be surrounded by neighborhood experts like Michael and Perry. We could tap into a community of people who had already done what we wanted to do, a built-in collection of consultants who happened to like having parties and celebrating their progress with a drink or two. If Traci and I dipped into our meager retirement savings, we could bump our budget up to a whopping five thousand dollars. I blurted all this out to Michael and Perry.

"I'd be happy to help you scout out houses," Michael said without hesitation.

"I can teach you how to plaster," Perry added, as if the whole thing was no big deal.

Even Eva seemed enthused, wagging her tail and glancing from Michael to Perry to me. She no longer seemed to be biding her time until she could attack. I felt like part of the gang.

There was one small problem. My summer in Flint was nearly over. I really missed Traci. I was running short of money. I longed to sleep in a real bed instead of a sleeping bag. I needed to write up my freelance stories, prep for the upcoming academic year at the university, and drywall the kitchen. (I also had to actually learn how to drywall since I'd never done it before.) It was clearly time to go. My return to Flint hadn't exactly gone according to plan. I had failed to buy a house. But I was optimistic. I could hunt for Carriage Town properties from San Francisco until I made it back to Flint. This could still work.

FIGURE 1. I attempt to enliven a family photo of my mom, my grandparents, and my older brother in front of our Civic Park home on the day my brother graduated from high school in June of 1972.

FIGURE 2. The vacant pink house in Carriage Town where I slept on the floor during the summer of 2009 was once owned by Charles W. Nash, an indentured servant who rose to become president of General Motors. (Photo by Fred R. Conrad/The New York Times)

FIGURE 3. Dan Kildee, the pied piper of the shrinking-city movement, wants Flint and other troubled urban areas across the country to accept the reality of decline and negative growth. (Photo by Gordon Young)

FIGURE 4. Another abandoned house that fell victim to arson on Jane Avenue in Flint's devastated East Side. Only a single residence remains on a block once filled with small homes built primarily for autoworkers and their families. (Photo by Gordon Young)

FIGURE 5. On a muggy summer day in 2009, candidates Dayne Walling and Brenda Clack momentarily join forces to judge a Kool-Aid-making contest during their battle to become the next mayor of Flint. (Photo by Gordon Young)

FIGURE 6. In 1954, more than a hundred thousand people crowded downtown Flint for a parade celebrating the fifty-millionth car produced by General Motors. A "milestone car"—a gold-colored Chevy with gold-plated parts—rolled off the assembly line to mark the occasion. (Photo courtesy of the *Flint Journal*)

FIGURE 7. The Art Deco splendor of the Mott Foundation Building is countered by the bland modernism of the abandoned Genesee Towers, the city's tallest building, as snow falls on downtown Flint in December of 2010. (Photo by Gordon Young)

Buick Motor Division—spanning an area over 300 acres and utilizing over 7,500,000 sq. ft. of floor space. This huge factory includes Car Assembly, Transmission, Sheet Metal, Drop Forge, Motor, Axle, Gray Iron Foundry, Engineering, Past Model Parts, Service Parts, and Shipping Plants.

FIGURE 8. A postcard exalts "Buick's Busy Acres," the massive factory complex with more than 7,500,000 square feet of floor space that helped Flint achieve one of the highest per capita income levels in the world. The ill-fated Saint John neighborhood is visible in the top right-hand corner.

FIGURE 9. A dead deer sprawls in front of an entrance to the demolished Buick factory complex, now one of the nation's largest brownfields, located in the heart of Flint. (Photo by Gerry Godin/All Things Buick)

FIGURE 10. Michael Freeman (left) and Perry Compton, along with
their dog, Eva, in the twelve-room Victorian that the couple purchased
in 1994 for $25,000. The house, built by a transplanted New York
businessman in 1872, had been chopped up into five apartments.
(Photo by Fred R. Conrad/The New York Times)

FIGURE 11. The entryway of Michael and Perry's Carriage Town home with its sweeping staircase and elaborate plasterwork. They estimate that they have spent more than $100,000 renovating the house. (Photo by Fred R. Conrad/The New York Times)

FIGURE 12. Dave and Judy Starr in the living room of their two-story Civic Park house, which is now worth less than the $14,500 they paid for it in 1968. "We're not going anywhere," Judy said. "This is our home." (Photo by Gordon Young)

FIGURE 13. Pastor Sherman McCathern at the altar of Joy Tabernacle Church in Civic Park, where he leads a congregation beset by crime, unemployment, and heartache. "I told God that if I can't help these people create jobs and opportunity, I can't stay here and just preach to people and get them all dressed up with no place to go," he said. "And that's what I believe God has promised me." (Photo by Gordon Young)

FIGURE 14. Throughout the city, abandoned houses like this one in Civic Park are ravaged by thieves known as scrappers in search of any metal they can resell—doorknobs, radiators, aluminum siding, but especially copper wiring and plumbing. (Photo by Gordon Young)

FIGURE 15. P-Nut (left) and Aaron (right) with me after a day spent painting P-Nut's new home in Civic Park, just a few blocks from the house where I grew up. (Photo by Sherman McCathern)

PART TWO

Quitters Never Win

Traci and I decided to celebrate my homecoming at the Peruvian restaurant two blocks from our house the night I flew back to San Francisco from Flint. It felt like I'd been gone a few years, and we were happy to be together again. It was an unusually warm evening without a trace of the typical late summer fog or wind to torment us. The streets were filled with healthy-looking Californians enjoying the weather as they strolled around in their straw fedoras, the latest ubiquitous fashion trend. Everyone seemed relaxed and carefree. We ate crab cakes and drank sangria at eight dollars a glass.

Traci had just started a new job at an architecture firm in Berkeley, even though it included low-level clerical duties at the reception desk, one of the indignities of starting a new career in the midst of the Great Recession. "I have to get someone to cover the phones if I want to go to the bathroom," she said.

"You're indispensable," I told her. "They can't function when you attend to your bodily functions."

She was also part of the marketing team that put together proposals for public buildings like libraries and recycling centers. She had a hand in drumming up the contracts that kept the firm in business. She took satisfaction in knowing that this work had visible results and was happy to be freed from the frustrating process of endlessly pitching freelance stories to cash-strapped editors. It was also a relief to have a steady paycheck and benefits. She figured she wouldn't be the part-time receptionist forever. This was a job that could lead to something better.

By the time dinner was over, we had made some decisions about Flint. I had been well aware of the city's dismal economic situation in the abstract, but now I'd seen it up close. I had a full understanding of how difficult it would be for us to find meaningful employment in the Vehicle City. Outside of the rare jobs that opened up at the Mott Foundation and a collection of local nonprofits, it was hard to imagine where we'd work. Competition was fierce for full-time teaching jobs at UM-Flint and Mott Community College. The city and county were letting workers go, not hiring them. We weren't the type to start a small business, especially in a city where businesses of any kind were an endangered species.

Though I sometimes complained that it wasn't as exciting as being a full-time journalist, it would have been foolish to give up my current job at the university. I had fun working with the staff at the school paper, teaching students how to write anecdotal leads in the classroom, and thinking deep thoughts about the future of journalism, even though no one really had a clue about where my chosen profession was headed. Besides, my teaching job gave me the time and just enough money to keep writing stories about places like Flint, to actually be a journalist instead of just a journalism professor. This is hardly a brilliant observation, but a summer in Flint had given me a new appreciation for my life in San Francisco.

It was clear that full-time residency in Flint was no longer a valid option for us. I had run into a litany of financial and emotional roadblocks during the summer, but they all boiled down to a fairly simple realization: the houses I could afford were too depressing or too dangerous to live in, and the houses that wouldn't require a Zoloft prescription and a shotgun were too expensive. I told Traci that there still might be a chance to somehow buy a little vacation house in Carriage Town, or a rental unit with a small studio that we could use for visits. I'd try to keep house hunting from afar, but it all seemed very improbable now that I was back in San Francisco, relaxing in a softly lit restaurant with candles on the tables and the sound of happy conversations humming around us. As much as my return to Flint had meant to me, I was glad to be home and looking forward to getting back to my old life.

I met up with Rich, the real-estate agent who inspired my quest for a Flint house, a week later for beers at the Latin American Club, where piñatas dangled from the ceiling and giant paintings of Chihuahuas looked down on us from the back wall. We hadn't talked much while I was gone, and he was eager to hear my take on the summer I'd spent in Flint, get a rundown on his pink house where I'd stayed, and catch up on a little local gossip. He was as upbeat as ever, but the exuberance I'd felt the previous spring while sitting in the same bar with him had disappeared. I told him I was just about ready to give up.

"Well, no one said it was going to be easy," he countered. "It's going to take a little sacrifice."

"That's easy for you to say," I responded. "You've actually got the money to pull off something like this."

"Well, not exactly," he said.

Over the next few hours, I learned that I'd made a lot of a assumptions about Rich in the short time I'd known him. He wasn't the well-off San Francisco real-estate agent I'd pegged him to be. He didn't own property in the city. He didn't even own a car. He rented a small apartment, and with the local market in the tank he wasn't selling a lot of expensive houses or high-priced condos.

His hold on the three Flint houses he owned was more tenuous than I'd imagined. He had bought the Nash House in 2005 for a whopping $72,000 with the same sort of no-money-down loan plus a high-interest second mortgage that Traci and I used to buy our house in Bernal Heights. The Nash would probably go for just $20,000 now. He had yet to find renters for it, which is why I was able to camp there, and at one point he was two years behind on his property taxes. Dan Kildee and the land bank could have easily ended up with the house. Then he had paid $22,000 for a duplex a few blocks away in 2007, but he'd only recently been able to rent half of it. The other half needed a lot of work, and the roof would have to be replaced soon. Again, he had fallen behind on the taxes at one point and had to pay interest and penalties to the county. "Why buy a second house when you hadn't even rented the first one yet?" I asked.

"Do you know how cool an original duplex is?" he responded. "They're very rare. I just love that house. I'd like to take my clothes off and roll around in it naked. It's so beautiful."

Okay, I'd clearly underestimated Rich's lusty attraction to historic homes. The same desire prompted him to buy a big, dilapidated two-story house on University Avenue across the street from Michael and Perry in 2008. He paid $6,250 in cash for it, and scrappers hit the place before he could secure it, making off with the light fixtures, door hardware, and even the built-in butler's pantry. The furnace didn't work and the brick chimney was collapsing. There was a dispute over who actually held title to the property. "I really couldn't afford to buy the last one," Rich said. "I really had to stretch."

On the back of a cocktail napkin, we tried to work out just how much the three houses had cost Rich over the years when you factored in the mortgage payments, utilities, repairs, and taxes. It all added up to well over $100,000, and Rich still had sizable mortgages left to pay off. I held up the napkin with my calculations scribbled in blue ink like it was a piece of evidence in court. "Why didn't you just buy a place in San Francisco instead?" I asked.

"I think Flint needs it more," he answered. "People might say I'm a fool, but too many people left Flint and never looked back. If every Flint expatriate did something to help, we could turn the city around."

Well, maybe. But how many people could fork over a hundred grand and risk financial ruin? I was struggling to commit just three thousand dollars. And having recently been immersed in the economics of Flint real estate, it was hard for me to imagine how this could work out financially for Rich during his lifetime. Even if he somehow rehabbed all the units and rented them tomorrow, he would never make back his investment unless property values reversed course and started to spike. I could see the city recovering someday, but it would be a very slow process. Rich, as usual, was thinking positive. "I'm preserving the architectural character of these great old houses in a neighborhood that's only going to improve," he said. "I'll get nice people to rent them. Then I'll buy some more."

He paused a minute, looking down at the glass in his hand. "People have this misconception that life is perfect," he said. "I've been able to keep this all going for a long time. Who else can say that?"

After a couple more beers, Rich told me something that helped me understand—in a pop psychology sort of way—what might be motivating him. After he finished eighth grade at Saint Mary's, the Catholic school we both attended on the East Side, he spent the summer preparing to go to Powers Catholic High School. It was a big jump for most kids, especially those who had spent their entire lives at small parish schools. (Powers was considered progressive. You didn't go to Mass every morning, confession every two weeks, or say the rosary on your lunch hour during May, as we had at Saint Mary's. You got detention, not a paddling from the nuns, when you did something wrong.) Saint Mary's kids were thrown into the citywide mix of well over 1,100 students, including a host of well-off non-Catholics fleeing the Flint public schools along with preppy suburbanites. Social status took on added importance, putting kids from the tough East Side, with its small houses built for autoworkers, at an automatic disadvantage. This was compounded for Rich when the bank foreclosed on his family home. He never learned the exact details, just that his father couldn't make the payments. Before school started, Rich's family moved into a trailer in the North End. "Losing your home is not a great way to start high school," Rich said.

We decided to abandon our beers and upgrade to margaritas.

Over the summer I'd learned that Rich's standing in Carriage Town wasn't as lofty as I'd expected, despite his financial and emotional commitment to the neighborhood. I'd often been greeted with polite silence when I brought him up with the various residents I got to know. Rich was apparently classified as a speculator, albeit a well-meaning one. He'd tangled with a few people on an online bulletin board, undiplomatically pointing out the flaws in their properties when they complained about the condition of his houses. It was another of the fissures in the Carriage Town foundation that I had discovered over time. It was a close-knit neighborhood, to be sure, but it was hardly united on all issues. There were internecine battles within the Carriage Town Neighborhood Association over how to deal with everything from code enforcement to the fate of several derelict properties owned by Hurley Hospital. Some of the rancor seemed fueled by nothing more than personality conflicts. In other words, it was a lot like any other neighborhood, but the stakes were higher. Carriage Town couldn't afford infighting if it hoped to survive. "There are so many forces aligned against us that we can't waste time bickering with each other," one resident told me, "but sometimes we just can't stop ourselves."

It had became clear that some homeowners weren't thrilled with Rich's vision of Flint's oldest neighborhood as a haven for student renters. I could understand their lack of enthusiasm because another of the unexpected effects of home ownership in San Francisco had been my growing unease with the number of rental houses on my block. There was no particular incident that sparked these feelings. It was almost subconscious. I began to notice that the worst-kept houses were rentals. They tended to have more people living in them, which meant more cars and fewer parking spaces.

Even though I'd been what I'd describe as a model renter during the nine years I'd spent in the same apartment on San Francisco's Potrero Hill before Traci and I moved in together, it just didn't compare to the attachment I felt for Bernal Heights now that I had half a million bucks invested in it. I picked up stray pieces of trash when I went for walks. I called the city about graffiti and the bizarre oddities that got dumped on surrounding streets—couches, garbage bags of old drywall, two thousand or so used Q-tips, plastic jugs containing odd-colored liquids that might be bodily in nature. I caught myself giving the stink eye to people who parked in front of my house to walk over to the bars and coffee shops on the main drag. I had to remind myself not to do it. I'd been on the receiving end of the same unjustified dirty looks when I parked in other neighborhoods. I had never understood it before. Now I did. As a member of the landed gentry, I felt my emotional and financial commitment gave me a proprietary claim over not just my home but the public thoroughfares surrounding it. I even waded into a stereotypical San Francisco controversy over the fate of a peeling, poorly executed 1970s-era mural—worthy of a C– in a high school art class—that sullied the nearby public library. I sided with a band of Audi-driving partisans who advocated painting over it. An equally vocal constituency of limousine liberals rallied to preserve it as a rich cultural artifact. To the barricades! Such are the petty distractions of a city with a median family income of more than $86,000, compared to less than $34,000 in Flint. When I was renting, none of this stuff would have concerned me. I thought I was doing my part simply by playing my Morrissey concert bootlegs at a reasonable volume and not tossing empties off the balcony.

So I could understand the aspirations of Carriage Town homesteaders who longed to see the neighborhood they had worked so hard to save transformed into an oasis of owner-occupied homes. At the same time, I thought Rich's approach was more realistic. He argued that Carriage Town just needed more good, decent people living there. It didn't matter if they were owners or renters. It needed the vibrancy that would only come with more residents.

I mentioned to Rich that he was a little like Dan Kildee. They both loved Flint. They both had a reality-based approach to improve the city but needed more money for it to work. And they were both underappreciated, to put it politely, by some of the very people they were trying to help. I meant it as a compliment, but Rich wasn't pleased with the comparison. It seemed he and many of the hard-core historic preservationists in Flint didn't like the way the land bank and other governmental agencies were rehabbing some of the houses in Carriage Town. Kildee failed to preserve the historic integrity of the structures by sometimes opting for cheaper drywall over plaster, vinyl windows instead of wood, and a host of other offenses. "He's destroying a lot of those houses, not saving them," Rich said. "They aren't historic properties once the land bank is done with them."

I thought I'd heard all the complaints about Kildee, but this was a new one I could add to the list. It was a nice counterpoint to the residents in other parts of the city who were griping that too many resources were being lavished on Carriage Town. It occurred to me that Flint wasn't just the toughest city in America, it was also the hardest to please.

We decided to call it a night. I was feeling depressed, which is unusual for me after a few drinks. I felt like my Flint adventure was really ending, right where it had all started. But Rich wasn't buying it.

"Keep looking," he said confidently as we shook hands on the sidewalk outside the bar. "You never know what might turn up."

I soon fell into my familiar routine of teaching classes, trolling for freelance work, and blogging about Flint. Rich had talked me into continuing my search for a house, but I was approaching it in a perfunctory manner by occasionally looking for possibilities online and checking in with a couple of local real-estate agents. One weekend in November, I called Michael Freeman to see if he had heard about any new houses that might be available in Carriage Town. The few options were too expensive, but toward the end of the conversation he mentioned for the first time that he and Perry owned a second house on University Avenue, just across Lyon Street from their place. He wondered if I would be interested in combining forces to fix it up.

It was a big, two-story house with eight rooms and more than 2,500 square feet. Like many of the houses in Carriage Town, it had a long history. It had been built around 1910 by a local grocery store owner. An insurance company had later set up shop in it, transforming the front porch into an ugly closed-in business entrance. A charity mission once had plans to turn it into a women's shelter but couldn't get the zoning approved.

A real-estate agent had occupied the house for several years. I recognized his name because he had lived near my family home in Civic Park—located a couple of miles to the northwest—when I was growing up. I remembered him as a friendly guy who used to hand out candy to the neighborhood kids at his office near the Balkan Bakery. He was married with a family, but Michael said he lived alone by the time he ended up in Carriage Town.

"I know him," I said. "My mom bought our house from him."

"Yeah, I think he may have committed suicide in the house," Michael said. "Or maybe it was the house next door."

After the suicide, the house was owned for many years by a woman who lived downstairs and rented out the upstairs apartment. She took pride in the house, doing the best she could to keep it in decent shape. She had three Rottweilers, the kind of dogs that made sense in a dangerous neighborhood. One day while she was at work they got out and were roaming the neighborhood. Michael was watching from his house when the police cornered the dogs in the yard and shot them, execution style. "It was the most horrifying thing I've ever seen," he said. When the woman came home, she found her dogs where the police had left them—wrapped in an old tarp in the parkway in front of her house. "She snapped after that," Michael said. "She started taking drugs and everything went to hell."

When the woman eventually moved, the house was taken over by a slumlord, and a succession of renters moved in and out as the property deteriorated. The chorus of yelling, fighting, and partying became a familiar soundtrack, often waking Michael and Perry at night and generally making their lives miserable. One evening they were having a dinner party with friends. They set the table with good china and candles. The wine was flowing, and everyone was having a good time. A window at one end of the dinner table looked directly out on the house across the street, and the conversation came to a halt when a man and a woman crashed through the back door, stumbled down the steps, and fell into the driveway. The woman was holding a horror-movie-size kitchen knife to the man's throat. "Don't you know I love you?" she screamed. "Why do you make me act this way?"

"I love you, too," he yelled back. "Please don't kill me."

Everyone at the table was staring out the window at the scene unfolding across the street. Michael got up and snapped the curtains closed. "Dinner theater is over," he announced, and they went back to their meals.

When the dinner-theater house came on the market in 2003, Michael and Perry bought it for $35,000. They certainly didn't have a lot of extra money lying around, given the expenses associated with fixing up their house, but they were determined to keep the property away from another slumlord and the chaos that would ensue. Michael had to borrow money from his dad to swing the deal, which included two fixed-rate mortgages. The house was costing them $620 a month, including insurance. They hoped to sell it to someone who would be a good neighbor, someone who cared about Carriage Town, but one deal fell through after the house had been gutted and other offers failed to materialize. They couldn't sell it, and they didn't have the money to fix it up and rent it. They were stuck with it.

Just when I had all but given up on a Flint house, here was an exciting possibility. The thought of joining forces with two experienced locals was much more appealing than tackling this on my own. They'd be right next door to keep an eye on things when I wasn't there. The house was big enough for a rental unit and a place for me and Traci. And it was Carriage Town, my adopted neighborhood, the source of my first byline in the *New York Times*.

Then Michael told me that the house needed $50,000 in work, along with another $25,000 if we wanted to replace all the old wood-frame windows, which would be nice but not absolutely necessary. My heart sank. It turned out that rehab projects in Flint weren't that much cheaper than restoration jobs in San Francisco. My assumption that the city's downtrodden carpenters, electricians, and plumbers would work for peanuts was a false one. This reality probably put every house in Carriage Town—even the junkers—out of my price range. Even if I split the cost with Michael and Perry, I couldn't come up with that kind of money.

But Michael had a solution. He ran down a few city and state low-interest loan programs that we could access. And the house would qualify for a tax break because it was in a historic district. I'd never even considered taking out another loan to buy a house in Flint, but Michael made a convincing case that we could cover the payments with rent money once the house was fixed up and we had tenants. He promised to send me a packet with all the documents he had on the house—a recent appraisal, a contractor's estimate for repairs, and a time line for rehabbing the house.

When the papers arrived the next week, I spread them all out on my living room floor. The list of repairs confirmed that the house was nothing more than a brick and wood shell that needed just about everything else to be installed—plumbing, wiring, gas lines, sinks, appliances, doors, and floors. But the time line and cost estimates charted a clear path to make it all happen. This was less a leap into the unknown than a well-organized plan for the future. I'd have two experienced partners. I paced around my San Francisco house, rubbing my hands together, talking endlessly about it with Traci, often when she was trying to read before bed. I sensed that she was wondering what would be worse at this point—buying a house in Flint or listening to me endlessly talk about buying a house in Flint. She was wary of taking out another loan, especially a loan with two people we didn't really know. In another city. On the other side of the country. And telling her about suicides and dog executions hadn't been a wise marketing strategy on my part. She demanded that I get some advice from a knowledgeable but impartial source. Once again, she was the voice of reason.

I called Michelle, our old landlord and the real-estate agent who had guided us through the gut-wrenching process of buying our house in San Francisco. I'd appreciated her blunt approach then, and I knew she wouldn't hesitate to give me an honest opinion on my plan to team up with two guys I didn't really know to rehab a derelict house that I'd never seen and which happened to be located in one of the worst real-estate markets in the country. She didn't disappoint. Before I even finished giving her the details, I could hear her groaning at the other end of the line. She sounded like she was painfully regaining consciousness after getting knocked out by a mugger.

"Okay, stop," she said before I could finish. She sounded disgusted. "Are you asking my advice?"

"Yes," I said.

"Do. Not. Do. This," she said, slowly and emphatically. "This is a *very* bad idea."

She launched into a seemingly endless list of everything that could go wrong. What if Michael and Perry broke up? What if they lost their jobs? Did I have enough money to cover the payments by myself? Who would pay for unexpected costs during the rehab? And there would be unexpected costs, lots of them. What happened if we couldn't rent the units? Did I know their credit rating? Had I run a background check on them? Were they convicted felons? Were they al-Qaeda operatives? (I made that last one up, but I had a feeling it might have crossed Michelle's mind.)

"I trust these guys," I said, surprised at how defensive I sounded.

"Why?" Michelle asked.

"Because they're, well, um, trustworthy," I answered feebly.

She repeated her advice before adding a couple dozen more reasons not to do it. If I insisted on pursuing it, she recommended talking to a real-estate attorney before I signed anything. I tracked one down in Flint and gave him the details without mentioning Michael and Perry by name. It seemed like he had compared notes with Michelle before he talked to me. He explained that he could draw up all sorts of agreements to map out what would happen when things went wrong, but ultimately the only asset I could gain if Michael and Perry didn't hold up their end of the deal was the house itself. And Michael and Perry had made it clear they didn't really want the house, so why would they make big sacrifices to hang on to it? A legal agreement wasn't going to change that reality.

"Oh boy," he said. "It sounds like you're the answer to all their problems. You're from San Francisco and you've got the money to take this house off their hands."

I explained that it wasn't like that. In fact, I didn't really have that much money either. "Then why are you thinking about investing in a house that's completely gutted and is worth less than the existing mortgage?" he asked.

Touché, fancy-pants lawyer. I didn't really know what else to say, but he did. "What's your address?" he asked.

"Why do you want it?"

"So I can send you a bill. I'll only charge you seventy-five dollars for a half hour, even though we talked for forty minutes."

I considered it another donation to help the Flint economy.

Despite these dire warnings, I did trust Michael and Perry. I believed their hearts were in the right place. They had invested a lot of money and effort into Carriage Town, and I was sure they weren't about to try to scam someone who might later own a house across the street from them. But I knew from experience all the unexpected costs that come with home ownership, so I understood that it would probably end up costing a lot more than $50,000 to make the house livable. And counting on steady, reliable renters in Flint to cover a mortgage payment was about as foolish as running a twenty-four-hour liquor store without bulletproof glass in the city. I huddled over my calculator and had numerous conversations with Michael as fall stretched into early winter, but I never got the numbers or the reassurances that this house made sense for me and Traci. No matter how I added it up, we were looking at loan payments, insurance, and expenses that would total around five hundred dollars a month for the next thirty years. This house, and the rest of Carriage Town, was out of our reach.

As disappointed as I was that I couldn't commit, I was more worried that I was letting down Michael and Perry. One of the most appealing things about the house was that I'd be helping out two people who had already sacrificed a lot for Flint. Michael told me it wasn't a problem.

"After living in Flint, you get very realistic," he told me after it was clear we couldn't work something out. "It would have been great if it happened, but I'm not upset that it didn't." I told him about the lawyer portraying me as a rich Californian about to get fleeced by a couple of Carriage Town con men. "We knew you didn't have any money," Michael said, laughing over the phone. "You may live in San Francisco now, but you still have Flint stink on you."

I took that as a compliment.

Burning Down the House

The fires started in late March of 2010, around the time Flint residents typically start fantasizing about the spring thaw. Like any city with widespread blight, Flint had an ongoing arson problem, but this was different. Sitting at my kitchen table in San Francisco, I watched a seemingly endless stream of shaky YouTube videos featuring Flint houses in flames while crowds watched from the street and neighbors frantically hosed down their roofs. I talked to nervous Flint residents who told me the sight of smoke plumes was now commonplace, along with an acrid, charred smell that wafted through the city. A friend of mine named Guy was one of them.

I met Guy through Flint Expatriates. He left insightful, depressingly funny comments on a few posts, and we started exchanging emails and phone calls. He was born and raised in Flint. Although Guy's grandfather had been a prominent Flint doctor, his father landed on the line at Chevy in the Hole, took to drinking, and ended up living in an apartment above Vechell's Lounge, a well-known bar near the factory.

Guy learned to play the organ and the piano growing up. He landed gigs at various VFW and union halls around Flint, found work in a band down in Houston, and eventually made his way to Las Vegas, where he joined the house band at the Dunes. The pay wasn't bad, and he had a room with two king-size beds at the casino hotel, but he saw no future in it. He returned to Flint and got a degree in psychology from the University of Michigan with nearly perfect grades. He took a creative writing class, and the professor was so impressed that he urged him to apply to the Iowa Writers' Workshop. But before long Guy was drinking heavily, just like his dad, and his marriage was on the rocks. He bounced around, living in Lansing for a while before returning to Flint in 1993 with his new wife, Maggie. He got sober, and they bought a 750-square-foot house on Arlington Street on the East Side, just a couple of blocks from Saint Mary's, the grade school I had attended.

Guy was a salesman at a mattress warehouse making seven dollars an hour, plus a little money on the side designing websites, a skill he had picked up on his own. He didn't have enough money to move. "I'm trapped on the East Side," he said during one of the long phone conversations we had when things were slow at the mattress store.

Flint had a way of intruding on our talks. One day a woman showed up at the warehouse. Guy thought he had a customer, but she was selling frozen meat out of a cooler in the backseat of her car, most likely stolen. "You wanna buy some steaks?" she asked.

"Do you accept plasma as payment?" Guy joked.

She didn't get it and left quickly. I guess when you're selling contraband T-bones, you don't have time to kid around.

"Man, that encounter pretty much sums up Flint," Guy said.

Guy thought of himself as someone who didn't scare easily. After all, he'd seen some weird shit in the neighborhood. There was the time the previous summer that a speeding car crashed into a neighbor's house, knocking it off the foundation. The male driver was draped over the engine block. His pregnant girlfriend was strapped into the passenger seat. They both survived, but the unborn baby did not. Guy detailed a host of other misfortunes that had befallen his street: a little boy drowning in a backyard pool, instances of child abuse in plain sight, neighbors drinking and fighting.

"When we first moved here, there were some GM retirees and a few other people on the block who kept their homes immaculate," Guy said. "But all those 'normal' people—for lack of a better term—either died or moved away. There's almost a complete absence of middle-class homeowners now. Almost everyone's renting, and it's like they're feral people. On warm summer days the street is a cacophony of profanity. It's just amazing how quickly the street declined."

There's no doubt Guy would have liked better neighbors—or the money to move—but he still maintained a large measure of sympathy for his fellow East Siders, even if they were making his life miserable and all but eliminating any value left in his house. "There's a prevalence of hopelessness coupled with contempt for authority in the neighborhood," he said. "There's just a lot of disillusionment. They never got a real piece of the American dream. And the piece they got is getting increasingly smaller."

Guy had a highly personal take on the arson spree. He and Maggie had been asleep one morning when they were awakened by pounding on their front door. Groggy, disoriented, and naked—Guy volunteered that he's not fond of pajamas—he jumped out of bed, thinking it was a break-in. "I'm not a gun nut, but I live on the East Side, so of course I have a shotgun," he said. "I was wondering if I was going to have to defend myself."

He threw on a pair of boxers and headed for the door. He could hear someone screaming for everyone to get out of the house. Guy opened the door, walked onto his front porch, and discovered that the two-story house next door, just fifteen feet away across the driveway, was fully engulfed by flames. Burning debris was floating down onto his house. He could feel the fire. It was so hot he smelled his hair starting to singe. A drunk man in his fifties had banged on the door. He was riding his bike home from a party and saw the fire. He had probably saved Guy and Maggie's lives. "Armageddon's happening on the other side of the driveway, and I'm in there sawing logs," Guy said. "Our bedroom window was open, smoke was billowing in, and we didn't even notice."

Maggie quickly joined him on the porch. Standing in his underwear, a wave of anxiety washed over him. He and his wife had three Chihuahuas, two cats, a blind Cocker Spaniel, and a German Shepherd named Buddy they had found on the street and nursed back to health. They were all in the house. He needed to get them out. And what about his computers? If they went up in flames, so did half his income. And there was the fact that he'd just paid off the house four months earlier and canceled the homeowners' insurance because it was too expensive. "I just had this overwhelming feeling that I was doomed," he said. "Everybody and their brother had just been laid off from the fire department, and I had no insurance. We were going to lose everything, and it was my fault. I was going to hate myself for the rest of my life, if I had one when it was all over."

Maybe all that time in Vegas had earned Guy a little luck, because the drunken bike rider had managed to call 911 on his cell phone. Guy could hear sirens in the distance. They were getting louder. The city's beleaguered fire department was on the way, which was hardly a sure thing in Flint. When the trucks rolled up, the neighbor's place was too far gone to save. The goal was to contain the blaze. Big sprinklers were used to soak Guy's house. He pulled himself together and jumped in his burgundy Dodge Dakota with bad bearings, baking in the driveway, and saved it from the fire. All his property was safe.

Guy knew how close he had come to losing everything, but it didn't give him a new outlook on life in Flint. "The fact that they saved our house and no one died is just amazing," he said. "But when people started burning down every empty building, it's still shocking. No one's more afraid than me. I live in fear all the time, because there doesn't appear to be any end to this. I don't see this getting better. Ever."

The city was burning, and it appeared to be connected with Mayor Walling's ongoing battle with the public safety unions over a new contract. Walling had held a press conference at 2 P.M. on March 24 to announce the layoff of forty-six police officers and twenty-three firefighters effective the next morning. He also promised to shutter two of the city's fire stations. The mayor complained that he was forced to take these drastic measures because the unions refused to make concessions that would ease the city's budget deficit. Raul Garcia, president of the firefighters' union, accused Walling of union busting and threatened to launch a recall effort against the mayor. "He doesn't care about the city," he said.

A half hour after Walling announced the layoffs, an abandoned house on West Second Avenue caught fire, then another on West Fourth Avenue, followed by still another blaze on Jane Avenue that injured two firefighters, including one scheduled to lose his job the next day. Nine vacant structures were torched in less than twenty-four hours. It was worse than Devil's Night, the infamous evening before Halloween that has traditionally been an arson extravaganza in Flint and Detroit.

In the two weeks following the layoffs, there were more than fifty suspected cases of arson in Flint. Most were in abandoned houses, but occupied dwellings were also targeted. "Thank God it's not summer yet, because I'm telling you if this continues through the summer, someone is going to get seriously hurt," Garcia told the *Flint Journal*.

It's typical for neighboring fire departments to pledge assistance when one is overwhelmed, but the suburbs, seeing no end in sight, were having second thoughts about these mutual-aid agreements. Firefighters in Burton responded to three Flint fires in the two days following the layoffs. When he got the fourth call for help, Burton's fire chief said no. After consulting with Burton's mayor, he sent a letter to Flint formally dropping out of the mutual-aid relationship. "I can't solve the city's problems," the chief told the local press in early April. "I have taxpayers in Burton who are my first priority. Those taxpayers are the ones that I will take care of." Clio and Davidson had already withdrawn support.

Four houses burned in Carriage Town, and a group of neighbors I had met the previous summer organized patrols to try to protect some of the city's oldest homes. Many of them took the fires personally. "Someone has it out for Carriage Town," said the president of the neighborhood association. Thankfully, Michael and Perry's homes were safe, as were Rich's. Sitting in front of my laptop reading about the latest fire, I was overcome by despair. At the same time, I couldn't help feeling relieved that the deal had fallen through, and I was not a Carriage Town homeowner. Flint was still stirring up a confusing jumble of emotions even though I was more than two thousand miles away.

Without explicitly blaming the fire department for torching houses, the mayor and other city officials responded with what could easily be interpreted as an accusation. "The point here is that this is a series of coordinated criminal attacks that are designed to scare the residents of this city," Walling said publicly. He claimed there was a "perverted political purpose" behind the fires. The city's director of public safety said, "I think it's someone that has knowledge of what they're doing, and I'll leave it at that. You can read between the lines." Union representatives vigorously denied the implication that firefighters were responsible for the fires.

The bitter labor dispute was just another reminder of the frustrating choices Flint was being forced to make. If anyone deserved good pay and benefits, it was Flint police and firefighters. They were on the frontlines of a dangerous city, struggling to maintain some sense of normalcy. Yet the mayor had to balance the budget, despite a shrinking tax base and decreasing help from the federal and state governments. There were only so many places he could make cuts. When Walling attempted to save money with a seemingly innocuous plan to reduce garbage collection to every other week, residents howled in protest over the smell, the hassle, and the jump in the local rat and skunk population. There was no simple, painless way to eliminate city services.

This was the ultimate curse of a shrinking city. The economic collapse and declining population actually necessitated more city services as crime and poverty skyrocketed. As Flint got smaller, it needed more money to manage the transformation from a thriving industrial powerhouse to something else. Instead, the city was being forced to slash its budget.

The labor negotiations had looked promising the previous fall, when Walling took office. With his first executive order, he cut his own salary by 5 percent, and he imposed furlough days on himself and his appointees to save money. The unions indicated that they were open to any ideas that would save the city money. "Everything's still on the table, and we're still going," one union leader declared. "Things seem to be moving in a positive direction."

I had covered a few labor negotiations over the years. Although the process can get messy, the fundamental disagreement is often quite simple, and this standoff was no different. Walling demanded a 15 percent overall reduction in some combination of wages, benefits, and pensions. The unions responded by offering cuts that Walling claimed didn't equal 15 percent. The expected public posturing ensued. The optimistic quotes in the local press disappeared. At one point, the union called the city's demands "crazy." And Garcia, the head of the firefighters' union, complained, "We've tried to negotiate in good faith. We've given them proposals, given them recommendations, and they responded to none." Walling eventually altered the city's position by asking for "double-digit" concessions, indicating that 10 percent was the new target, but as the weeks dragged by there was no agreement.

As in numerous other labor battles around the country, pension and healthcare benefits posed a major roadblock to a new contract. Typical of many local and state government pension plans, retired city workers in Flint receive monthly pension payments for the rest of their lives, along with certain guaranteed healthcare benefits. The exact pension amount is determined by a formula based on the employee's salary and overtime, years on the job, and a negotiated percentage in the labor agreement. The higher the percentage, the higher the pension payments.

I learned that Flint had approximately 3,000 retirees and only 750 active employees, down from more than 1,100 in 2008. The city devoted a staggering $32 million each year to retiree pension and healthcare costs, more than 20 percent of its total annual budget. A dip in the stock market, where pension funds were invested, meant the city was forced to kick in more money. Rising healthcare costs also increased the city's contribution. Both had happened frequently in recent years. Although city workers covered a portion of their pension and healthcare costs, it was a set amount that couldn't go up until a new contract was negotiated, regardless of rising costs.

It's not uncommon in negotiations for a union to accept freezes or cuts in wages, healthcare, and other benefits in exchange for enhanced pension rewards down the line. That means workers don't get pay or benefit increases while they are on the job, but they reap bigger monthly pension payments once they retire.

This kind of deal often looked good on the front end for a city. The immediate cost of a public employee stayed the same or even decreased. The mayor looked tough by announcing that the union made concessions. The union appeared reasonable and understanding. The city budget might shrink. But while it created short-term savings, these compromises could leave a legacy cost that would haunt a city for decades. As workers retired, many of them relatively young after logging the twenty-three years needed for Flint cops and firefighters to be fully vested, the increased pension costs started to eat away at the initial savings. Not to be morbid, but the longer the retirees lived—often far from Flint, perhaps in a Florida retirement community—the more it cost the city. Over time, the increased pension benefits in a contract could end up costing far more than the initial savings from wage and benefit freezes or cuts. It's known as kicking the can down the road.

Flint was already having trouble covering its existing pension and healthcare obligations. The unfunded liability was $170 million for pensions and $774 million for healthcare and other retirement benefits. That's the amount the city estimated it would eventually have to pay out that it didn't currently have on hand. It worked out to nearly $10,000 in unfunded liability for every Flint resident. For comparison, the unfunded liability per capita in a prosperous community like Ann Arbor, which was roughly the same size as Flint, was less than $2,000.

Generous lifetime pension and healthcare plans were a big reason that Flint was devoting 70 percent of its general fund each year to public safety. That didn't leave much money for the city's other well-documented needs. It helped explain why Flint couldn't handle the basic functions of a city government, like mowing parks, fixing potholes, or boarding up abandoned schools.

When the hopeful tone of the early negotiations had all but disappeared, Walling opted for layoffs rather than making further concessions. "I firmly believe that I'm in the right on this," Walling told me when I called him to talk about the negotiations. "Our need for services is high, so those people who choose to work for the city need to do it under terms that the citizens can pay for. Otherwise, move to Texas or Colorado and see how you do there. We just don't have the ability to pay for a Cadillac pension plan when most people in this community have a hard time paying their car loan off each month."

With the layoffs, the number of Flint cops dipped to 145, compared to 225 three years earlier. There were times when there wasn't a single officer patrolling the streets. A union leader said trying to fight crime in Flint with a force that small was "like putting a Band-Aid on a bazooka wound on a person's chest."

Unfortunately, the mayor and the union leader were both right.

In April, with fires raging across the city, the nation's taxpayers helped address Flint's arson problem. Dale Kildee, Flint's longtime congressional representative, helped secure a $6.7 million federal grant to rehire thirty-nine firefighters and reopen the two closed fire stations for two years. The grant was part of the federal stimulus program and administered by FEMA, which confirmed what many residents had long suspected: Flint was a disaster area.

Firefighters wrote the grant application, and the money eliminated one of Walling's key negotiating tools—the threat of layoffs. To keep the money, the city could not reduce fire staffing levels for two years. But the mayor was quick to frame the development in flattering political terms. "This will bring our firefighting force up to a level higher than it was when I was elected," he said.

From the time the firefighters were laid off in late March until they returned in May, there were more than 150 arson cases in Flint, a threefold increase over past years. When the firefighters were back on the job, the number of arsons dipped, but they hardly disappeared.

It's hard to say what the perfect background would be for someone with the overwhelming task of catching the arsonists burning down Flint, but Sergeant Lenny Jaskulka of the Michigan State Police Fire Investigation Unit came close. Big, bulky, and imposing, the former Army Ranger with an accounting degree looked like a white version of Mike Singletary, the Chicago Bear linebacker and one-time San Francisco Forty-Niners head coach who was known for his intensity. Jaskulka grew up near the Mexican Village neighborhood in Detroit, so he had one big advantage—the shit that happened in Flint wasn't all that unusual to him. "I remember the tanks rolling down Michigan Avenue in 1967 during the riots. I remember my mom being scared to death, my dad not being able to go to work because they closed the GM plant," he said. "And I remember every New Year's Eve it sounding like Beirut, and the city burning every Halloween. So the situation in Flint is nothing new. To me, it's a normal urban environment."

Flint was home to a variety of arsonists with an array of techniques, motivations, and combustible calling cards. While there is much nuance when it comes to arson, the root cause in Flint is obvious to Jaskulka: abandoned houses equal fires. "A city with this many empty buildings is like having a strip mall with eight candy stores, no workers, and no locks across the street from an elementary school," he said. "It's just too hard to resist."

Jaskulka, who had worked closely with the local police on suspicious fires for the past decade, often drew on the bland, stilted language of police reports when he described the "individuals" who burn buildings, but he frequently went off script and opted for terms like "lowlifes" or "numb-nuts" or "morons" to describe arsonists. There are gang members engaged in "retribution or initiation" who are partial to Molotov cocktails. There are jobless guys bored after a night of drinking who remember that they've got lighters in their pockets. (Jaskulka once caught three "idiots" who fell into this category with the help of a witness who described one of them as a "big fat white weeble wobble.") There are property owners in desperate financial situations just looking for a way out or actively engaged in insurance fraud. And then there are the scorned lovers seeking revenge after a bad breakup. "The ex-girlfriend sees her old boyfriend with another girl, gets pissed, and tosses a cocktail," Jaskulka told me. "These are the easiest to solve because the house is usually occupied, and the victim usually wants to talk: 'I know the bitch who did this!' There's a story you can build off. There are people you can bring in for interviews and catch them lying on videotape in an interview room."

A decade of dealing with all these "knotheads" had helped Jaskulka identify some fundamental patterns of life in Flint: "There are a few predictable ways of conflict resolution in this city. One is throwing Molotovs; the next is a drive-by shooting; and the last one is homicide."

Jaskulka seemed to have more sympathy for homeowners surrounded by blight who engaged in what he called "urban renewal." They can't get the city or the land bank to tear down or even board up an abandoned house in their neighborhood, so they take matters into their own hands. "They've got crack whores going in and out of the house next door, or they've got drug deals going down all day and night," Jaskulka said. "Their kids can't go outside and play. They don't feel safe. So they get fed up and make the problem go away by burning down the house themselves."

But even these well-intentioned fires, if that's the way to describe them, often lead to bigger problems. The fires can get out of control and spread to other houses or divert firefighters from a blaze in an occupied dwelling elsewhere. And what if the abandoned house—referred to as an "a-band" by the police and fire departments—isn't empty? "You have ten feet of debris that's collapsed into the basement after the fire, and a witness saying I can't find this person and they were turning tricks out of this house, or someone was squatting in there," Jaskulka explained. "The city has to bring a backhoe out. The state police have to bring a cadaver dog down from Lansing. We have to dig the whole thing out. It takes a couple days of full-time work, but how do you not justify it? You have to dig there. That happens more than you can possibly imagine."

But the suspect causing many of the fires on Flint's East Side did not fall into any of these categories. Jaskulka said he had identified a classic serial arsonist he believed was responsible for more than twenty fires. A disgruntled ex-girlfriend tipped him off that the suspect frequently left his house and returned home just as fires broke out in the neighborhood, allowing him to sit on his front porch and watch neighbors, firefighters, and cops scramble to respond. He tended to start fires after he drank, but he didn't always have the money to buy booze, so it was tough to detect a pattern. He's a sexual predator, according to his rap sheet, which fits FBI profiles of arsonists, who tend to be white males with a history of troubled relationships and financial problems. Jaskulka described him as "a spider spinning a web of fires."

"Why don't you arrest him?" I asked.

"We can't charge him with nothing but hearsay," he answered. "Unless we catch him in the act, or get an eyewitness, or a video of him starting the fire, we can't touch him."

And with the bare-bones staffing levels at the fire and police departments, there was no chance of twenty-four-hour surveillance on the suspect.

It was another frustrating reminder that some of the city's agonizing battles could be won by simply throwing more money into the mix. More money to tear down abandoned buildings that are beyond repair. More money to hire cops to curb the crime that inevitably comes with economic collapse. And more money to sit and watch an arsonist who, at some point, would be compelled to start another fire, to feel the power of watching a city respond to him with sirens and commotion and heartache. If Jaskulka could sit and watch, he was sure he'd eventually catch this guy in the act.

I asked Jaskulka about the persistent rumor that firefighters themselves were burning houses in response to the stalled contract negotiations, station closings, and layoffs. I didn't expect him to address the accusation head on. I figured he'd circle the public safety wagons by expressing outrage or belittling the claim, which I didn't believe anyway. But Jaskulka surprised me. He said he thought the rumor was true. "It's similar to when a baby or a two-year-old does not get his way. He creates a temper tantrum long enough for you to give in," he said. "In this case, professionals who are facing massive layoffs with the city take it upon themselves to make a point in the news media by lighting up the city."

Jaskulka pointed out that from the day of the layoffs to the day firefighters were rehired with FEMA funding there was a big spike in fires compared to the same period in past years. There were close to ten fires burning day and night in the areas where fire stations were closed. In addition to the volume and location of fires, the nature of the blazes was suspicious. Amateur firebugs and Molotov tossers tend to start fires on the outer edge of a structure—on a porch or near a window. They rarely put themselves in danger, always leaving themselves a clear escape route. These fires consume the building more slowly, and the fire tends to be visible fairly quickly, giving neighbors the opportunity to call 911 sooner and firefighters a better chance of containing the blaze. During the layoffs, the fires were often set in multiple spots throughout the structure, including the center of the basement and the first floor, ensuring that it would take longer to spot the fire and increasing the chance of an inward collapse of the structure. Once that happened, there was really nothing to save. "We in the fire service, whether it's the fire department or fire investigators, know how to bring a building down," Jaskulka said. "When the fire department arrived on all of these fires, they were fully rockin' and rollin'."

But none of this meant that Jaskulka was going to be filing charges against firefighters. "I have to have an eyewitness, or I have to have physical evidence that puts one of these individuals there. All I have is conjecture," he said. "There was a definite pattern, and there was also a definite motive to set the houses on fire. If it quacks like a duck and looks like a duck, it's a duck. But I need more than that to go to court."

Lieutenant Mark Kovach, a firefighter with twenty years' experience and the vice president of the Flint Firefighters Union, Local 352, was blunt when I contacted him about Jaskulka's theory. "That's bullshit," he said. "No one has ever investigated a single Flint firefighter for any arson cases." Trent Farnsworth, the union president, scoffed at the charges. "If a firefighter was found starting these fires, I'd resign my position," he vowed.

Despite the denials, even the possibility that some of the very people risking their lives to put out fires in Flint were also starting them was another indication of how far the city had fallen. Despite the need for unity in the face of overwhelming obstacles, Flint was divided and fractured. Like my friend Guy, I was starting to doubt if it could ever be made whole again.

Emotional Rescue

This story should probably end here. I'd been warned repeatedly and explicitly by friends and strangers alike that my desire to buy a house in Flint made no sense. Sadly, the topic had lost its appeal at Zeitgeist, where not even the sunny spring weather and excessive amounts of alcohol could sustain it. After toying with the idea of joining a local Elks Lodge en masse and taking it over, the basketball crowd was now fixated on the prospect of somehow renting or buying a small garage or empty warehouse in San Francisco and transforming it into our own "Gentleman's Club," outfitted with old chairs, couches, stereo equipment, and a big-screen TV so we could hang out, watch sports, and make cocktails. (No one mentioned that hundreds of bars throughout the city could fulfill this fantasy for a lot less money and hassle.) I'd try to steer the conversation back to Flint by describing the latest act of desperation in the city, but I could tell that the interest was now merely polite. The Zeitgeist gang had moved on to a new unattainable goal. God, fate, economics, and that lawyer back in Flint who cost me seventy-five bucks had delivered a clear message: nice try, but give it up.

But my friend M.G., whose father had immigrated from Iran and settled in Los Angeles, had an uncanny ability to keep me from completely abandoning my muddled desire to somehow reclaim a part of Flint. "My dad has always told me that you just go and do things and then something else happens," M.G. said as he sat across the battered picnic table in Zeitgeist's grimy outdoor patio one Saturday. "You change the landscape. If you're walking in a field, you start walking in the hills, and the end result is going to be different. Sometimes things get worse, but a lot of times things get better." Bar logic at its best. I interpreted this vague, Zenlike bit of advice—imported from Persia via La-La Land—as a hint that maybe it wasn't time to walk away from the dream of a Flint house just yet. Then I got up to buy another round of Bloody Marys.

My blog was soon serving as a high-tech Ouija board, sending me cyber signals that my business in the Vehicle City wasn't finished. In rapid succession, several friends and acquaintances who had grown up with me in the Civic Park neighborhood got in touch after reading Flint Expatriates. We exchanged stories about buying Wacky Packs at the corner store, tangling with various local bullies—one of whom was now serving a life sentence for murder—and playing street hockey with a tennis ball dipped in gasoline and set on fire. (Adolescent boys with a touch of pyromania can be very creative.) A lot of happy memories came flooding back.

I'd toured Civic Park the previous summer when I visited John and Christine, the couple who still lived on my old block. It looked rough compared to the 1970s and '80s. I was stunned by its rundown condition. It seemed dangerous, and I didn't consider it a viable place to buy a house. But I had grown more comfortable with the neighborhood as the summer progressed, and I attended campaign events in the area. I bought fresh-baked bread at the Balkan Bakery, which was still in business about a block from my childhood home. Crime was a problem, but I learned it was not as bad as many Flint neighborhoods that stretched to the north toward my high school.

Though the sight of childhood landmarks in their current state of decay had been depressing at first, I came to view them as reassuring reminders that Flint hadn't been completely transformed into something unrecognizable. I spotted houses and street corners and even trees that I remembered fondly. The faint outlines of a strike zone painted on the brick wall of Civic Park School triggered memories of countless pickup baseball games. I still considered Civic Park "my neighborhood."

From my research, I knew there was no shortage of houses well within my meager price range. And I certainly had the emotional connection to the neighborhood. If I was going to take another shot at buying a house, Civic Park seemed like an obvious place to focus my efforts. This variation on my plan was probably as far-fetched as the others, but as the end of the school year approached, I started organizing my return to Flint. Traci's only request was that I make it a shorter visit this time around. Neither of us wanted to spend another summer apart. I invited her to come along, but she used work as an excuse to stay behind in San Francisco. She was getting more marketing responsibilities and was no longer doubling as the receptionist at the architecture firm. I didn't blame her for declining. I knew that Flint would not be high on my list of vacation spots if I hadn't grown up there.

Slate, my great enabler, came through again with an assignment to profile Dan Kildee. I now had funding for the trip, sort of. The eight hundred dollars I'd make wouldn't even cover airfare and living expenses, but I've already shown that financial planning isn't necessarily my strong suit.

Rich had finally managed to find a renter for the Nash House, which would help him put a dent in the back taxes he owed, so my pink domicile in Carriage Town was no longer available. But if Flint had anything, it was abundant housing options, and a new home away from home quickly presented itself, courtesy of a writer I had met in Flint. It seemed like another sign that I was on the right path.

Jan taught at UM-Flint and had published numerous poems, essays, and a novel. I wrote about her in Flint Expatriates, then she wrote about me in *East Village Magazine*, a lovable, long-running Flint oddity that often topped out at eight pages with poetry sharing space with ads for Vern's Collision and Big John Steak and Onion, a legendary local fast-food joint. We'd met for beers and cheeseburgers with some of her students at the Torch bar the previous summer.

Jan and her husband, Ted, proved that there was no predictable pattern for how people ended up in Flint. They had first met in Tonga in the midseventies. Jan, a former reporter and the daughter of an evangelical preacher in Ohio, was a Peace Corps volunteer. Ted was a consultant hired by Peace Corps headquarters in Washington, D.C., to train new arrivals. They didn't meet under ideal circumstances. A volunteer Jan knew was murdered in Tonga by another Peace Corps volunteer. Ted was asked to provide counseling. He was eight years older than Jan, and they hit it off almost immediately. Their brief Polynesian romance ended when Ted flew home about four months later, but it had been memorable for both of them.

After the Peace Corps, Jan attended the University of Michigan in Ann Arbor to work on a master's degree in social work. She got an internship with a social services agency in Flint in 1980. The layoffs were really hitting home by then, and the city was becoming a place where things only got worse, never better. "It was pretty damn bad in Flint, so we were seeing lots of substance abuse, spousal abuse, child abuse, severe depression," Jan told me. "People think this is crazy, but I liked the town and I liked the people. Maybe it's the writer in me. It was so much more interesting than Ann Arbor." (If only fifty thousand more people with advanced degrees felt the same way.)

Jan was offered a full-time position at the Flint social service agency in August of 1981, the same time I was enduring two-a-day preseason high school soccer practices in the Michigan heat. The job paid $14,000 a year. She happily accepted, moving into a second-floor apartment two blocks from Central High School and a short walk from downtown. Believe it or not, there was a thriving band of writers in Flint at the time. They congregated at Hat's Pub downtown for raucous literary readings. "I just fell in love with that whole scene," she said. "Everybody used to just get trashed back then, so I cut my teeth as a writer by reciting poems to drunks."

Inspired, she got an MFA in writing from a low-residency graduate program in North Carolina and landed a full-time teaching gig at UM-Flint. She fell in love with another Hat's regular, a poet who also taught at the university, and they eventually got married. By the late nineties, they had been together nearly twenty years. The Hat's Pub days were long gone. The bar had been torn down and replaced with a parking deck, the sort of utilitarian effort to "improve" downtown that had become all too typical. Jan and her husband began to drift apart.

Around this time, she began working on a novel based on her Peace Corps experience. A professional journalist happened to be writing a nonfiction account of the murder. He interviewed Jan for his book, and they were soon exchanging information. When the journalist tried to interview Ted, he got an unusual request. Ted would talk to him if the journalist would give him Jan's email address. Jan was sitting in her office at the university in 2000 when she got an email with "Ted Nelson" in the subject heading. They hadn't talked or written in more than two decades. "My blood pressure shot up a little bit when I saw it, because I had very vivid memories of this fellow from Tonga," she said.

Ted was divorced and had three older children. He lived in Southern California and was doing well running a business that made trophies and plaques. He had an anachronistic little retail store on Las Palmas Avenue in Hollywood, near the Scientology headquarters, but he did most of his business wholesale. The big seller was a gold statuette that looked suspiciously like an Oscar, but for copyright reasons Ted called them Superstars. They were so popular he had bought a factory to pump them out by the thousands. Jan and Ted started talking, but they didn't see each other until Jan's marriage officially ended about six months later. It was like they picked up where they'd left off so long ago in Tonga. They wanted to have a life together, but there were some obvious logistical issues to work out. "It was one thing to walk away from my marriage, but I didn't want to just walk away from Flint," Jan said. "People were telling me this was my big opportunity to get the hell out of this armpit, you know? But I didn't feel that way about it. I had deep roots in Flint. To this day it's hard to explain to people who aren't from here, but Flint has a big hold on me."

Ted came up with the solution. He suggested buying a house together in Flint, keeping his apartment in Southern California, and splitting their time between the two incongruous locations. In 2003 they closed on a two-story Colonial with three bedrooms, hardwood floors, and a fireplace for $140,000. It was in a nice part of town off East Court Street where "the four hundred"—Flint's elite—had lived when my mom was in high school. Ted could keep tabs on his business back in California out of a spare bedroom on the second floor. During the summer and academic breaks, Jan and Ted lived in an apartment in San Pedro on a hill overlooking the Los Angeles harbor. It was a fitting location. "I think of Pedro as the Flint of Los Angeles," Jan joked. They were bicoastal, sort of, dividing their time between the shores of the Pacific and the Great Lake State. They were happy.

Jan was living a variation on the life I was trying to create. More than anybody else, she understood my attraction to Flint, just as I understood her need to escape to California for long stretches of time. Living in Flint was hard work. So when I mentioned that I was hunting around for a place to rent that summer, she offered up her house and threw in the use of her red Honda. She set a ridiculously low price, which seemed more like a token charge, so I could keep my pride. I sensed that Jan thought I was on some sort of misguided spiritual journey, and she wanted to help me along. There were some conditions. I had to care for the family pets. This being Flint, my mind raced through the litany of typical security animals employed by the locals—Rottweilers, Pit Bulls, German Shepherds, Komodo dragons. Instead, I got two sweet cats named Joey and Cinder, whose only bad habits were their desire to sleep in bed with me.

Jan and Ted took me out to a sushi place in Flint Township near the Genesee Valley Mall on the warm June night that I arrived in Flint.

They were leaving for San Pedro the next morning, so they gave me a rundown on the house and briefed me on the neighbors. Near the end of the meal, Ted told me a story about the hard-drinking poet Charles Bukowski, memorably portrayed by Mickey Rourke in the movie *Barfly*. There used to be a bookstore near Ted's trophy shop in Hollywood that specialized in Bukowski's work. The poet frequently showed up to sign copies and give readings. Ted got to know him and discovered they both lived in San Pedro. One day Ted gave Bukowski a ride home from the bookstore. They were stuck in rush-hour traffic on the 110, surrounded by hazy sunlight and smog. Bukowski, surveying the car-bound humanity around him, said, "Hey, I just wrote the greatest poem ever created. Wanna hear it?"

Ted, who has a dry sense of humor and is not easily impressed, declined, knowing that he'd end up hearing it anyway.

"Too bad," Bukowski said. "Here it is . . ." He paused dramatically before reciting his latest masterpiece: "Life, fuck it!"

According to Ted, the terse poem remains unpublished, but I couldn't help thinking it very well could be the unofficial motto of Flint. It's the perfect response to so many things that have happened to the place over the years. And it's often all you can really say in response to the latest calamity.

17

Get Real

Dan Kildee was driving with his knees and talking with his hands as his black Chrysler pushed eighty miles per hour on a stretch of I-69 near East Lansing about a week after I returned to Flint in June of 2010. I was in the passenger seat, working up a sweat as I frantically took notes for my *Slate* story and tried to fight off the onset of car sickness. We passed a familiar Michigan tableau—a dead deer sprawled across the edge of our lane—and Kildee adjusted accordingly without touching the steering wheel. But it was the eye contact that really got me nervous. "The shrinking-city concept is a little like a pear tree," Kildee said, locking eyes with me despite the increasingly heavy traffic. "If you want it to bear fruit, you can't let it get overgrown with unsustainable branches. You have to clear away the dead branches to save the rest of the tree."

He changed lanes and started laughing. "Okay, that was one of my weakest metaphors," he admitted, "but you get the idea."

We were headed for an annual gathering of progressives called the Michigan Summit. Van Jones, President Obama's short-lived green jobs advisor, was scheduled to deliver the keynote, and Kildee was participating in a panel devoted to one of the great imponderables—"The Future of Michigan Cities." It was yet another chance to trumpet what could be viewed as his commonsense approach to urban planning in an age of decline or, conversely, a radically un-American idea that embraces defeat and limited horizons.

Though he was still approaching the subject of shrinking cities with an almost evangelical zeal, a lot had changed since I met Kildee a year earlier. He had resigned as county treasurer and land-bank chief, but expanded his reach by creating the Center for Community Progress, a well-funded nonprofit dedicated to helping cities across the country implement variations on the model he had created in Michigan, where there were already more than forty local land banks. Many of the cities Kildee was assisting were not shrinking, but they were still looking for ways to combat speculators and pockets of blight. He now split time between his home in Flint Township and a Connecticut Avenue condo in Washington, D.C., which just might be the escapist dream of all Flint politicians.

To keep things interesting, Kildee had also toyed with a run for governor, but dropped the idea when significant union support failed to materialize. Of course, it was common knowledge that Kildee was likely to run for Congress if aging Uncle Dale decided to retire. A high school buddy of Dan's told me that the two Kildees even joke about it. Dan will ask his uncle how he's feeling, and the congressman will feign suspicion and respond, "Hmm, why do you ask, Dan?"

Kildee was already working with several state and local governments to implement his ideas in cities like Detroit, Buffalo, Cleveland, New Orleans, Little Rock, and Minneapolis. He and Community Progress had consulted with the Ohio legislature on land-bank legislation that had recently passed with bipartisan support. A Republican state representative from Philadelphia was currently guiding a land-bank bill through the Pennsylvania legislature after working closely with Kildee, who envisioned his work expanding to the West and the Sunbelt, as once-booming cities dealt with rampant foreclosures and declining populations.

If there was any doubt, the Great Recession had proved that what happened in Flint was not an isolated incident. "The truth of the matter is that cities are fragile organisms, and any of them could be one corporate boardroom decision away from becoming the next Flint," he warned as we approached the Michigan State University campus. "There was a time when Flint was a growing, vibrant, wealthy town, and we had absolute certainty that it would never end. A lot of cities have that same certainty now, but they should know they aren't bulletproof."

There was a certain irony in the notion that a guy from Flint—a factory town that practically invented the concept of planned obsolescence and grew prosperous on General Motors' rapacious lust for an ever-expanding market share—might successfully export the notion that cities can save themselves by repurposing land and accepting negative growth.

Flint mayor Dayne Walling was also in East Lansing, the same bustling town where he went to college, and participating in the panel discussion with Kildee. Walling spoke first, laying out an inclusive vision for Flint that stressed improving the quality of life in *all* districts, quickly distancing himself from the shrinking-city plan. Though some abandoned homes would need to be eliminated, he saw Flint as a place that could be all things to all people, a city with a dense downtown, suburban-style homes with big lots in certain neighborhoods, and just about everything in between.

He calmly reiterated his desire to update the city's master plan, which hadn't happened since 1960, with input from *all* the citizens of Flint. The master plan details the city's goals for land use, housing, infrastructure, parks, open space, economic development, and historic preservation. It's not an easy process for growing cities, but it's even tougher for a shrinking city like Flint, where the inspired ideas earnestly debated in urban-planning seminars collide with the dirty reality of local politics in a time of scarcity. There would be winners and losers. Not all Flint's roughly seventy-five neighborhoods would get everything residents wanted or needed. And if Kildee had anything to say about it, certain areas would be targeted as higher-density redevelopment zones, and others would be designated as greener, less populated sections. There was a real danger of the process degenerating into a turf war, with neighborhood leaders fighting it out for dwindling resources and voters promising retribution for any politician who failed to deliver the goods.

Walling had secured a federal grant to fund the process, which would take two to three years to complete. He had already held planning sessions in every ward to get feedback. Predictably, public safety and economic development emerged as the top two concerns among residents.

Walling delivered a reasoned, measured presentation guaranteed not to offend anyone or establish any controversial new policies. Just what you'd expect from a young mayor overseeing a fractured city and facing a reelection campaign in just over a year. He earned polite applause.

Kildee was next. Speaking without notes and exuding his typical confidence, he frequently worked bursts of loud applause out of the audience of policy wonks, community organizers, and union officials. "We need a system that doesn't treat urban land like it's a baseball card to be bought and sold by people who watch infomercials," he declared. He deplored local governments "doing back flips" to subsidize business development in suburban areas instead of reinvesting in urban areas. After praising Walling's efforts, he delicately hinted that to fix a place like Flint, local leaders will have to risk offending some voters with unrealistic expectations. "The tough part of all this is having the courage to paint a picture of what a successful city looks like and not simply attempt to create a replica of what it was in 1950," he said. But the standing ovation came when he endorsed a regional approach to solving the problems facing cities in decline. "The City of Flint built Genesee County by importing cash and exporting products around the world for decades," he said. "The shoe is now on the other foot. The economic model we've developed takes some of that wealth back to restore the city. And by doing that, the entire region improves."

Kildee had also found a receptive audience at the federal level after he helped draft a transition memo for the new Housing and Urban Development secretary, Shaun Donovan. Shortly after he got Community Progress up and running, he was offered a job at HUD. He turned it down. "It was pretty clear to me that I'd gotten used to being able to speak my own mind and follow my own policy instincts," he said. "It would have been hard for me to do that in a relatively senior level at HUD."

You don't have to spend much time with Kildee for him to illustrate this point. In the car on the way back to Flint, he labeled a local state senator who opposed his views a "moron." He pointed out that while he agreed with Dayne Walling on a lot of things, they had very different approaches. "I think the problem is leadership," he said. "Let's not pander to people by telling them things that make them feel good but are not true. Don't make them think we're going to rebuild every neighborhood, because we're not." He described the speech by Van Jones, which was long on laughs but short on substance, as "sort of interesting but kind of like something you'd hear in eighth grade." (The lack of rigor hadn't stopped Kildee from snapping a smartphone photo of Jones during the speech and posting it to his Facebook page.)

Despite his outspokenness, Kildee still had the ear of Obama administration officials. He mentioned that a few weeks earlier Derek Douglas, the special assistant to the president for urban affairs, had summoned him to the White House to talk shop for a couple of hours. "That's like going to Carnegie Hall for me," Kildee said, beaming. "I lived my whole life basically doing recitals, and now I have a chance to be in a place where really important policy is being made."

After the session, Kildee realized he wasn't going to be escorted out. He had a security badge, so he decided to go on a twenty-minute self-guided tour. "I'm this kid from Flint, but here I am at the White House," he said. "I just walked around like I knew where I was going."

A few weeks later, I met up with Kildee again. We walked over to the long-vacant Durant Hotel, now fully engulfed by the renovation process to convert it into apartments and retail space that Kildee had orchestrated as head of the land bank. He called the construction workers by name, shook hands with them, and smiled when he wasn't gazing up at the building itself. A foreman was summoned as a guide, hardhats were issued, and we walked through the main entrance, stepping around construction equipment. The grand ballroom, where my mom attended various dances and the dinner that was the culmination of her etiquette lessons, looked majestic despite the table saws and stray lumber scattered about. Many of the apartments on the upper floors were nearly completed, outfitted with shimmering stainless steel appliances, dark-wood cabinets, and granite countertops. It was fancy. The prices would be a little high for Flint but still endearingly cheap compared to San Francisco. Two bedrooms and 1,139 square feet would cost $875 a month in the Durant. Kildee, his dark suit now coated with a light layer of drywall dust, looked like a new father staring at his kid in the hospital nursery. "Wow," he said at one point. "It's almost finished." That was as close to speechless as I'd ever seen him.

Kildee and I then made the short drive to the East Side and walked around the neighborhood where his family used to live, the streets where he played as a child before moving to Civic Park. We stopped on Jane Avenue between Minnesota and Iowa Avenues. There was only one occupied house on the street. The rest were burned out or abandoned. Big, mature trees, some with fire-singed branches, cast gloomy shadows over the block. The street had become an unfortunate tour stop for journalists from all over the world seeking to visually document Flint's decline. Kildee's father and his uncle Dale had grown up on the same street a few blocks west in the house his grandmother lived in from 1934 until her death in 1994. "She was never going to leave that place," he told me. "That's where she raised her kids."

Kildee walked across an overgrown yard and onto the rickety porch of a little bungalow with white vinyl siding—if it were aluminum it would have been stripped long ago. All the windows and doors were boarded. It was owned by the land bank. "As soon as I walked up to this house, I remembered it from fifteen, twenty years ago," Kildee said, sounding wistful. "I remember knocking on this door during a campaign and having the woman who lived here tell me about my family, who just lived a couple blocks down. She told me stories about my uncle Ken, who died before I was two or three years old. My son's named after him."

He stood on the porch, his hands stuffed into his pockets, surveying the blight surrounding him. "What's interesting is that all through that period, so many people stayed in this neighborhood," he said "Until the eighties or so, it was a pretty stable place."

A middle-aged man—looking like he either just rolled out of bed or hadn't been to sleep yet—ambled unsteadily down the sidewalk and stopped in front of the house. He startled me because there are moments in Flint's sparsely populated neighborhoods, lulled by the sound of birds, the rustle of trees, and not much else, when you forget there are still people around, that this is still a semifunctioning city. As usual, Kildee had drawn an audience, even on one of Flint's empty streets. The guy didn't know Kildee, but it was likely that anyone in a suit standing on the porch of an abandoned house indicated some level of authority. He glanced at me in my Levis and short-sleeved shirt, decided I was not the one to talk to, and fixed his tired gaze on Kildee, who was giving him a closed-mouth smile. "Somebody needs to fix these houses up, not just let them fall down!" the man said emphatically. "Put some goddamned money into them so people can live there again!"

Kildee looked at the guy with his patented sympathetic expression and nodded his head, which easily could have been interpreted by the uninitiated as agreement but certainly wasn't in this case. Satisfied that his point had been made, the guy moved on down the sidewalk, awkwardly stepping over a dead tree limb blocking his path. "Fix them up!" he yelled without looking back, pointing into the air for emphasis as he waded into the shadows.

Kildee walked down the steps and into the yard, still taking in the scenery. It was the first time I'd seen him pass up an opportunity to give his shrinking-city pitch. Maybe he was too caught up in memories to deliver it. Or maybe he was fantasizing about what the block would look like with no houses at all, just grass and the nice shady trees that had survived the fires.

"I think he was talking to the wrong guy," I said.

"Definitely," Kildee answered. He stopped in the middle of the overgrown yard to elaborate. "Look, I'm a Flint kid, so I'm trying not to come off as some sort of an academic, but you've got to be able to have a serious, intelligent, fact-based discussion about this stuff in order to really come to the right conclusions. What ends up happening is that it becomes just an emotional issue. We've got to save Flint. We've got to get people back here and return Flint to what it was, and nothing short of that is going to be acceptable. To me, that's a prescription for disaster."

Kildee needed to get back to his office for a conference call with a group of planners and city officials from Buffalo. Or maybe it was Stockton. Either way, I knew they had their own local versions of Jane Avenue—an abandoned byway with a rich history and an uncertain future. And Kildee was eager to offer them an untested but well-articulated plan to deal with all those troubled streets.

18

Living Large

It was easy to settle into life at Jan and Ted's house. I was lord of the manor. Unlike my previous home away from home in Carriage Town, this place had chairs and couches and beds and hot water. But I discovered that the relative luxury of life off East Court was not exactly conducive to house hunting or writing. For one thing, there were books everywhere, which was a constant distraction. Then there was the fifty-five-inch flat screen in the living room. It was huge. I felt like I was in Michael Moore's private screening room. And the World Cup was under way, so I found myself trying to search for houses online while South Africa battled Mexico in crystal-clear high def. The sound of those simultaneously hypnotic and annoying vuvuzelas at the stadiums echoed through the house. I was procrastinating as much in Flint as I did back in San Francisco, padding around the house in my pajamas, eating pretzels even though I wasn't hungry, and conducting an unofficial head count of Ted's fake Oscars, which decorated every room. I guess it was a sign of how comfortable I felt in Flint.

Jan had left a note detailing a family tradition that she hoped I could fulfill for her. Whenever she was in Flint on the solstice marking the first day of summer, she would go outside and ring an antique bell her father had purchased for her mother in San Francisco's Chinatown years ago. So on the night of June 21, I sat in the backyard and waited for the darkest point of the night, as instructed by Jan. The little bell was surprisingly loud when it rang out in the quiet neighborhood. I bailed a little early because the mosquitoes were clearly out to get me, but I'd done my duty. I walked across the lawn in my bare feet and headed inside to hunt for some calamine lotion, feeling like I was creating fresh memories of Flint, that my life here wasn't confined to a neat block of time in the seventies and eighties.

Another night I was sitting in the living room reading. Both cats were nearby, giving me the stare-down, as was their wont when it was time to go to bed. I looked outside and spotted fireflies pinging around the yard. Somehow I'd missed them the previous summer, or maybe they were elitists, confining themselves to Flint's better neighborhoods. Who could blame them? I was just about to Skype Traci on my laptop, so I called her and walked outside, holding the computer so she could experience a cyber version of a warm summer night in Flint, with fireflies dancing in the yards of houses that were, thankfully, still occupied. I know this sounds like a scene from a depressing short story in the *New Yorker*, something Richard Ford might cook up, but it was an unexpectedly happy moment.

"I've never seen fireflies before," Traci said over the tinny laptop speakers as I stood in the yard, looking at her happy face glowing in the night. "I've only read about them."

"See, Flint's still got something to offer," I said, wishing Traci were really there with me. "Fireflies and firearms."

It was a strange sensation to inhabit a place with so many vivid memories, a place I longed to be part of, without anyone I cared about to share it with me. Almost every person I had ever been close to in Flint was gone, although a few of them had settled in nearby suburbs. I kept thinking I would run into some old friends on the street, but aside from seeing my grade school basketball coach in a restaurant, it never happened. I wondered if this was what it was like to be so old that you'd outlived everyone you knew from childhood.

So I was relieved when my good friend Mark drove up from Grosse Pointe one weekend. We'd had numerous adventures together growing up in Flint, often involving failed attempts to impress girls at the Copa. He came from a good Flint family. His grandparents had been sought-after interior decorators back in the days when Flint residents sought out interior decorators. They belonged to the Flint Golf Club, where I toiled as a caddy, and did a lot of work for various wealthy scions of the Mott family. In college, Mark had even dated one Mott descendant named Bunny or Khaki or some other name straight out of the *Official Preppy Handbook*. She was cute and seemed to really like him, but

Mark admitted that the relationship foundered because she was a Christian Scientist and didn't drink. "I grew up in Flint," Mark explained to me, still slightly exasperated by the situation more than twenty years later. "What the hell were we supposed to do when we went out if there was no drinking?"

Mark and I more or less covered old ground during his visit. We cooked out on the grill in the backyard one night and watched the Tigers game on the massive television. We headed to the Torch for beers and cheeseburgers the next night. Around eleven, Congressman Dale Kildee showed up in his trademark dark suit, similar in cut and style to the one he wore when I was his intern in the eighties. He ordered a drink, shook hands with us, and skillfully pretended to remember who I was. Not bad for an eighty-year-old guy. We headed to Angelo's for Coney Islands and shakes afterward. The East Side diner was nearly empty.

"This place used to be packed on a Saturday night," I blurted out to the waitress, who looked as hard-bitten as the waitresses I remembered as a kid. (The gender-neutral term "server" is not in vogue at Angelo's.)

"So I've heard," she said, slapping the bill on the table. "That doesn't happen much anymore, but at least you can get a seat right away now."

I wondered if this was what passed for positive thinking in Flint.

On Sunday, Mark and I toured his grandparents' old neighborhood. We slowly rolled up and down the street. There were a few abandoned houses and the charred remains of a big two-story that was probably the victim of an arsonist. We stopped in front of the house where Mark's mom grew up, and I jumped out to take a picture. A neighbor's door immediately flew open. A big white guy stepped out onto his front porch.

"What the fuck are you guys doing?" he asked, sounding more exasperated than angry. He looked tired.

"We're just taking a picture of the old neighborhood," I yelled back, embarrassed that I'd needlessly alarmed another nervous Flint resident.

He turned and walked slowly back inside his house. As we were driving away, I looked back and saw him watching us through his front window. An encounter like this might have angered me the previous summer, prompting me to declare that this was still my city and I had a right to be here. But I understood the place better now. I didn't blame the guy. He was probably just trying to unwind on a Sunday morning, hoping for a chance to let his guard down. I wondered if he ever wanted to quote Bukowski and just say "Life, fuck it!" and escape to California for a few weeks of relaxation in an apartment overlooking the Pacific, like Jan and Ted.

It seemed like a good time to end our Sunday drive in Flint. Mark needed to get back to his wife and young son in Grosse Pointe. "I'm really glad my grandparents aren't around to see this," he said as we passed another burned-out house, turned the corner, and drove away.

Fading Murals

I had a plan for figuring out if it made sense to buy a house in Civic Park. My goal was to discover someone who was maintaining a home despite the challenges facing my old neighborhood. A holdout. A dreamer. I needed to find inspiration. My friends John and Christine were obvious examples of residents who hadn't given up hope, but I wanted to know if there were more people like them, other diehards fighting to ensure that the neighborhood had a future.

I would drive through Civic Park until I spotted a house in good condition. Then I'd just go up, knock on the door and try to talk with the owner. If there was no answer, I'd track down a phone number and call to set up an interview. I figured this was the best way to get the unvarnished truth about life in the neighborhood. Numerous friends pointed out that this was not the safest plan, but I figured if I couldn't find people who felt comfortable having a conversation with me, then Civic Park was no place to buy a house.

Like the rest of Flint, Civic Park had an elaborate history. Only a few miles northwest of downtown, it is one of the country's first subdivisions and one of the largest districts listed on the National Historic Register. The development began in 1917 as a private venture to create housing for autoworkers and their families flooding the city. After World War I, the project was taken over directly by GM, which formed the Modern Housing Corporation to avoid the embarrassment of shop rats living in tents and tar-paper shacks surrounding the factories. The company had real concerns that substandard living conditions would hurt its ability to recruit and retain workers.

The creation of Civic Park shows how fast and loose life was in an industrial boomtown. This was not an era that required elaborate environmental impact reports or a time-consuming public approval process for a massive housing development. It also provides yet another illustration of Charles Stewart Mott's power and influence.

One morning in 1917, a survey crew headed by a twenty-six-year-old named Charles Branch was preparing lots for new houses on the far East Side. The workers were surprised when a well-polished automobile cut across the empty field, stopping near the surveying equipment, and none other than Charlie Sugar stepped out and started a conversation with Branch.

Mott: "Did you read in the paper last night that we were going to put 10,000 men to work at Buick and Chevrolet?"

Branch: "Yes, I did."

Mott: "When I woke up this morning I thought of something. Where are we going to put them? How soon can you start building ten thousand houses?"

Branch: "I can send out a surveying crew in the morning to make a boundary survey if I know where to send them."

That's how Branch was hired to create the initial plat and street design of Civic Park. A more modest goal of one thousand houses was soon established, but they needed to be built as quickly as possible. A work camp that would rival many small towns was created to accommodate 4,600 workers. There were ninety-six bunkhouses and two commissaries that could feed 1,500 at a single sitting, along with barbershops, shoe repair shops, and several open-air theaters. A railroad line was built to carry two thousand tons of materials from the Chevy plant to Civic Park. At one point, trains left the supply station every six minutes, twenty-four hours a day. Five sawmills cut hemlock and yellow pine around the clock. In just nine months between 1919 and 1920, GM built 950 houses of varying design on 280 acres of farmland, a staggering accomplishment that rivals the pace of new construction in places like Las Vegas and Phoenix during the more recent housing bubble. It was not unusual for a new home to be completed in seven hours from start to finish.

More than two dozen variations on eight different models were available to homeowners, including the New England Colonial, the Civic Park Saltbox, and the Urban Traditional. "A typical home had five or six rooms, a slate roof, an open porch and a basement," reads the historic-site marker. "Curved streets, planned park areas and tree-lined boulevards added to the attractiveness of the community."

Bassett Place, named after a former Buick president, is one of those curved streets. My childhood home sits midblock. It was not built until the late twenties, after the initial Civic Park construction spree. It faces a sprawling park, one of the last projects completed by GM's Modern Housing Corporation, with baseball diamonds, tennis courts, and a stretch of woods once filled with trails perfect for BMX bike riding and illicit cigarette smoking.

I hadn't intended to start my search on my old street. It was probably just muscle memory that led me back to Bassett Place. Over the winter, I had checked the property records and connected with the current owner to try and arrange an official visit. The phone conversation had been awkward. "You're from California and you want me to let you inside of my house?" she'd asked. "I'll have to call you back on that." She never did. Who could blame her? I had given up on ever seeing the inside, but now I noticed there was no car in the driveway. I called the number that was saved in my cell phone. No answer. I parked across the street and stared at the house. Thanks to the dull utility of aluminum siding, it was surprisingly unchanged since the day we moved out twenty-five years earlier. I noticed a familiar chip in the wood steps leading to the screened-in front porch. I called the number again. Still no answer. There didn't appear to be anyone home.

I had a sudden urge to see the small square of lawn in back where I played football as a kid, the chain-link fence I jumped in the winter to save time getting to the Dupont Street bus. I wondered if the tree where I used to read my Encyclopedia Brown books nestled in the comfortable crook of two big branches was still standing. I wanted to catch a glimpse of the Flint I remembered. I knew this was probably a mistake. I was bound to be disappointed. I was starting to regain my sense of familiarity with Flint, shedding some of the trepidation I'd felt the previous summer. I wasn't sure if that was such a good thing. I hesitated, then got out of the car and headed for the driveway. I'd just take a quick look.

Lingering uninvited in the yard of a house in Flint is not a wise move, but it was all so instantly familiar that my nervousness disappeared in the June heat. There was the tree. There was the fence. There was the pint-sized, makeshift football field with a flowerbed doubling as the sideline. But I was surprised to see something I had completely forgotten—the peeling remnants of a mural on the side of the neighbor's garage. My sister had painted it in the midseventies, an escapist desert landscape with an orange sun setting over a purple mesa surrounded by golden sands and the occasional cactus. It was similar in style and temperament to the airbrushed scenes adorning many customized vans in Flint at a time when Earth, Wind & Fire was battling the Eagles for supremacy on car radios and eight-track tape decks throughout the city, another reflection of Flint's racial divide.

The garage, listing badly and engulfed in shrubbery, hadn't been painted in more than three decades. It once belonged to our neighbor, a stylish elderly woman named Mrs. Procunier. I played gin rummy with her on Tuesday nights when I was a kid. We would sit at a little table in her kitchen, taking turns dealing while she worked her way through a pack of Parliaments and I polished off the Brach's candy she supplied. I also mowed her lawn, shoveled her snow, and bought her cigarettes at the nearby Double D Market, now a vacant lot dotted with fast-growing ghetto palms across the street from the recently shuttered Civic Park School. To allow me to procure smokes at such a tender age, she wrote a note on a piece of scrap paper in her perfect cursive: "Gordie Young has permission to purchase cigarettes for me. He is my employee."

Mrs. Procunier also signed off on my sister's plan to paint the mural. She didn't seem thrilled with the idea, but she was kindhearted. After all, she had forgiven me for almost burning the garage to the ground during my extended flirtation with pyromania. (Take a lighter and a can of Lysol and you've got yourself a flame thrower.) She didn't live long after the mural was completed. She enjoyed a cigarette the day she died of pneumonia, perhaps one purchased by me. She bequeathed our family two thousand dollars and a light blue Buick LeSabre in her will.

Dan Kildee's younger brother Mike and his wife then moved into the house. They drove a Renault Alliance and made out in their backyard, which made them seem wildly exotic. As if to counteract Mrs. Procunier's unhealthy smoking habit, Mike was an avid runner who put up a basketball hoop on the garage. I remember him telling me once when we were shooting baskets that he thought the mural was pretty cool.

In one of my recent conversations with Dan, I had asked for his verdict on Civic Park. He'd spent the bulk of his childhood just five blocks away on Genesee Street. "That neighborhood was at the tipping point about eight years ago, and it tipped," he said, frowning. "The wrong way," he added unnecessarily.

My old neighborhood was clearly in the crosshairs of a revolutionary urban-planning experiment. The shrinking-city concept is a rational approach for a punch-drunk municipality with few options, but standing in my old backyard in a neighborhood on the edge of extinction, despite its historic status, I felt the emotional reluctance of many to embrace the new approach. As I looked at the decaying mural my sister painted in the twilight of Flint's glory years, I understood how agonizing it was for a city to cut its losses and let go of the past, to walk away from so many memories. It felt like accepting defeat.

Back in my car, I drove the streets of Civic Park, window down to better appreciate the beautiful weather, passing familiar landmarks, or what was left of them. My pal Jerry's house on Delmar Avenue was now a vacant lot. Another friend's home on the same block was abandoned, but the railroad ties his dad used to define their flowerbeds in the seventies were still visible. The two-story on the corner of Humboldt and West Dayton—known as "the bachelors' house" because four young guys who were very popular with the ladies lived there—looked like it had been hit by a tornado. The windows were broken, and the front door was wide open, affording a view of the living room where numerous parties had raged. A couple of blocks away, *Rivethead* author Ben Hamper's old house had seen better days. I slowed down for properties that seemed promising, only to discover that they were gutted, nothing more than shells. This was going to be harder than I thought. Blight was in abundant supply; a well-maintained Dutch Colonial defying time, the elements, and complex global economic trends was not.

But while the perfect house was difficult to spot, I was certainly attracting a lot of attention. Judging from the icy stares I got from the few people I passed on the street, I was a highly suspicious character. White guy, short hair, Ray-Bans. There were two obvious possibilities—cop or misguided suburbanite trolling for drugs. The pessimistic might add a third option—a random, crazy muthafucka. I felt the urge to yell out the window, "It's okay, I used to live here." After all, I regularly covered these same streets by foot, bike, and skateboard as a kid. I knew these houses. I'd scouted all the shortcuts and gaps in backyard fences. I still remembered where the unfriendly dogs once lived.

I didn't get too excited when I spotted an impressive wooden sign in the yard of a corner house proclaiming, "Welcome to Milbourne Avenue Block Club / Working Together for a Better Neighborhood." I knew that well-intentioned block clubs frequently couldn't compete with the forces of decline in Flint. These signs were scattered around the city, often acting as tombstones for blocks that didn't make it.

But Milbourne between West Dayton and West Hamilton wasn't dead yet. The curbs lining the street were painted white. Many residents had planted red flowers in the parkway between street and sidewalk. Closer inspection revealed that the flowers were fake, indicating a thrifty pragmatism, a realism that might ensure long-term survival. There was only one vacant lot. A few houses were abandoned, but only a couple were boarded, burned out, or obviously empty. The occupied homes were painted and well kept. Yards were mowed. The random trash that littered so many other blocks was nowhere to be found. A TV news crew looking to capture the decline of Civic Park wouldn't shoot on this block.

And there were actual people visible on the street.

An older black couple sat on lawn chairs in the driveway of an immaculate yellow house. A statue of the Virgin Mary looked out over the front yard. The walkway to the steps was covered in black Astroturf and flanked with running lights. The front of the house was decorated with black shutters and one of those eagles you'd expect to find in an Ethan Allen catalog. If not for the bars on the first-floor windows, it looked like a typical suburban house. Down the street, a woman on her hands and knees was planting flowers. Real ones. At another house, a man on a tall ladder was trimming a tree with a handsaw.

I drove slowly down the street, wondering if I was engaging in magical thinking. Was I looking so hard for signs of hope that I was inventing them? I checked out two adjoining blocks just to make sure; they were shabby, abandoned, and empty. They resembled a movie set after production had shut down.

I looped back around to Milbourne. Instead of a single house, I'd stumbled on almost an entire block making a stand against seemingly inexorable decline. I stopped the car and basked in a little of the useless nostalgia I'd vowed to avoid. With the humidity building as the afternoon stretched toward evening and the birds chirping from the trees above, this could have easily been a typical Civic Park street on a hot summer day in the seventies. It could have been the Flint I remembered.

I noticed two black women—one older and holding a small dog, the other younger with short, bleached hair—watching me from the side porch of the gray house with the block-club sign in the yard. Though I was excited to find their street, they didn't seem thrilled to discover me surveying the situation. I walked over, introduced myself, and asked if they had time to talk. They agreed with a shrug.

I checked out the house as I walked up the driveway. The shingles needed a fresh coat of paint, but the planters near the forbidding wrought-iron security door were filled with healthy flowers. There were new eavestroughs on one section of the roof. It seemed like a house owned by people who still cared but were short on funds.

I took a seat at a glass-top patio table with Betsy, who was just shy of her seventieth birthday, and her forty-three-year-old daughter, Delarie. Betsy had tinted wireless glasses and was wearing a black T-shirt. She looked comfortable on the shady porch, holding a little black Yorkipoo named Quasi on her lap. "There's a lot of drugs and gangs in the neighborhood since you lived here," Betsy said, sounding tired and touching the silver cross she wore on a chain around her neck. "But our block is a lot quieter."

Delarie had a beautiful smile and seemed ten years younger than me, but we had both graduated from Flint high schools in 1984. We ran though a list of people we might know but failed to find a connection, illustrating the gulf between a white Catholic school kid and a black public school student. But like many conversations I had with Flintoids, the initial, practical suspicion quickly evaporated. Once they trusted you, Flint residents were anything but guarded. Betsy and Delarie seemed somewhat bemused by my enthusiasm for the block, agreeing that Milbourne was better than most in the neighborhood but tempering my exuberance with the perspective that comes with being an actual resident. "Civic Park has really gone downhill, but I have hope," Delarie said. "This street is trying to help make up for the rest of the neighborhood."

Betsy and her family ended up here almost by accident. She was living about a mile to the east when she spotted a rent-to-own sign in the yard of the house on a trip to the Double D Market to buy groceries in 1991. She liked the oversize lot—a perfect place for her eleven grandchildren and five great-grandchildren to play. "I prayed to God to give me this house with a big yard, and it worked out," she said. "I like my corner."

The house became a gathering spot for family and neighborhood kids. There was room for an above-ground pool, a swing set, a trampoline, and a badminton net. Betsy was known as "Granny" to the children; Delarie was "Mama," regardless of whether they were relatives or not. But the kids grew up, and then the board of education closed Civic Park School in response to dwindling enrollment and budget cuts. "I really miss hearing little kids in the neighborhood," Betsy said. "Sometimes I feel lost and alone without them."

Delarie added, "They made it seem normal."

Delarie raised two boys in the neighborhood. She rented a house across the street—now abandoned—for several years before moving in with her mom. The boys were eighteen and twenty-three now and still lived with them. The youngest was working on his GED, hoping to join the army. If all went well, he would be in boot camp at Fort Bennington in July. "He had some trouble in school," she explained. "I'm trying to save him, because if you stay around here you can get bitter."

Betsy had moved to Flint from Mississippi in search of opportunity when she was thirty-five. She joined her sister, who had already migrated north. Betsy's time in Flint had not been easy. She was working at a restaurant and lounge on New Year's Eve many years ago when she slipped while carrying a container of hot grease and suffered severe burns. She underwent five skin-graft surgeries on her neck and face. Although she won a $2.5 million judgment against the restaurant, she was never able to collect. "The restaurant didn't have that kind of money," she explained.

Betsy's husband had died in 2007, not long after he retired from GM. The day of the funeral, she was sitting with Quasi when the puppy put its paws on her chest and Betsy felt a sharp pain. After a visit to the doctor, she was diagnosed with breast cancer. Betsy had children in North Carolina and Georgia who wanted her to move in with them, but she was undecided. "I'm a survivor, but I'm not sure I can take care of this house," she said. "Then again, I'm used to having a place of my own. All I'd have is a room at my kid's house. I'm not sure which direction I'll go. I'm just not sure if I'll stay in Flint."

Delarie was the only one of six children still living in Flint. "I'll stay here as long as my mom stays," she said. "I see this block as the soul of the neighborhood. Every night you hear shots from the other streets, but not on our street. But I still don't leave home without my gun. I just feel better carrying it."

She showed me her nine-millimeter handgun, a black Taurus Ultra Slim she kept loaded with hollow-point bullets. She carried it in a small holster on her waist. The gun shattered the reassuring sense of normalcy that had enveloped me, the feeling that Civic Park wasn't that far removed from the place where I grew up, a neighborhood where three people could spend a pleasant afternoon sitting on the porch and talking without the need for firearms. She left the gun on the table, and it was distracting. I kept glancing at it.

"She's concerned about my safety," Betsy explained, sensing my discomfort.

"I'm concerned about *my* safety, too," Delarie added.

I asked what they thought of Dan Kildee's shrinking-city concept. It got a cold reaction, even from two residents who might leave the city to escape its problems. "There are parts of Flint where you can sit on your porch and see empty lots for two or three blocks," Betsy said. "I don't want that to happen here. That's not going to help me. That's just going to make me an easier target."

Delarie repeated a persistent rumor. "You know the land bank is burning down houses all over the city to get rid of them."

As so often happened in Flint, the glimmer of hope I had felt just twenty minutes earlier was fading away. Betsy and Delarie exhibited the contradictory feelings I discovered practically everywhere in the city. They defended their block and the memories they had created there. They were proud of this place. But they were also weary, and it was clear that it might not take all that much for them to join the Flint diaspora, to head to North Carolina or Georgia or Mississippi and leave the challenges of Civic Park behind.

"But what's happening on this block to make it better?" I asked, trying to get back to a positive topic. "Why's Milbourne different from all the other blocks?"

Betsy told me that a black congregation had taken over the once all-white church just around the corner. Community Presbyterian had given way to Joy Tabernacle. The pastor was named Sherman McCathern. "He's doing everything he can to help," she said. "And Dave Starr runs the block club. He's trying hard, too. You should meet both of them."

It turned out I was in luck. There was a block-club meeting scheduled for the next day.

20

Gun Club

Dave Starr looked grandfatherly, with his gray hair and glasses, as he tapped a crooked stick on the edge of a patio table in his backyard and announced, "The meeting of the Milbourne Avenue Block Club is officially called to order." The friendly sixty-eight-year-old was the first white guy I'd seen in Civic Park. With his well-worn jeans, flannel shirt, and red suspenders, he appeared to be an easy mark in a tough neighborhood. But looks can be deceiving.

Dave has his Yahoo account set up to automatically append to each of his emails two concise lines that reveal a great deal about his past and present life:

Retired Shop Rat—14,647 days in a GM Plant
45ACP: Don't leave home without it.

The first commemorates the more than forty years he spent working at Buick, starting on the line before becoming a factory electrician. The second references the ammo for his gun, a stainless steel Dan Wesson .45 caliber semiautomatic CBOB. The C stands for "Commander," meaning the barrel is shortened to 4.25 inches. The modification reduces accuracy, but within the seven-yard "defense zone" where he would be forced to use the gun it's not going to matter. BOB is short for "bobtail" and refers to the rounded handle, making it easier to stash and retrieve from a tight space, like a pocket or a waistband. He bought it online for $925. It was an upgrade from the cheaper Springfield .45 he also owns.

169

It was a Thursday at dusk, and eight residents of the block had gathered for the first meeting of the summer. I'd called Dave earlier to see if I could attend, explaining that I was a Civic Park native looking to buy a house. He seemed unconvinced but was happy to have me sit in on the meeting. I drove over with a bag of cherries for everyone to eat.

Betsy was there, having made the short walk down the street from her house on the corner, and I was happy to see a familiar face. Dave had set up a big industrial fan powered by an orange extension cord snaking into the garage, so an artificial breeze stirred the warm summer air. Dave's wife, Judy, served lemonade. Some of us sat in lawn chairs, and a few took seats on a low cement-block wall that surrounded a deep hole taking up half the yard. I wondered if Dave was building a bomb shelter but was afraid to ask.

The meeting could be compartmentalized into a discussion of three forces conspiring to thwart Milbourne Avenue's progress—nature, economics, and local government in the form of Flint City Hall and the land bank. Unlike the economy, vegetation grows fast in Michigan during the summer, and the abandoned houses presented a constant landscaping challenge. Many of the land-bank houses in the area had wild, overgrown yards. And the city's failure to mow the street medians on nearby West Hamilton Avenue had recently caused a traffic accident. "What are we going to do about these high weeds?" asked a neighbor who had lived in the nice yellow house up the street with her husband since 1977. "Those weeds scare me. It's like they've got plans to become trees!"

But restraining weeds with delusions of grandeur and other improvement projects, such as repainting the curbs on the street, cost money the block club members didn't necessarily have. There was a long discussion of the best way to voice their concerns with the city and the land bank to get things cleaned up. Dave, working on his third cigarette in less than an hour, didn't bother to hide his dislike of both government entities. "I want to go down there and tell them to start doing their job," he said. "I can't mow grass that's three feet high by myself." Another neighbor, who had lived up the street since 1976 and had stylish blond dreadlocks, gently cut him off. "Dave, just leave them alone and we'll do what we can do," she said, pointing out that she had a brother-in-law with land-bank connections who might be able to help them out.

After the meeting broke up, everyone drifted out to the sidewalk to talk in the gathering darkness. There had been no grand decisions made, but the simple fact that a group of neighbors had come together and made modest plans for the future of Civic Park seemed like an accomplishment. It was the sort of basic, fundamental act that was missing in so many parts of the city. I asked Dave if he would mind giving me a personal tour of the neighborhood the next day. He said he had a doctor's appointment, but he'd be glad to help me out later in the week. The streetlights began to flicker on, my old signal to get home for the night when I was a kid. It still applied. I was nervous about being in the neighborhood after dark. I said my goodbyes and headed to my car.

When I returned to the Starrs' pale yellow house with dark shutters a few days later, Dave seemed fidgety. We were standing in his living room, which was outfitted with his and hers La-Z-Boys, a collection of family photos, and some impressive NASCAR collectibles, including a wall display of Matchbox-size cars and a few dozen commemorative plates devoted to various drivers. I could hear Judy putting dishes away in the kitchen. I noticed Dave wasn't smoking and wondered if that was the problem. In a way, it was.

"I got some bad news at the doctor the other day," he said. "I've got lung cancer."

The cancer was stage one and attacking the lower lobe of his right lung. He would need surgery sometime that summer.

I told him I was sorry, unsure of what else to say. I suggested that we cancel the tour, that we could do it later, but he brushed it aside. Judy came in, and we sat down in the living room. A gray cat appeared, eyeing me suspiciously. "That's Jinx," Dave said. "Someone dumped her across the street, and she ended up in our garage one day. Two Pit Bulls were ripping the siding off trying to get at her. I went after the Pit Bulls with a two-by-four and she came inside and decided to stay." There were three other cats somewhere in the house, reluctant to make an appearance. "Jinx seems to think it's his job to protect me," Dave added. "He sleeps in the hallway and keeps all the other cats from bothering me at night."

Under the watchful eye of Jinx, I asked them to tell me how they'd met and ended up living in Civic Park. Judy was a twenty-one-year-old beauty-school student when she went out on her first date with Dave. They'd been set up by Dave's sister, who was a classmate of Judy's. They went to a drive-in movie, and after it was over they sat in the driveway of Judy's parents and talked until dawn. "This was a deal where you meet someone and you know that's the person you want to spend the rest of your life with," Judy said. "I don't know how you know, but you just do." It was the same feeling I had after my first date with Traci, although we were in our thirties when it happened.

Dave and Judy got married about a year later in the cafeteria of Saint Michael's school because the parish was in the process of building a new church. I knew this spot well. It was where I ate lunch in first and second grades before the school closed. I also worked bingo there with my mom to help offset the tuition at my Catholic high school, selling cake, candy, and pop to elderly, chain-smoking players. It was now a "warming center" run by Catholic Charities, not to be confused with a homeless shelter. Families who still had a place to live but couldn't afford to pay their heating bills could come there in the winter for warmth.

They moved into the house on Milbourne when Civic Park was almost exclusively a white neighborhood. A black pediatrician was the only nonwhite resident on the tree-lined block. Their classic two-story New England Colonial has a steeply pitched roof and is modeled on the style favored by the Puritans. It cost $14,500, and they made a $450 down payment. Their mortgage was $123 a month. "At the time I couldn't figure out how we could come up with that kind of money every month, but we did," Dave told me. He figured the house was worth less now than it was when they bought it in 1968. He was not wrong.

For a time, Judy worked as a beautician, but she gave that up after a son and daughter were born. Civic Park was a good place to raise a family. There were kids everywhere. The school was just a few blocks away. Haskell Community Center, with its playground, pool, and bowling alley, was nearby. There was baseball in the summer and skating in the winter at Bassett Park. But as Flint's economic fortunes declined, Civic Park began to change. The number of rental houses increased, and abandoned homes became more common. Crime flourished, and security bars and home alarm systems became a necessity in a neighborhood where residents used to leave their doors unlocked.

Civic Park also morphed from a white neighborhood to a black neighborhood. Dave can't even remember when they became the only white family on the block, the Caucasian equivalent of their long-ago neighbor, the black pediatrician. But though white flight was commonplace in Civic Park and the rest of Flint, the changing racial demographics didn't bother Dave and Judy. "I just figured they're people just like everybody else," Dave said. "Maybe it was my upbringing or my Catholic school background, but I've always been taught to see the person, not the skin color. We have wonderful neighbors. Really nice people."

Their friends and family didn't always have such an enlightened outlook. White neighbors confided that they were moving because the blacks were taking over, destroying property values. "I grew up in a prejudiced household," Judy said. "My dad pressured us to move. At one point he said to me, 'I don't know why you're living there with all those niggers.'"

Judy is slight and soft-spoken with short gray hair and glasses. She likes sweatshirts with pastel designs—seashells and starfish and the like—that you'd find at craft fairs. But you can tell when something doesn't sit right with her. "I just told my dad, 'Too bad. We're not going anywhere. This is our home.'"

Dave and Judy's devotion to Milbourne hasn't come without its share of heartache and tragedy, however. In 1996, after both children had moved out, Judy was working at McDonald's to earn extra money. She had to be there at 4 A.M. to prep and open the restaurant. One morning she went out to the car for work and didn't notice the teenage boy who lived across the street sitting on his front porch. He'd had problems with drinking and drugs, and his parents sometimes locked him out when he missed his curfew, hoping to teach him a lesson. "It was a tough-love thing," Judy explained. As Judy unlocked the car in the predawn darkness, he came up behind her, swung her to the ground, and slammed her face into the concrete. He apparently planned to steal the car. "The only thing I remember is lying on the ground and begging him not to kill me," Judy said.

The car alarm went off and woke up Dave. "I looked out the bedroom window," he said. "I could see the car in the driveway with the door open, and I could hear her moaning. I raced down there and found her face down with blood all over the place." Dave called 911, and the police caught the boy hiding under the deck behind his house. The police told Dave he was crying when they found him, afraid that he'd killed Judy. "He almost did," Dave said.

Judy's jaw was broken in three places. Her eye socket was fractured. She was taken to the University of Michigan Hospital in Ann Arbor for seven hours of surgery. She endured eighteen months of medical procedures. She consulted a denture specialist because her gums, teeth, and jaw were so damaged. Dave installed a hospital bed in the living room and prepared Campbell's Chunky Soup in a blender for Judy to eat. The neighborhood kids all made get-well cards for her and brought them over. "The people on the block showed they were more than just neighbors," Dave said. "They were our friends."

At the same time, Dave realized the neighborhood might be too dangerous for them to stay any longer. His daughter urged them to move. He asked Judy if it was time to leave. "I don't know where and I don't know how, but if you don't want to live here anymore, we'll go," he told her.

"This is my home, and I will not be driven from it," she answered without hesitation.

"She may not act like it, but she's one tough lady," Dave told me.

But Judy's determination couldn't completely erase the aftereffects of the attack. Her vision was damaged and she had trouble focusing in one eye, but the psychological scars were more insidious. For several months, she wouldn't leave the house, even to go into the backyard, without a baseball bat. "I'd try to feel comfortable, but sometimes I had this fear, you know," she said. "But this is our home. I wasn't going to walk away from it."

I understood her devotion, even though my mom had always described our family as a band of gypsies, comfortable anywhere yet never fully settled in one spot. We are allegedly drifters with a yearning for the open road. My mom certainly took that approach to life. Her failed marriages to two navy pilots ensured a peripatetic lifestyle. My brother was born in Flint. One sister was born in Jacksonville, Florida, and another in Olathe, Kansas. I was conceived in a Quonset hut at Hunter's Point Shipyard in San Francisco when my dad's carrier was in drydock and born in San Diego. I've certainly moved around a lot as an adult. Yet I'm the kid in our family who spent the most time in one spot, and that spot was Flint. I share Judy's attachment to this troubled spot on the Michigan map.

The conversation soon drifted to lighter fare. We talked about professional wrestling and NASCAR. Judy's favorite driver is Jeff Gordon. Dave's favorite driver is anyone other than Jeff Gordon. "Sometimes in a race I'll try to jinx him," Dave said, narrowing his eyes and wiggling his fingers in the direction of the television. "Once or twice he's had an accident right after I did it." Dave was smiling. Judy was not. She shook her head and stood up.

"Let's go for that walk," she said, selecting an official red and black Jeff Gordon jacket from the coat rack. "You got the pistol?"

"Right here," Dave answered, pulling his shirt back to reveal his .45 sticking out of the front pocket of his Wrangler jeans. He looked at me and added, "It's mostly for the Pit Bulls." I wasn't sure if this was meant to be reassuring.

Dave locked the door and Judy, who was intent on actually getting a little exercise, quickly pulled ahead of us as we walked north up Milbourne toward West Dayton. Dave was more intent on explication, pausing frequently to deliver commentary, gossip, and insight, like an earnest tour guide at the Civil War battle sites he's fond of visiting on vacations. In fact, we only made it as far as the white house with the aluminum siding next door before he stopped. It was more or less abandoned, although it was hard to tell from the outside. The house was tidy, with curtains in the windows. Dave explained that it had been a rental owned by a woman in Detroit. One day while the tenants were out, scrappers broke in and stole the copper pipes. Dave had noticed the front door open and water running out of the house. The owner didn't want to pay to fix the plumbing, so the renter moved out. Rumor on the street was that the owner's son was a truck driver, and he sometimes crashed at the house, even though there was no water. The electricity was still on, and Dave worried about the house catching fire. Not exactly an unusual story in Flint, except that the owner had paid $65,000 for the house on a land contract in 2007. "No idea why someone would pay so much for this house," Dave said. "It's insane."

We caught up to Judy halfway down the street in front of a light blue house that appeared to be occupied despite an addition in back that was collapsing. Dave said the owner had flown to the Philippines several months ago. "He married a lady there, if you know what I mean," Dave said, raising an eyebrow and giving me a half smile.

"How'd they meet?" I asked, unsure where this was going.

"Mail-order bride," he clarified. "I guess she's having trouble getting into the country, so he went there. He said he's coming back with her someday, but I kind of doubt it."

Judy jumped in. "Have you ever seen that show *Hoarders?*" she asked. "That's what he's like. There's a little pathway to get through the house. That's it. He doesn't throw anything away."

We stood on the sidewalk for a few seconds, staring at the house. I tried to imagine the owner bringing his new wife back to Flint, to the alleged wealth and promise of America. It was hard to envision the scenario ending well.

Down the street, three black men were huddled over the engine of a van parked on the street. One glanced up at us standing on the sidewalk, smiled, and called out: "Hey, Mr. Starr, come and see what I've done with the car."

"That's Anthony," Dave said to me. "A great guy."

Anthony and his wife, Tabitha, had rented a house on the block for twenty years and were hoping to buy it from their landlord. Anthony had a light blue Chevy Lumina in the driveway that he'd been working on. He'd swapped out the fuse panel and found a replacement hood in a slightly paler shade of blue. He was excited about the car, even though it was just the kind of blandly unreliable make and model that helped hasten GM's decline. Anthony walked us around the Chevy, pointing out improvements. "That's why I love this street," Dave said as we walked away. "Anthony gives me some hope. The guy even shovels my driveway and rakes my leaves when we're not home."

We passed an empty rental house owned by a speculator in California before reaching the corner of Milbourne and West Dayton. Joy Tabernacle came into view across the street. Six church members, all young black men, were out sweeping and cleaning the parking lot. But the yards of houses across from the church were littered with tires and an impressive variety of junk. One house looked like you could knock it over with a feather. It was owned by a guy in Nevada. We rounded the next corner and walked down North Chevrolet Avenue, a major thoroughfare of Civic Park that runs all the way to Chevy in the Hole. Nearly every house on the block was abandoned. I pointed out an occupied home across the street, the yard filled with kids' toys and a brightly colored plastic clubhouse. "Hey, at least there's some kids left in the neighborhood," I said, but Dave frowned. "I hear a lot of domestic violence calls on the scanner from that place in the summer," said Dave, who regularly monitors his two police scanners. "Fights and stuff."

We passed a vacant lot landscaped with Hennessey cognac bottles and several trees scorched by fire. "Drug house," Dave said matter-of-factly. "A crowd gathered to watch it burn, and they cheered when the walls came down. They were happy to see it go."

At another vacant lot, he paused again. "A car doing about a hundred hit the house that used to be here during a car chase. Knocked it right off the foundation. I heard the boom and came over. The car was upside down in the yard. Two dead."

We came to the corner of West Hamilton and North Chevrolet Avenues, an intersection I had crossed every day on my "commute" to Saint Mike's in second grade. My mom had to be at the hospital at six for work, so I woke up on my own during the school year. She would set an alarm on the stove to signal when it was time for me to ride my bike to Dupont Street and catch the city bus to school. Now there was an all-too-familiar shrine of plastic flowers, balloons, stuffed animals, and homemade signs for a little girl killed in a car accident at the corner. "We tried to get a light put in here, but the city said there wasn't enough traffic to justify it," Dave said.

There were no visible cars. In fact, there wasn't another person in sight. We kept walking and came to the corner of West Hamilton and Milbourne. We had only circled a single block but had already passed nearly twenty abandoned houses. I noticed a cracked slab of sidewalk inscribed "W. B. Brown & Sons 1917." It dated back to the creation of the neighborhood. It was hard to believe it had survived. Nearby, in red spray paint on an adjacent square of concrete, another makeshift memorial read "R.I.P. Quack."

"Probably a gangbanger," Dave said.

"Who liked Donald Duck," I said, a desperate attempt at humor. The sun had hidden behind a cloud, and Dave's travelogue of death, decay, and mayhem was making me depressed.

"Or a doctor," Judy said without smiling. I couldn't tell if she was serious. Then she added, "Our street is supposed to be up for new sidewalks soon. We're next on the city list."

"Yeah, right," Dave said, and they both laughed at the notion that Milbourne Avenue would be the recipient of infrastructure improvements anytime soon. Gallows humor. Given the archeological evidence at our feet proving that some sections of the sidewalk hadn't been replaced in more than ninety years, I could see why they weren't optimistic.

We headed down West Hamilton for another block and turned on Proctor. To the uninitiated, it might look similar to Dave and Judy's block. But it quickly became clear that almost all the houses were abandoned. Many had yellow C/P symbols spray-painted on the front, indicating that the water and gas pipes had been capped. Thieves had made off with every scrap of aluminum siding. There were thirty old tires piled in one driveway. It was uncomfortably quiet—a character in a suspense movie might describe it as "too quiet." There was suddenly a sense of danger. Dave told me that their mail carrier tried to hit streets like this bright and early in the summer, before the gangbangers and the Pit Bulls woke up. "I'm telling you, our block of Milbourne is like a tropical paradise in a sea of blight," Dave said, then he paused as if searching for a more thoroughly superlative metaphor, but a sour look washed over his face. "Whew, smell that?" he asked. "The skunks got out of control when Walling cut the garbage pickup."

Like many Flint residents I had come to know, conversations with Dave often looped back to Mayor Dayne Walling and Dan Kildee. The verdict was seldom positive. Walling's attempt to help balance the city budget by reducing garbage collection to once every two weeks in late March had united the city in opposition to the measure. Blacks and whites, liberals and conservatives, labor and management, Michigan State and University of Michigan fans alike formed an unlikely alliance against the measure. The only constituency that seemed to endorse the move were skunks and rats, and they didn't vote. Walling had reverted to weekly garbage collection after the withering public outcry and the realization that the move hadn't saved any money because city garbage collectors had to work overtime to collect all the extra trash every two weeks.

We passed several vacant houses, none of them boarded or secured, all owned by the land bank. Dave pointed this out, shaking his head. "Kildee was in the paper the other day complaining that Detroit wasn't doing a good job of keeping property away from speculators," he said. "Some of the worst houses in Flint are land-bank properties. They're as bad as speculators."

I noticed that Judy was frowning, too. It was unclear whether it was from the skunk smell or the mere mention of Kildee's name. We looped back around to Milbourne, passed Betsy's corner house, and stopped at the lone vacant lot on the block. "Now, Gordon, are you familiar with the hip-hop band the Dayton Family?" Dave asked rather formally.

I couldn't help but laugh. I didn't take Dave Starr to be a fan of Flint's foremost gangsta rap act, creators of classic songs like "How Many Niggas You Know?" "Sex, Drugs, Money & Murder," and "U Can't Fuck with Us." Despite numerous struggles with the law in the nineties, the founding members of the Dayton Family—Ira "Bootleg" Dorsey, Raheen "Shoestring" Peterson, and Matt "Backstabba" Hinkle—managed to produce a gold album and capture the essence and humor of the Vehicle City in its declining years with songs like "Welcome to Flint":

> In Flint, we ain't never been scared to die slim
> 'cause we been there ever since they closed GM
> Welcome to Flint Town, it's nutty and wild,
> niggas love to murder execution style.

The members of the Dayton Family grew up about seven blocks to the east near Bonbright Street, but Shoestring's mom was renting the house that once stood on this vacant lot on Milbourne when the band was searching for a spot to shoot a video for their song "Ghetto." In the video, the house has a mailbox indicating it's on Dayton Street. Apparently, Milbourne didn't carry the same street cred. Before we moved on, Dave offered up a concise musical critique. "You know, rap used to be more about telling a story," he said. "It grew out of guys on the street corner just telling stories. I think it's lost some of that now. It's not as good."

Flint is a place where strange things can happen, but I have to admit I never expected to be walking the streets of Civic Park, discussing the evolution of hip-hop with a retired white shop rat. But the conversation was certainly instructive. If I had any doubts that Dave Starr understood the particular dynamics of his neighborhood, they were gone now. He certainly wasn't living in the past. His eyes were wide open.

When we got back to the house, I asked Dave about the backyard construction project I had wondered about during the block-club meeting. It turned out he wasn't building a bomb shelter. He was in the middle stages of creating what would be a three-thousand-gallon pond with a filtration system and a cascading waterfall. He'd been working on it since 2007 and planned to fill it with water lilies and other plants. He hadn't decided if he would stock it with koi or smaller, double-tailed wakin goldfish. "One of my neighbors suggested catfish," Dave said, smiling. "I think he's looking forward to a cookout or something. We may have to consider it if the economy keeps going like this."

His enthusiasm built as he detailed the work that was left to be done, but he finally paused as he surveyed the cement-block retaining wall, the deep hole, and the high mound of dirt near his garage. "I planned to get a lot done this summer, but this cancer thing might slow me down."

I asked how much the pond would cost from start to finish. He figured about eight thousand dollars. I tried not to look surprised. It could end up costing more than his house was worth. Dave looked at me as if he knew what I was thinking.

"Some people might think we're old-fashioned or strange, but this is not just a house where we live. This is our home, and we're going to take care of it," he said. "You can either run away from your problems or you can stay and fight."

Bargaining with God

It took me a few weeks to catch up with Sherman McCathern, the pastor of Joy Tabernacle Church, which was located within shouting distance of the corner house where Betsy and her daughter lived. I'd heard positive reviews of his work in the neighborhood at the block-club meeting. He had only been in Civic Park for about a year, but he'd already established himself as a stabilizing force. When we met, he made it clear that it was no accident the two of us were sitting in his well-ordered office behind the sanctuary.

"It's providence that you're here," he said. "These things don't happen by accident."

I had my doubts that God had brought me to Civic Park, but McCathern told me I should have more faith. After all, the Almighty had more or less given him this building, the first permanent home of the nondenominational church he had founded shortly after the 9/11 terrorist attacks. "Let me tell you a story about how God works," he said.

McCathern said that God had woken him with a message early one morning in January of 2009. The pastor needed to drive over to the corner of West Dayton Street and North Chevrolet Avenue. This wasn't just a vague notion that he should head to the heart of Civic Park. This was God telling him to do something. Immediately. "I got up and came over here, and my whole life changed," McCathern said. "I knew then that for whatever reason I'd been born, and for whatever reason I'd gone through everything that I'd gone through in my life, it was at this particular place that it would all come to fruition."

McCathern, a tall, imposing fifty-five-year-old black man with a shaved head and an unwavering gaze, found himself standing in the crumbling parking lot of Community Presbyterian Church. For decades, the sturdy blond-brick structure with stone trim, a bell tower, and elaborate stained-glass windows had been a reliable, unifying presence in Civic Park. It was built shortly after the neighborhood was created, and the congregation climbed to 1,600 in the sixties. Even my family, steeped in Catholic tradition, occasionally went to the Friday night fish fry in the basement. I probably wore one of my Notre Dame football T-shirts. "They aren't so bad . . . for Protestants," my mom said to me, only half jokingly, as we walked home from one of the dinners.

But as the neighborhood changed, the church failed to change with it. Reverend Timm High, a thirty-three-year-old from Minnesota fresh out of the seminary, tried to diversify the congregation when he became pastor in 1986. The only African American connected with the church at the time was the custodian. High had numerous ideas to change the situation. He wanted to take over a nearby ice cream parlor to give teenagers jobs and teach them business skills. He suggested purchasing empty houses, rehabbing them, and helping local residents buy them on land contracts. It would forge a bond with the community and help slow the rapid decay of Civic Park. He met stiff resistance from many longtime members of the church. "There was almost an attitude that they wanted to turn back the clock to the 1950s," High told me when I called him to talk about the church. "That's a hard mentality to over-come. I tried, but I couldn't do it."

High, married with two children, also experienced the consequences of living near the church. His house was robbed twice. On one occa-sion, burglars severely beat the family dog, a Norwegian Elkhound named Thor. "They must have used a bat," High said. "The dog was never really the same after that."

High left in 1995 to run a church near Syracuse, New York. Despite it all, he doesn't regret his stay in Flint. "I'll always be grateful that I lived there," he said, echoing the loyalty many people feel toward the city after they leave. His replacement, an engaging, energetic young black woman from Chicago, didn't have much luck connecting with the neighborhood either. The dwindling white congregation typically drove in from other neighborhoods or the suburbs on Sundays. Even today, some older black residents of Civic Park refer to Community Presbyterian simply as "the white church."

The Presbytery of Lake Huron, the church's governing body in Saginaw, finally closed Community Presbyterian on New Year's Eve in 2008, when there were fewer than one hundred active members. The church was having trouble paying its heating bills. It was put up for sale. At one point, the asking price was $100,000, an astounding sum that indicated just how out of touch with Civic Park the church hierarchy was.

I was eager to learn how the scenario had played out that left McCathern in control of an overpriced church. I was clearly the target audience for any story about someone acquiring Flint property against all odds. But the pastor knew how to build suspense. He wanted to fill me in with some background details first. He told me he'd traveled a long and often troubled path to end up in Civic Park. He grew up in Pontiac, a blue-collar factory town located roughly halfway between Flint and Detroit, and his early biography could easily have been lived out in the Vehicle City. His father was just sixteen when he traveled north from rural Tennessee to work in a GM plant. He was a drinker and a gambler, but he always supported his family. McCathern was born in the projects, but when he was ten the family moved to a predominantly white housing development in Pontiac called Herrington Hills. It was not unlike a more recent version of Civic Park.

"Were you happy to move to a better part of town?" I asked.

"I went through culture shock when we moved," McCathern answered. "It was an extremely nice neighborhood, but it was hard for me to reconcile it with life back in the projects. That's when the desire to help people who are struggling was really instilled in me."

McCathern's grandfather had been a minister back in Tennessee, and McCathern knew early on that he wanted to follow in his footsteps. After high school, he enrolled in the American Baptist College in Nashville, graduating in 1978. It was the first time he'd ever been away from home. He tried his first beer and his first cigarette while studying to be a minister. Unfortunately, he didn't stop there. In addition to a bachelor of arts degree, McCathern picked up a drug habit in college after experimenting with cocaine. Despite his growing addiction, he founded a church in Nashville and ran it for three years before realizing he had to get help. He resigned and, using money he inherited when his father died, checked himself into Hazelden, an elite treatment center near Minneapolis favored by celebrities.

Life after rehab included several relapses, as it often does, but McCathern eventually landed in Little Rock, Arkansas, clean and sober. I lived in the city at the same time when I was working as a reporter. We discovered that we knew some of the same people. (McCathern indicated that this was another sign from God that our paths were meant to cross.) He pastored at a local church and got a job as a case manager for a nonprofit working with teenagers and young adults involved in the city's burgeoning gang and drug scene. In 1992, he was shot three times at a convenience store in an apparent robbery, although McCathern speculates it may have been a gang initiation ritual. He survived only to relapse and start smoking crack. He ran into trouble with the law and decided to resign from his church and the nonprofit. He and his wife of many years divorced.

After another stint in rehab, this time in Nashville, McCathern got an offer from an old college friend to work on anti–youth violence initiatives in Racine, Wisconsin. It was a chance to do meaningful work again, and McCathern was able to avoid falling into his old drug habit. He was on vacation visiting his mother in Pontiac when he heard from a college classmate, who asked if he was interested in being an interim pastor at a church in Flint. McCathern decided to move back home with his mother, commute to Flint for his work at the church, and earn extra money as a substitute teacher in Pontiac. When the church passed over McCathern to select a new permanent pastor, a few members asked him to start his own church. Joy Tabernacle was born.

Finding a permanent home for the new church was a struggle. The small congregation first met at the YWCA in downtown Flint. McCathern baptized new members in the pool where countless Flint kids had learned to swim. In the first year, the congregation grew to sixty members. Joy shared space with the New Testament Full Gospel Church in the fall of 2002, but two months later the 122-year-old church burned to the ground.

The predominantly white First Church of the Brethren invited Joy to hold services at its building, and the two congregations worked together for two years. Eventually, Joy relocated yet again to an annex property of Morning Star Baptist Church. It happened to be located next to New Paths, an alternative sentencing program that nonviolent offenders could pursue in lieu of jail time. Just as he had in Little Rock and Racine, McCathern began working with troubled young men, many of them with criminal records and few job skills. He offered them free meals every Friday, and they were welcomed at Sunday services. McCathern estimates that more than half of his congregation left the church because they did not want to associate with New Paths. "It was very discouraging," he said. "This is the most trying ministry I've ever been involved with. Flint is the most trying city I've ever lived in. It's hard to raise the hopes of people who have to live in an environment that has five or six or seven abandoned houses on every block."

All the while, he was still hoping for a church building of his own. He looked at a few overpriced, run-down buildings that would have cost a fortune to rehab. A real estate agent told him about Community Presbyterian, but he hadn't given it much thought because of the price tag. He reconsidered after he got that message from God.

McCathern didn't have much money, but he wasn't particularly worried. God had told him the church was his. He just had to figure out a way to make it happen. He started by befriending Richard "Rick" McClellan, the white caretaker left behind to keep an eye on things. Rick's parents had been longtime members of Community Presbyterian. He had grown up in the church, and at that time he was literally living in it, sleeping on a couch in the study, a small, book-lined room just off the pastor's current office. Rick's seventeen-year-old Chihuahua, Sera, named after the Doris Day hit song "Que Sera, Sera," kept him company, along with a cat named Boo. His black Ford pickup was typically the only vehicle in the parking lot. He cleaned the church, answered the rare phone call, and monitored the alarm system, although he sometimes forgot to turn it on when he left. During the day, he also made money selling antiques around Flint.

Rick took an instant liking to McCathern when he spotted him snapping photos of the church one day. "He was just a friendly, approachable person," Rick told me when I tracked him down a few weeks after meeting McCathern. "I was hoping he got the church from the very beginning." Rick gave the pastor a tour and was surprised to discover that he was terrified of Boo and all other felines. He could handle working with gangbangers and welcomed the chance to minister to some of Flint's most marginalized citizens, but his empathy had limits. "Cats are sneaky," McCathern told him, "and I don't like sneaky."

The pastor was amazed at the pristine condition of the church. He took it as a sign that God was watching over the place. In a neighborhood marked by destruction and decay, not a single one of the stained-glass windows had been broken. The church had never been robbed or vandalized. Rick admitted that he didn't even bother to lock the ground-level windows of the church. He said that he talked to a neighborhood guy about a month after the church closed, who told him that the local crack dealers protected the church because they knew it had helped the community over the years. "It was strangely reassuring," said Rick, who sometimes took bike rides around the neighborhood.

Before long, McCathern asked if he could bring his congregation over to look at the church. Rick readily agreed. More than one hundred people showed up. "I probably could have been fired for doing it, but I trusted them," Rick said. "I guess I wasn't such a great caretaker."

The pastor talked Rick into allowing his congregation to start fixing up the church. They trimmed the shrubs, patched the roof, polished the floors, and painted the drab beige walls in the basement a more inviting bluish green color, which happened to be one of Rick's favorites. They even resurfaced the parking lot. "I just knew it was all going to work out, so I didn't mind putting some money into the church before I technically owned it," McCathern explained. The final step was for Rick to give the pastor his own key, the alarm code, and permission to hold a service. (There is some dispute about whether McCathern was supposed to get final approval from the higher-ups in Saginaw, but it never happened.) For the first time in decades, the church was packed on a Sunday, this time with more African Americans than had ever stepped foot inside Community Presbyterian during its long history.

Word filtered back to Presbyterian headquarters that a large black congregation was holding services in the church. Rick soon got a call. Instead of trying to hide anything, he lobbied for the pastor, detailing all the work he'd done and what a great steward of the church he would be. He became the pastor's biggest supporter.

On the surface, Rick McClellan and Sherman McCathern were an unlikely duo. One was a white remnant of the old Civic Park, a solitary reminder of the days when Community Presbyterian was a thriving part of the neighborhood, who was now camped out in the empty church with his dog and cat. The other was a gregarious African American minister with a checkered past determined to find a home for his flock and somehow revive Civic Park at the same time. But there were some similarities. Their last names were almost interchangeable; they were nearly the exact same age; and, if you really wanted to stretch it, they both had shaved heads. And then there was a more unlikely connection between the two men. Both had started what could only be described as race riots at roughly the same time when they were in high school, certainly a bond that few people share.

Rick attended Northwestern, Flint's newest high school, which was located on the northern edge of the city, right next door to my Catholic high school. When he enrolled in the late sixties, the neighborhood and the school were largely white. By his senior year, in a testament to the profound impact of white flight in Flint, the racial demographics had been reversed. "White people just started selling their houses like crazy after a few black people moved into the neighborhood," Rick remembered.

As the editor of *Paw Prints*, the school newspaper, Rick was disturbed by the Ku Klux Klan flyers that were regularly tucked under the windshield wipers of cars in the school parking lot during the day. They were similar to the racist propaganda that I remember seeing on telephone poles around the city at the time. In February of 1972, he decided to write an editorial denouncing the Klan and encouraging white students not to give in to racial hatred. "A crusade should be initiated which would make the atmosphere in schools one where writing distributed by such a corrupt organization as the Ku Klux Klan would only be laughed at by its recipients," Rick wrote. He tore the top off one of the flyers and used it as a headline so readers would know what kind of rhetoric he was condemning. He was aiming for an edgy collage effect that would clearly not resemble the other stories in the paper. "I was trying to be a little too creative," he told me. "When it printed you couldn't tell it was ripped from the flyer. It just looked like a regular headline." It read: "White Youth Fight Back—The United Ku Klux Klan Is With You."

The paper was distributed during third hour, and some black students were so enraged by the headline that they didn't bother to read the editorial. Fights started throughout the school, even as the principal appealed for calm over the public address system. A group of angry students headed for the room where the newspaper was put together, looking for Rick. As luck would have it, he was in Florida visiting his grandparents that week, completely unaware of the havoc his editorial had unintentionally provoked.

On Monday, the fighting intensified inside the school. "Two white students apparently were shoved into a classroom in one wing of the building later in the afternoon and beaten by black students," reported the *Flint Journal*, in its typical one-sided fashion. None of the articles on the unrest mention white students attacking black classmates. "Chairs and tables in the room were overturned and a blackboard was shattered. A large pool of blood was discovered on the floor, with a trail of blood along the wall of the hallway toward the main lobby." A rock fight broke out among students who left the school grounds at lunchtime. Police were called to the school to help restore order.

Over the next few days, the situation calmed down, partly because of the police presence and partly because roughly two-thirds of the students didn't show up for the rest of the week. But a week after the editorial ran, violence broke out at Beecher, a racially mixed high school in Mount Morris Township, just a few miles from Northwestern. There were fights and a few fires started at the school. Police were called in, and Beecher High was closed briefly. The most devastating result of the racial unrest was the suicide of Paul L. Cabell Jr., a twenty-six-year-old black assistant principal at Beecher who had worked tirelessly to resolve racial tension at the school. He killed himself in the study of his home with a small-gauge shotgun. "No one . . . can comprehend the continuous agony that this situation presents," he wrote in a suicide note.

Rick returned from Florida and learned that the school district had transferred him to Southwestern High School for his own safety. He had no idea why, but when he figured out what had happened, he made the decision to return to Northwestern. He had many friends at the school, both black and white. He didn't want to abandon the newspaper, which he loved. "The people who knew me didn't have a problem with the article," he explained. "And the people who didn't know me didn't know what I looked like, so it was fine. I didn't have any problems."

The details of the race riot Pastor McCathern started at roughly the same time are a little hazy. He's more of a big-picture man than someone who attends to details. His son is a student at Michigan State, and McCathern told me he once accidentally bought him a maize and blue University of Michigan T-shirt as a present. In the Great Lake State, that's the equivalent of offering an Israeli flag to a Palestinian as a housewarming gift. The pastor laughs about it now, pointing out that the important thing was that his son was in college. It didn't matter which one. He admitted that he has a spotty memory. "Dates elude me," he explained, which is why he can't recall exactly when he started the race riot. It was sometime during football season in the fall of 1970.

At the time, Pontiac was making national headlines over efforts by white residents to stop court-ordered busing to integrate the city's highly segregated public school system. According to a suit filed by the NAACP in 1969, Pontiac schools were either 90 percent white or 90 percent black. The showdown in Pontiac made Flint's struggle to promote integration seem mild-mannered by comparison. Members of the American Nazi Party were arrested at antibusing rallies. Klansmen were eventually convicted of dynamiting empty school buses. A thirty-six-year-old housewife named Irene McCabe led a high-profile march to Washington to lobby for a constitutional amendment banning busing. She was welcomed at the Capitol steps by Gerald Ford, then the House minority leader from Michigan. The next day, McCabe met with an advisor to President Richard Nixon. "Pontiac is the new South," one Michigan state legislator said at the time. "I'm frankly ashamed to say right now that I am a citizen of this city." But the antibusing fervor was political gold for Alabama governor George Wallace. He used it as a wedge issue to win Michigan's Democratic presidential primary in the fall of 1972.

In this tension-filled setting, McCathern was emerging as a student leader in high school, becoming what he described as "a defender of the people." This was evident at a high school football game when a black student wandered down from the hillside where spectators sat and started mingling with the players. The coach, who was white, confronted the student and told him to get off the sideline. They started arguing. McCathern said he ran down to protect the student, and the coach punched McCathern in the stomach. "I'll never forget that day," McCathern said. "After he hit me, all the black kids ran down the hill to get the coach, and all the white kids ran down the hill to protect him." When it was all over, McCathern was kicked out of school for several months. He was eventually readmitted and graduated with his class at Pontiac Northern in the spring of 1972, the same time Rick was graduating from Flint Northwestern.

But neither the unlikely symmetry between Sherman McCathern and Rick McClellan nor the quirk of fate—or divine intervention—that had brought them together could ensure that Community Presbyterian would become Joy Tabernacle. In the midst of the Great Recession, the pastor had no luck getting a loan, so he made an offer to buy the church building on a land contract with a small down payment. It was rejected. To make matters worse, another congregation was also interested in the property. McCathern prayed for guidance, offering to hold free Christmas dinners every year if God could somehow deliver the church to him. (He said he often "negotiated" in this manner with the Almighty.) McCathern decided to make the biggest offer he could with a promise to make additional payments in the future. The vast majority of Joy Tabernacle's congregation was unemployed. Many were trying to rebuild their lives after addiction, prison, and a host of other tragic circumstances. But the members had raised fifteen thousand dollars to buy the church. It was nowhere near the asking price, but it was the best they could do.

McCathern's real-estate agent telephoned and told him he had some news, but then abruptly ended the call. He wanted to confirm that he had the details right. He called back and told the pastor that his offer had been accepted. McCathern was ecstatic, but he cautiously asked about the additional payments he was sure would be looming down the line. That's when the news got even better. No additional payments were necessary. Neither was a mortgage. Joy owned the church out-right, along with everything in it, including the plates in the kitchen, the collection of choir robes, a massive pipe organ, and the computers, files, and assorted office supplies left behind.

Pastor McCathern invited the former members of Community Pres-byterian, who had scattered to other churches, to return to Civic Park for a special celebration at Joy Tabernacle. In a way, it was also a long overdue ceremony to mark the transformation that had taken place in Civic Park over the past four decades, and a chance to chart a course for the future of the neighborhood. It had the feel of both a baptism and a funeral, and crosscurrents of hope and sadness filled the church. Two dozen members of Community Presbyterian were there, some of them in their eighties and nineties. Most likely, it would be the last time they'd spend a Sunday in the church. Mayor Dayne Walling attended, declaring that October 11, 2009, was Joy Tabernacle Church Day. (In a testament to what a small town Flint had become, Dan Kildee's wife covered the event for the *Flint Journal*.) Rick McClellan stood at the altar and handed an ornate candle to Pastor McCathern, a literal and figurative passing of the torch. Rick's elderly parents, Elmer and Jeanne, were there. During the ceremony, the pastor noticed that Jeanne was crying. He walked over to her and gently asked if she wanted to speak. She took the microphone. "We knew the church was closing someday, and we'd always hoped that a new church would take over that would treasure the place the way we always have," she said. "This is exactly what we've dreamed of."

As he finished the story, the pastor was smiling. "After hearing all that," he said to me, "you can't tell me God doesn't have a plan for all of us."

One of the church deacons stuck his head in the office and reminded McCathern of an upcoming appointment. The pastor invited me back for the Sunday service as he walked me out of the building. Having been required to attend Mass every morning for a long stretch of grade school, I had developed a built-in aversion to formal religious ceremonies. I was a cultural Catholic, at best. I would have made an exception for Joy Tabernacle, but I was returning to San Francisco soon and my schedule was getting tight. There were houses to inspect and decisions to make. I also needed to finish my profile of Dan Kildee, which was proving surprisingly difficult because I couldn't condense it to the assigned length of one thousand words. I had overreported the story in a big way, mainly because I just liked hanging around Flint and talking to people.

"Don't worry," McCathern said. "There'll be another chance. You'll be spending a lot more time in Flint."

I had my doubts, but the pastor seemed very sure of himself.

Psycho Killer

Shortly before returning to Flint in the summer of 2010, I read an online story about the most recent murder in the city. The police had found David Motley's body near the base of a tree in a shady yard at the corner of Leith and Dexter Streets in the northeast corner of Flint early on the morning of May 24. The thirty-one-year-old had left a house party the night before, intending to walk to a nearby liquor store and meet up with a friend. He was stabbed to death on his way there. Motley was at a distinct disadvantage in any late-night confrontation. He'd had several surgeries on his leg and walked with a limp. "He was in no condition to be fighting or running," said his mother, who described her son as "a kid at heart."

It was another murder of another black man in a city consistently ranked one of the most dangerous in the country. Another senseless death. Temperatures had climbed to nearly ninety degrees the day Motley died, and hot weather meant the number of killings would increase, in keeping with Flint's seasonally adjusted murder rate. I wrote in my blog that there were four murders in the first three months of 2010, when it was just too cold to do much of anything, including kill people. The spring thaw prompted eight murders in April. Motley was one of eleven killed in May. He died the same day that a nineteen-year-old kid was found shot to death in the middle of Bonbright Street. No matter how comfortable I had become in Flint, the killings were a reminder that the city was a place where bad things happened all too often. Flint was on pace to break its all-time record of sixty-one murders in a single year, set back in 1986, the year my mom moved to Florida.

But it wasn't until early August that Motley's death took on a more sinister aspect, if it's possible for a murder to grow worse over time. He was apparently the first victim of what came to be known in the national media as the "Flint Serial Slasher." A task force made up of local police departments, the state police, and the FBI announced that at least thirteen men, all but one African Americans, had been stabbed by a muscular white man with a goatee, a stud in his left ear, and a baseball cap. Over the spring and summer, while I scouted for houses in Civic Park, ten attacks had taken place in Flint, three in nearby Burton. Five men, including Motley, had died. The killer typically preyed on black men who appeared vulnerable—old, disabled, or small in stature. He often asked for directions or posed as a motorist having trouble, sometimes attacking victims as they peered under the hood of his green and gold SUV. In some cases, the killer didn't bother with subterfuge; he just walked up to someone and started stabbing. "I think that he's hunting," said one Flint police lieutenant.

A populace conditioned by constant disappointment was still caught off guard by the city's latest calamity. "It is just crazy that this could happen here," one Flint resident, identified as a nineteen-year-old babysitter, told USA Today. I felt the same way. My reaction wasn't logical, but I believed Flint's catalog of bad juju made it immune to a serial killer, that fate would not impose such a pointless affliction on a place that had already suffered so much. That the killer often took advantage of black men willing to help out a white stranger in some of the city's toughest neighborhoods was especially cruel. A goddamned serial killer. What next? A catastrophic flood caused by a tsunami from Lake Huron? An outbreak of the Ebola virus? An invading army from Canada? Flint just couldn't catch a break.

Of course, once I gave it a little more thought, Flint was obviously fertile ground for a roving, senseless murderer. The budget cuts and layoffs had left it with just 145 police officers, far fewer than most cities of comparable size, let alone one with stratospheric levels of crime and poverty. Officers no longer investigated burglaries in person; the victim could call in details or visit the station to file a report. I noticed that cars often stopped at red lights, especially in the more deserted areas, then ran them if there was no oncoming traffic. Not a huge deal in the grand scheme of things, but it added to the general feeling of lawlessness in the city. I started running lights too, telling myself there was a good reason drivers didn't want to be stranded at a lonely intersection. It made you vulnerable.

Though the presence of a serial killer added a new element of fear to the city, it did nothing to jumpstart the labor negotiations with the police and fire departments that remained stalled after nearly a year. The union continued to argue that Flint needed more cops on the street. Walling continued to counter that he would gladly hire more once the union made concessions and he had the money to do it. The mayor never dropped his outwardly positive attitude, even though it was increasingly unconvincing. "Now that we have a very good description of the suspect because of the cooperation we've had from the surviving victims, there will be people organizing all across this community to try and identify this individual," the mayor announced. "We've been through a lot, but we're still working together." As that quote illustrates, it's just not that easy for a politician to put a positive spin on a racially motivated serial killer.

The case took a strange turn when the serial killer appeared to leave town. A suspect matching the description, right down to the SUV, attacked three nonwhite men in Leesburg, Virginia, stabbing two and hitting the other in the head with a hammer. That was followed by another stabbing in Toledo, Ohio. These far-flung incidents prompted a tipster to call the task force and identify Elias Abuelazam as a possible suspect. Abuelazam wasn't exactly your typical Flintoid, able to keep a low profile and blend in as he went about his grisly work. He was a six-foot-five, 280-pound Israeli citizen with a green card. The thirty-three-year-old worked at a local convenience store—affectionately referred to as a "party store" in Flint and Detroit—and lived with an uncle on Flint's East Side. He had recently traveled to Virginia and Ohio. He drove a 1996 green and gold Chevy Blazer.

Police arrested Abuelazam at around 10 P.M. on August 11 at the Atlanta airport. He was chatting on his cell phone, just minutes from boarding a flight to Tel Aviv. A few hours later back in Flint, the FBI woke up a victim who had been stabbed by the serial killer in July. Three of his organs had been cut, and he had a long scar from chest to groin from the surgery that saved his life. The agents showed him a photo of Abuelazam. He made a positive identification, and Abuelazam was extradited back to Michigan to stand trial.

In a way, Walling was proved right. The community had pulled together. But with all the layoffs and cutbacks, the city needed help from the state police and the FBI to catch the alleged killer. "Now everyone can breathe a sigh of relief," the mayor said. But the serial killer had victimized the entire city, not just the men he attacked. Even after Abuelazam's arrest, something had changed. If there was any doubt beforehand, now it was clear that almost anything could happen in Flint, even things you never expected.

It was an uncomfortable realization, given the high tolerance for crime I developed while growing up in Flint. There was the time in grade school when I woke to the sound of yelling downstairs. My siblings were all away at college, and it was just my mom and me in the house. I left my second-floor bedroom and headed down to the kitchen, where my mom was hovering near the back door with a frying pan raised over her head. The window on the top half of the door had been smashed, and a disembodied arm was reaching in, trying to unlock the deadbolt.

"I just called the police," my mom shouted, with more resolve than panic. She didn't scare easily. "They're on their way."

"Good for you," answered the owner of the arm, hidden behind the door in the dark, as he continued to grapple with the lock.

The police arrived and made an arrest. The guy was too high to offer much resistance, and he clearly wasn't a criminal mastermind. He was freshly paroled from Jackson State Prison. For rape. One of the cops came inside to make sure we were okay. He told us the suspect claimed my mom was his girlfriend, and they'd simply had a little spat.

"He's not my type," my mom responded.

Despite what had just transpired, we all had a good laugh over that one in the living room. Typical 3 A.M. humor in Flint.

Another example: On a Sunday morning when I was in high school, I woke up to a loud racket downstairs. My mom was at work, and I figured it was my brother, who had come home after college in search of a teaching job. As a joke, I grabbed an old croquet mallet that had been floating around the house for years and headed down the stairs. I thought it would be hilarious if I scared my brother and then used the excuse that I thought he was a burglar. The stairwell was enclosed, so I tiptoed down and then leaped around the corner into the dining room, the mallet raised over my head, and let out a blood-curdling scream. I was face to face with an actual thief, not my brother, who had gone out early to play basketball. My little joke must have been convincing, because the burglar—who looked to be a high school kid about my age—screamed in terror, *Home Alone*–style, dropped the bag he was stuffing with my grandmother's hand-me-down silver, and ran out the

front door. Without thinking, I chased him down the street in my boxers with the mallet, perhaps the most unthreatening and unlikely
weapon you could wield in Flint. I stopped when I realized the last thing
I wanted to do was actually catch this guy and get my ass kicked in my
underwear.

One more: There was a stretch of Hamilton Avenue near Bonbright
between our house and my grandparents' where kids regularly shot at
cars as they passed in the night. Or at least it seemed like a regular
occurrence because it happened to us twice. The first time the shot blew
out the passenger side window, spraying glass into my face. The cops
said it was just a pellet gun. Nothing to worry about. The second time
left an entrance and exit wound in our rear bumper. Either that was the
world's most powerful pellet, or someone was shooting real bullets. We
opted for an inconvenient but safer alternative route after the second
incident. But that was too much hassle, so we quickly returned to the
Hamilton Avenue route and took a few precautions when driving
through the shooting gallery. My mom would hunch low over the steering wheel and floor it; everyone else in the car would lie down or slide
to the floorboards. We joked about it at first, but then it became second
nature. My elderly grandmother, who always rode in the backseat,
would simply ease herself into a reclining position in midsentence, like
she was lying down on the couch to watch a little TV, and continue
talking until we'd gone a few blocks and everyone could sit up again.
Ho hum.

Throw in the various petty crimes that happened over the years—
several bike thefts, the family car stolen out of the driveway, a few
random beatings by unknown groups of kids—and you have what I
would consider a fairly typical experience with the criminal element in
Flint during the seventies and eighties. Unsettling when it happened, but
nothing to get too upset about. Lots of friends had better (that is, worse)
stories. It didn't dawn on me that it might be a little weird, a little
unhealthy, until I started having conversations in college with kids from
placid places like Chevy Chase or White Plains. Traci, who grew up in
Anacortes, Washington, gateway to the serene beauty of the San Juan
Islands, gets a look of profound distress when I relate these stories. She
doesn't think they're funny. Instead of laughing, she gives me a hug and
tells me it's all okay.

If I needed more visceral proof that growing up in this environment
might have some unwelcome psychological side effects—the kind
of rich life experience that keeps therapists in business—I got it that

summer. I was driving down Hamilton Avenue, and I felt myself involuntarily slumping behind the wheel as I rolled by Bonbright, where the family car had been fired upon more than thirty years earlier. It was the middle of the day. The neighborhood felt abandoned, more lonely than menacing. There wasn't a person in sight. But I still stayed low and stepped on the gas, even as I told myself how silly I was acting.

I realized that I took a perverse pride in these stories. They imbued me with a measure of toughness that I certainly didn't possess. It's a variation on a guy from Buffalo bragging about the horrible weather he endures. Or a New Yorker's strange habit of telling you she pays three thousand dollars a month for a rat-infested studio with no kitchen and she likes it! But the serial killer was a wake-up call. This was no joke. Did I really want to return to the scene of the crime with Traci by my side? Was I willing to trade the old stories—burnished by time into comically self-aggrandizing anecdotes stripped of all fear—for the reality of present-day Flint, where hulking Israelis with knives roamed the streets, where I could easily end up a character in a new batch of violent tales that might not have such a happy ending?

I thought about all this as I cleared out of Jan and Ted's comfortable home, said goodbye to the cats, and saluted the majestic flat-screen television. My profile of Dan Kildee was finally complete. I had easily found several houses in Civic Park that were cheap enough for me to afford. Many properties were in about the same condition as our house in San Francisco when Traci and I moved in. They needed a good cleaning and some fresh paint. Eventually, they'd require some big-ticket repairs, but they weren't in danger of collapsing anytime soon. And unlike our San Francisco house, they had good bones. If you looked hard enough, you could still find classic Civic Park Saltboxes, Colonials, and Bungalows with the original woodwork, plaster walls, and wood floors still intact, albeit in a slightly battered state.

But as I drove to the airport to fly back to San Francisco, I was as undecided as ever.

PART THREE

23

Winter Wonderland

Back in San Francisco, I once again became mired in my typical decision-making process, a routine that didn't really involve deciding anything. I endlessly mulled over the pros and cons of a Civic Park house, making lists on legal pads and jotting down various financial scenarios with the help of a calculator. Then I did it all over again. And again. It was similar to the way I hunted for a set of lost keys, looking in the same spots as if the keys would magically appear during the third or fourth round. I paced around the house, reciting various action plans, then countering them with alternative approaches. I was good at taking all sides in an argument. Out loud. Traci, who had seen this movie before, would point her index finger at the side of her head, twirling it in the universal symbol for crazy, and softly announce, "Cuckoo, cuckoo, cuckoo."

I had a Google Alert set up for the Vehicle City, and each morning I read through everything written about Flint, searching for blog material. Unbidden, I read excerpts aloud to Traci while she tried to eat breakfast or get ready for work at the architecture firm. We had a small house; there was no escape. One day I found myself outside the closed bathroom door, laptop in hand, expounding loudly on the latest odd-ball crime I'd discovered—a guy accidentally shooting himself in the crotch or some other nonsense the *Flint Journal* never failed to unearth, despite its diminished reporting staff. Through the closed door, Traci declared, "This bathroom is a Flint-free zone, similar to a no-ho zone." Other times she would simply give me the talk-to-the-hand gesture and declare, as sternly as possible for someone raised in a calm, rational household, "No more Flint today. That's it." (Our cats, Sergio and Purdy, seemed more interested, provided I fed them before subjecting them to the latest arcane news from the birthplace of GM.)

Finally, Traci staged the equivalent of an intervention on a fall afternoon just after I began teaching again at the university. We were walking along the trails of Bernal Hill near our house, taking in the spectacular views of the city in all directions. Dogs of various sizes, shapes, and pedigrees frolicked around us. I spotted a huge, vicious-looking mutt with wild eyes and a muzzle.

"Now that's the kind of dog we'd need in Flint," I said.

"The muzzle would come in handy around here when you start talking about Flint," Traci said, putting her arm around my shoulder. "Let's talk about you not talking about Flint anymore."

When Traci resorts to sarcasm, I know it's serious. We stood at the top of the hill looking at the tall downtown buildings in the distance. She told me that she understood my devotion to Flint. It was similar to the attachment she felt to her hometown in the San Juan Islands of northern Washington. A part of her wanted to get back to small-town life—a simpler, less expensive existence. She missed real seasons and warm summers. She admitted that I'd initially done a great job selling our possible return to Flint. We could get out of the rat race and make a difference in a place that needed help. With a laugh, she confessed that geography had made it very appealing in the abstract. Michigan is a warm, fuzzy-looking mitten of a state surrounded by the beautiful blue of the Great Lakes, those landlocked oceans of the Midwest. But while the Wolverine State photographs well from a satellite, the close-ups can be disturbing. My tales of murder, arson, poverty, and general lawlessness had convinced Traci that Flint wasn't the small town she had in mind. And my frequent descriptions of the city's economic free fall had led her to question just what the two of us could do to change its downward trajectory. She was getting tired of our life revolving around Flint. I couldn't blame her.

Obviously, I was having a hard time letting go now that I'd rediscovered my hometown. It was like I lived there, except I didn't. I was wearing out my welcome in my current home by obsessing about my old home and the possibility of a future home. I was becoming the real-estate equivalent of a model-train enthusiast or a Trekkie. This had to stop.

But just when I thought Traci was wisely cutting off all access to Flint, she made a surprising suggestion. I'd been telling her how much I wanted to experience the city in wintertime again. I hadn't seen snow in my hometown since 1986. "Go back one more time when school gets out in December," she said. "Spend some time with your new friends. Play in the snow."

I was relieved. I wouldn't have to quit Flint cold turkey. It would be like a farewell tour, of sorts. Then I couldn't stop myself; I had to push it. "And if I happened to finally find a house that might make sense for us, like a rental or something, you'd still be open to it?" I asked, like an idiot.

She paused, her eyes following a blimp that was floating over Candlestick Park to the southeast. The Forty-Niners were playing that day. She turned back and gave me an exasperated smile. "Sure, but it's hard to imagine finding the perfect house in Flint," she said. We watched as the blimp began to slowly turn back toward us. "The important thing is that you make a decision. Then it's over. For good." It was clear what she thought the outcome of this visit to Flint should be.

Housing quickly presented itself, as usual. A few months earlier I'd exchanged emails with a childhood friend who had read my Flint blog. Duane and I hadn't talked or corresponded in any way since the day we graduated from high school in 1984, but some clichés are true—people in the Midwest are loyal, generous, and friendly. I mentioned that I was planning a trip in December, and he instantly invited me to stay at his place. Duane had grown up on Delaware Avenue in the heart of the crumbling East Side. Now he lived on Paradise Drive—I'm not kidding— in a Hawaiian-themed subdivision in Grand Blanc. Big, sprawling houses with ridiculously abundant wall outlets but no panhandlers or late-night shootouts. He had a yard the size of many San Francisco parks and a nice spare bedroom. When the quarter ended at the university for Christmas break, I happily headed to the very suburbs I'd grown up resenting.

Duane and I seamlessly picked up where we had left off nearly thirty years earlier. The shared experience of the Flint Catholic school system—the sports, the nuns, the corporal punishment—is a strong bond indeed. Without much hesitation, we were filling each other in on our lives with the sort of embarrassing detail that I'd probably never share with my closest friends in San Francisco. I admitted all my anxieties about my mortgage and my eccentric desire to buy a house in Flint. He raised his eyebrows slightly when I told him how much Traci and I had paid for a San Francisco house that was smaller than his garage—as close as a polite, unflappable Midwesterner who had perfect attendance in high school would come to saying, "Damn, you're crazy, Gordo!"

In turn, he filled me in on his housing situation. He'd gone through a rough divorce. His ex-wife had pushed hard at one point to have their dear departed dog disinterred from the backyard so she could lay him to rest at the house she now shared with her new husband, who happened to be her boss at work. That's why Duane was living alone in this sprawling, perfectly ordered house. He was underwater on the mortgage. The bank wouldn't refinance or modify the loan, and Duane didn't think it was right to walk away. He'd stay put for now. He had managed to hang on to a good engineering job with an auto parts manufacturer, so he could easily make the payments.

For two weeks, I spent most days in Flint looking at houses or just roaming the city in the Chevy Cavalier Duane loaned me. At night, the two of us talked about Flint, family, and life. We drank beer and watched sports. Duane filled me in on his hilarious business trips to India to help foreign automakers fine-tune their heating and cooling systems. One night I helped him rewrite his online dating profile, the first step in finding someone besides me to spend time in the house with him. At least I was putting my writing skills to good use.

The frigid weather brought back a whole new set of memories. I left the house with wet hair one morning, and it froze almost instantly, just like it had when I walked from my house to the bus stop for school in the morning. The winter smell of cold air and car exhaust was unexpectedly pleasant. Duane and I shoveled out the driveway one morning, reminding me of my first low-paying job in Flint. I'm sure this nostalgic embrace of freezing, crappy weather would have been short-lived if I had to face five months of it, but I was happy to feel the inside of my nose freezing and my lips getting chapped. I was having fun wallowing in the familiar.

And even though it wasn't supposed to be the primary purpose of my visit, I couldn't help thinking that there was a still a chance a Flint house might present itself to me now that I was no longer officially looking for one. After all, Traci and I hadn't landed a house in San Francisco until we'd decided it would never happen.

24

Home on the Range

On a clear morning cold enough to numb my face after a couple of minutes outside, I was standing at a workbench with Dave Starr in his relatively warm basement on Milbourne Avenue. Judy, his wife, was upstairs assembling a miniature Carole Towne Christmas Village in the dining room, as she did every holiday season. I could hear her moving around on the worn carpet directly above us. Dave's task was less festive, but he approached it with equal enthusiasm. He was showing me how to make bullets. Or, more precisely, we were making cartridges or rounds. The bullet is actually just the little pointy part at the end, Dave told me. I had a lot to learn.

Dave and Judy's house may have been filled with fraying, well-used furniture, but what it lacked in contemporary style was trumped by organization. The basement corner devoted to munitions and weaponry was no exception. Plastic containers labeled "Dirty," "Decapped," and "Clean" were filled with .45 brass casings and stacked neatly on a metal shelf next to the workbench. There was a Cabela's Model 400 Vibratory Case Tumbler, a vaguely sexual name for a device that uses mulched corncobs to clean and shine spent bullet casings. Dave showed me a few shiny examples to prove how well it worked.

The Lee turret press he used to make new rounds out of the casings was mounted on the edge of the workbench. It had a container at the top filled with Winchester 231 gunpowder, a series of rotating dies, and a long handle, sort of like a low-key slot machine before the one-armed bandit went digital. With the first crank, the spent primer—an impact-sensitive chemical that explodes when hit by the firing pin, igniting the powder and firing the bullet—was removed, the casing was resized, and a fresh primer was inserted. Then five grains of powder were loaded into the casing, and Dave set the actual bullet in the casing by hand. On the final crank, the casing was crimped to hold the bullet in place, creating a new round that was ready to use. It was quick, and efficient. I was expecting something more delicate and time consuming. Dave pointed out, somewhat wistfully, that there was a more expensive press that completed the whole process with a single crank of the handle.

"Do you save money by making your own rounds?" I asked.

"That's the idea," Dave said, "but you just end up shooting more, so it doesn't make much difference."

Dave had undergone cancer surgery to remove the lower lobe of his right lung shortly after I met him at the block-club meeting the previous summer. He recovered in the hospital for five days. It was the first time Judy had spent the night alone in the house since they were married. She slept with the .45 on the bedside table and a round in the chamber. "I would like to have a Taser, but I hear they're illegal," Judy told me when we were back upstairs. "Dave always wants me to go out shooting with him, but I don't like guns."

Dave's back had been sore since the surgery, and he wanted to see how it felt to shoot again. He invited me to go along when I called to tell him I was back in Flint for a few weeks. He told me he'd only had to draw the gun once, when he crossed paths with a neighbor's Rottweiler on one of his fitness walks. Thankfully, the dog's owner had emerged from his house, shouting, "Don't shoot, don't shoot!" I had never shot a gun of any kind in my life, which was probably somewhat unusual for a Flint native. Even Traci had shot BB guns as a kid, and her parents had guns in the house when they both briefly worked for U.S. Customs. I thought knowing something about firearms would come in handy if I ever became a Civic Park property owner.

Guns have always seemed like a bad idea to me. I've never heard a convincing argument that makes me think America wouldn't be a better place without them. And it's hard to imagine that the founding fathers would have been pleased with the public's easy access to semiautomatic weapons and armor-piercing bullets. So it was odd how excited I was about going to the range with Dave. I even brought my camera along, planning to have Dave take my picture popping off a few rounds. Maybe somebody could take a photo of us together. I'd post it on the blog. Two real Flintoids getting in a little target practice. It seemed like a surefire way to establish some Flint street cred and distance myself from San Francisco, where voters banned the sale or possession of handguns in 2005, only to see the measure thrown out by the courts.

One of the unexpected fringe benefits of Flint's decline is that you seldom have to wait for anything. Traffic jams are rare. Service at bars and restaurants is generally brisk, given that there are few customers and the wait staff really need the money. But that pattern was broken at Advanced Ranges on Center Road, just across Flint's eastern border in Burton. On a punishingly cold afternoon, there was a forty-five-minute wait. (Note to would-be Flint entrepreneurs: Guns!)

The cavernous, fluorescently lit lobby was decorated with taxidermied deer trophies, a bear in a Santa hat rising up on its hind legs, and a depressed-looking moose head decorated with tinsel. He appeared to be wondering how it had come to this. A flyer on the bulletin board announced classes in "Japanese Swordsmanship" taught every Monday from 6 to 8 P.M. by Victoria Van Fleet and John Solomon, who sounded like a couple in a romance novel. A girl about five years old in a pink coat stood on a chair watching shooters in the range through a viewing window. My gun lust was already starting to fade. Even though we were separated from the range by a thick wall, it was loud. How many times had I read about somebody describing gunshots as little pops similar to low-grade firecrackers? Liars, apparently.

Although several ex-girlfriends and my mother would probably disagree, I'm fairly easy-going. I like to think there aren't many things that get me irritated or even angry. I'm not a complainer. But there is one thing I don't like, and that is loud noises. I figured the noise-canceling headphones Dave brought along would solve that problem.

The range was a cramped, low-ceilinged affair. I foolishly assumed it would be just the two of us, but I counted close to eighteen men firing away or waiting their turn as I stared through the viewing window over the little girl's shoulder. Since I've already admitted my problem with loud noises, I should probably come clean and confess I also have an ever so slight issue with confined spaces. And crowds. I mean, I'm not a full-blown claustrophobic or anything. I ride elevators. I go to concerts. But I was getting cold and clammy. I rationalized that the cubicle walls separating the lanes would provide a modicum of privacy.

Lane 2 finally opened up. We stepped into a small antechamber to put on our headphones before using a second door to enter the range. Now it was really loud, even with the headphones. You had to yell to be heard over the constant crack of gunshots. Dave was talking to me, but it sounded like he was underwater. The range was dimly lit for a space designed to facilitate the safe discharge of firearms.

To our left, in lane 1, a fastidious older guy with gray hair, a nice leather jacket, pressed jeans, and cowboy boots was calmly firing a very big gun. He looked like a tidier version of Willie Nelson. To our right, in lane 3, an instructor dressed in black was barking instructions at a middle-aged student with a mustache: "Body armor drill! Stand by! Fight!" On command, the student fired away. Spent shells were flying out of the various lanes, bouncing off the linoleum. An attendant walked the floor, sweeping them up into a dustpan, a strangely domestic activity given the setting.

Dave shot first, calmly emptying the magazine. I tried to stop the involuntary shudder I experienced each time he fired. I watched him insert a fresh magazine for me and lay the gun on a counter padded with short pile carpet. He turned and shook his head, a smile on his face. "Pathetic!" he shouted. "I'm out of practice." He crouched down and gathered up his spent shells to polish up back at home and use again.

It was my turn. A fog of paranoia enveloped me as I picked up the gun. The .45 felt heavy and awkward in my hand. Theoretically, I was more capable of protecting myself at that moment than at any other point in my life, given that it was the first time I'd held a loaded weapon. Yet I felt extremely vulnerable. I realized I could easily kill someone now, or kill myself. And that there were a dozen or so men in close proximity who could kill me. It was a magnified version of the queasy sensation I once had on a camping trip in the Sierras with three friends when we stood on the vertiginous ledge of a rock face towering above a mountain lake, except now the crystalline view was replaced by hot, smoky air and a shadowy target in the distance.

A discharged shell from another shooter popped over the low barrier separating the lanes and bounced off the top of my head. I jumped like a cat. I turned my head to glance back at Dave, forgetting the sports truism I learned in seventh-grade basketball: where your head goes, your body will follow. I had inadvertently swung my arm and the gun to the left as I turned. I was aiming in the general direction of Willie Nelson in lane 1, although he didn't know it. Dave, an uncertain look on his face, waved both hands like he was fanning me. Obviously, he wanted me to keep the gun pointed at the target.

A voice in my head finally cut through the doubt. "Pay attention and shoot the fucking gun!" But just as I raised the .45 toward the target, the guy in lane 1 fired. Or was that me? Had I just accidentally shot the gun? I heard muffled shouting, but I couldn't tell if it was the training session next door or someone yelling at me for missing the target so badly.

I decided to just get it over with. I aimed in the general direction of the target and started firing. I was surprised by the kick of the gun and the heat generated by the shots. In addition to shaking, I was also sweating up a storm. And I discovered that it actually hurt to fire a gun. My left hand was aching. I emptied the magazine with no idea how close I had come to the target. As I put the gun on the counter, I noticed a rivulet of blood running from my thumb, down my forearm, and onto my shirt sleeve. It was all becoming clear. Shooting was painful because I had been improperly gripping the .45 in such abject terror that each time I fired, the slide on top of the gun popped back against my thumb like a piston.

I should mention that I also have a slight issue with blood. It's primarily confined to blood tests. A few years back I stupidly glanced at the blood being drawn into the syringe and went into full-blown shock. I had to get a shot of adrenaline while I was sprawled on the lab floor. Another time I passed out during a blood test, and when I came to I was literally choking the doctor and two assistants were trying to pull me off him. So being covered in blood wasn't exactly offsetting the disorientation brought on by the loud noises and cramped quarters. But I tried to think positive. With a mixture of embarrassment and relief, I realized that this was a handy excuse to exit the range.

"Band-Aid," I yelled to Dave, holding my thumb up for him to see, inadvertently dripping blood onto the front of my shirt in the process. He frowned and nodded his head. I worried that the attendant would think I shot myself, so I hustled out the door while Dave got ready to shoot again.

I started to explain the situation to the middle-aged woman behind the counter in the lobby. She was very understanding. She handed me three Band-Aids, and I awkwardly tried to apply one without dripping blood on the counter. "You should go to the bathroom and wash it first," she said, talking very slowly and pantomiming the motions of lathering up your hands with soap. "Use warm water but not too hot. Then pat it dry with a paper towel, real gently."

Why was she talking to me like a child? She probably figured that if I couldn't shoot a gun without cutting myself, I might not know how to wash my hands properly. I got the sense that she considered me mentally deficient as I stood in front of her, bloody, shaking, and jabbering. There was a burly guy behind her in a camouflage hunting shirt who looked away when I made eye contact. I wished I hadn't worn my cowboy shirt with the pearl buttons. I worried that it made me look like a city slicker. Or a kid in the fifties. And now it was pretty much ruined anyway. It had cost me thirty bucks at an alleged thrift store in San Francisco.

In the bathroom, I looked in the mirror. There was blood on the front of my shirt and all over the left sleeve. My face glistened with oil and sweat. There was a quarter-size flake of dried blood that looked like an unattractive birthmark on my chin. A dark peninsula of sweat stretched from each armpit all the way to my belt. I wondered if I was the first person to sweat out his pants pockets. Disgusting, yet impressive. When I sweat, I don't mess around.

What I needed was a shower, a couple of drinks, and a nap. But I still had my foolish pride. I washed up and headed back to the range. While I was gone, Dave had managed to cut his hand loading a magazine. When I picked up the gun to shoot, the handle was covered in fresh blood, but I persevered and emptied another magazine. When I had finished, Dave signaled that he was ready to go. He was not into Band-Aids. He just kept wiping his palm on his jeans, so we both left the range decorated with blood stains.

Back in the car, Dave was in good spirits. His back was feeling fine, despite the surgery. He spread the targets out on the seat between us to reveal that most of the shots were close to the center of the target, including mine. "You did good," he said. "A few low shots, but that's just you overcompensating for the kick. You feel the gun popping up, so you aim low."

I decided to stop pretending with Dave. I told him how nervous the whole thing made me. I hadn't expected the gun to kick so much. It was so loud in there, and I felt kind of claustrophobic. I hesitated and then told him that when I was holding the gun, it dawned on me that I could kill somebody at the range, and they could all kill me.

Dave glanced over at me when I stopped talking. The guy was a Vietnam veteran. He had slaved away in the shop for decades. He fought off Rottweilers on afternoon strolls. This was supposed to be a fun outing, not an existential struggle that might lead to therapy. He was probably wondering what kind of a wacko he was driving around with in his car. Or worrying that I was about to start crying.

"Well, I probably shouldn't tell you, but that was a fairly low target load," he said as he put the key in the ignition. "The gun wasn't kicking much at all. The rounds I keep in the gun when it's at the house will really belt you."

"Oh," I said.

"Hey, want a Life Saver?" he asked, rubbing his bloody hand on his jeans and fishing a roll out of his pocket. "They're my new cigarettes after the cancer. Not as good, but a lot cheaper." Dave had been a two-pack-a-day smoker, and he laughed and said the "silver lining" of having cancer was that it would save him four thousand dollars a year on smokes.

I took a Life Saver, feeling like I was in some sort of commercial gone awry. As we pulled out of the parking lot, Dave launched into a story about the time he shot an elephant gun and it almost dislocated his shoulder.

Just another day in Flint.

25

California Dreamin'

When I called Pastor Sherman McCathern to tell him I was back in town and wanted to take him up on his invitation to attend services at Joy Tabernacle, he wasn't surprised. "I knew you were meant to get more involved with the congregation," he said. "But you should come by before Sunday. I've got something to show you."

That's how I wound up standing in a cold, damp Dutch Colonial in Civic Park as McCathern—all six feet two of him—prepared to pull up a long strip of nasty beige carpet from the living room floor with his bare hands. There was no heat in the abandoned house, but McCathern wasn't wearing a winter coat, just a casual slate-colored jacket that matched his well-pressed dress slacks. You could see his breath as he worked his hands under the edge of the carpet and the worn padding beneath it to get a better grip.

"We can take care of that for you, Pastor," said one of the three church members who were clearing debris and making initial repairs to the house. "You don't have to do that. It's on our list." Unlike McCathern, they were dressed for construction work in December, with gloves, hats, and thick coats. I was wearing a heavy parka specially purchased for this trip to Flint, along with a sweater and scarf. I had my ski thermals on under my pants, and I was still freezing my ass off. All my years in California had made me vulnerable to weather like this. I wasn't sure I could still officially call myself a Michigander.

"Oh no, I've got it," McCathern assured him before he popped up, taking the carpet with him and filling the empty living room with a cloud of dust. There was coughing and waving of hands, but McCathern wasn't bothered. "Look at these floors!" he exclaimed. "They're in great shape! Can you guys clean them up to look like that?" He turned and pointed at an unexpectedly well-polished banister leading upstairs. It appeared to be the only untarnished thing left in the house. It was practically gleaming in the dim light.

"Sure," one of the workers said, glancing at the other two, who nodded their heads in tentative affirmation.

The house had huge holes knocked in the walls and ceiling, a suspect roof, and a near complete absence of plumbing, courtesy of house scrappers. The front door was nailed shut from the inside with two-by-fours. The kitchen and upstairs bathroom needed a complete renovation. Then again, things could have been worse. The windows were still there, and they were relatively new, a few still covered with tattered, rose-colored curtains that cast an eerie light. The exterior cedar shingles were in decent shape. I'd grown used to quickly estimating the rehab cost of various Flint houses I'd looked at over the past eighteen months. This one looked like twenty thousand dollars, at least. But for Pastor McCathern, it was worth far more than the sum of its parts. It was another sign from God. "This place is remarkably well preserved," he said. "I think it's providence that it was spared."

Joy Tabernacle had recently purchased the burnt-orange and pale yellow house on the corner of West Dayton Street and Milbourne just off the church parking lot from the Genesee County Land Bank for five hundred dollars. From the front porch, I could see the Starrs' home in the distance. McCathern planned to transform the house into the Civic Park Heritage Museum.

"This is America's history, right here," he said, pointing at the spot where he had just pulled up the carpet. "The auto industry started right here. Just look at the street names. Chevrolet Avenue! This place means something! But what's happening? They're selling Flint off on the Internet. I'm sorry, but I'm just not used to America saying forget history. I want this house to be a place where people remember what Flint means to this country!"

He had shifted into preaching mode, which was not unusual, and I realized I was standing in a straight line with the three church members facing the pastor, who was backlit by the living room windows, his arms outstretched and a look of profound distress on his face. "Why don't Flint and the rest of the country recognize this for what it is? A piece of history! What's missing from this picture? Why can't the city find . . . " He paused, searching for the right words. "What they called? Marketing people! Why can't they find *marketing people* to promote this history?" We all stood in silence for a few seconds, our breath blowing into the center of the room, staring at the newly exposed hardwood floor, contemplating another question about Flint that none of us was capable of answering.

The Civic Park Heritage Museum was just one of the ways McCathern was attempting to revive the housing stock surrounding Joy Tabernacle. As we walked back to the church, he pointed out an abandoned house across the street, explaining that it had been wide open to the elements after thieves had worked it over. Church members had boarded up the windows and doors, cleared the debris in the yard, and spruced up the place as best they could. It looked about as nice as a vacant house could look. "Some guy in Ohio owns it, but we commandeered it," he explained. "We're going to take this neighborhood back. You can quote me on that."

For a while, McCathern had forged an unlikely alliance with a California speculator who owned another house near the church. It had been vandalized by scrappers, and the pastor agreed to make repairs and keep an eye on the place until the owner, the CEO of a software company and one-time president of the chamber of commerce in Seaside, a little town near Monterey, could rent it. Then the house was vandalized yet again, a common occurrence in Civic Park. After all, there's no better time to hit a house than just after renovations. The relationship broke down over squabbles about the cost of more repairs. "He thought I was trying to rip him off like everybody else had," McCathern said. "I told him only God can protect an empty house from scrappers in Flint, and I'm not God. But he was from California, and he just didn't realize what he'd gotten himself into buying a house in this city." The pastor was still watching over the house, making sure it was secure, but he hadn't talked to the owner in months.

(I eventually tracked down the owner of the house in California. He had an accent like the German filmmaker Werner Herzog. He basically confirmed the pastor's version of events. He owned two other properties in Flint. None was rented and all had fallen victim to vandals. At one point, he said he had secured more than two million dollars in financing from investors to buy a hundred Flint houses, rehab them, then rent them out. But he claimed it was impossible to find people he could trust who were willing to work for ten dollars an hour. The financing for the deal eventually fell through. "Flint seemed like a place with low risk and the potential for high rewards," he told me. "It seemed like it was at the bottom and could only go up. But my entire experience with the city has been a nightmare.")

McCathern had tried and failed to work out an arrangement with the owner of yet another abandoned house less than a block away who lived in Alaska. There were several other absentee landlords with empty properties near the church that he had tried to contact without success. The entire time-consuming process was like herding cats, and McCathern hated cats. Cities with more resources could aggressively cite speculators for code violations to try and force compliance, but Flint, constantly struggling to erase a budget deficit, had just two housing inspectors for the entire city. As long as homeowners paid their taxes, it was unlikely they would hear from the city about the condition of their properties. "This is just some little investment for these speculators," the pastor said. "I don't think they understand that people have to live near their abandoned houses."

He sounded like he was channeling Dan Kildee, but McCathern had mixed feelings about the land bank. He didn't understand why the agency was so reluctant to turn over houses to people like him who had big and often noble plans but small bank accounts. McCathern felt the whole process of obtaining the structure that he hoped to turn into a museum had been needlessly complicated. "Sometimes I feel like a one-man army because the land bank doesn't seem to have any plan for all the houses they control in Civic Park," he said.

Back at the church, we settled into his small office, which was connected to the study where Rick McClellan had slept when he was the caretaker of the church. "His little dog had a few accidents in there," the pastor said, "so we had to have the carpet cleaned." McCathern had a big desk, but it was clear he didn't like to stay behind it for too long. He fidgeted and straightened various office supplies as he described what he was doing when he wasn't trying to prop up the housing market. Much of it involved his attempts to raise the economic fortunes of his flock. "I told God that if I can't help these people create jobs and opportunity, I can't stay here and just preach to people and get them all dressed up with no place to go," he said. "And that's what I believe God has promised me."

He had no shortage of plans, but many were proving difficult to implement. The church was home to a direct-care training program that had helped nearly thirty members get certified as nurses' assistants and caregivers, but the goal was to get sixty to eighty enrolled. McCathern was hoping to set up the computer room he inherited from Community Presbyterian—filled with several aging PCs—as a place where the congregation could get computer training, create résumés, and search for jobs, but he admitted that he was unfamiliar with technology and the room wasn't being used yet. His efforts to get churchgoers into a Baker College work-study program to earn degrees and certifications in areas like home weatherization had run into problems; the program requirements were too lofty for members of the congregation who were eager to learn but had low reading levels and lacked high school diplomas. McCathern was trying to set up a pilot program with lower entrance standards. He had also contacted various social service agencies to partner with them in various ways, but the city and county governments often proved as daunting as the out-of-town speculators. McCathern had managed to connect with someone at the Charles Stewart Mott Foundation, the ultimate Flint funding source for people trying to make a difference, but he couldn't remember the guy's name. "I do need to find his card and call him," he said as he rummaged through his desk drawer.

I realized that McCathern's strengths—the boldness, optimism, and energy that enabled him to turn his life around, secure a beautiful church for a song, and raise the spirits of a congregation conditioned by misfortune—were not necessarily suited for the plodding, detailed, and often frustrating work of navigating bureaucracies. This was not a man hardwired to master the minutia of grant writing or sweet-talk the board members of a nonprofit that might fund one of his many projects. Pastor McCathern was built for inspiring people, making deals with God, commandeering houses, and ripping up old carpet. "I don't know if some of these people really understand the essence of what we're trying to do here," he said. "We're out in the field in the middle of a crisis. We don't have time to sit in meetings all day."

The first crisis had come less than a month after the congregation moved into the church in the fall of 2009. Two women and a man were shot to death as they sat in a van at 4:30 on a Sunday morning about a mile from Joy Tabernacle. They were parked in an alley behind an unlicensed after-hours club that was once home to a popular pizza joint where my family often ate and my sister worked as a waitress. None of the victims attended Joy Tabernacle, but two dozen of their relatives did, and the triple homicide devastated the church. McCathern organized an antiviolence rally, an event that has become all too typical in American cities, and a photo ran in the *Flint Journal* of him hugging the nineteen-year-old son of one of the victims. "It's an undeclared war in our streets," McCathern told the press. Other murders had touched the church since then, and it seemed likely there would be more.

If I needed a more immediate example of how crime, tragedy, and possibly redemption intersected at Joy Tabernacle, I soon got one as I sat talking to McCathern. A young-looking twenty-year-old guy dressed in black jeans, a black hoodie, and a pair of Air Jordans stuck his head into the office and smiled at the pastor. "Steve, come in here, I want you to meet someone," the pastor said enthusiastically. We shook hands and made our introductions. Steve was shy and unfailingly polite. He was trying to grow a beard, but it didn't seem to be working. He sat down and before long was casually narrating his life story.

Steve was a Civic Park kid, just like me, but a lifetime apart. He had never met his father, and his mother "would drink every day if she could afford it," so Steve spent a lot of time with his grandmother. "I'm a granny's boy," he said.

He'd had behavioral problems early on, culminating in an incident at school when he was in fifth grade. He was sent to the principal's office for the quaint offense of shooting spitballs. He decided impulsively to make a run for it, and when the principal grabbed him by the shirt, Steve snapped. "I started knocking pictures off the wall and messing up his desk," he said. "Then I grabbed a bat he had in there and started swinging. He called the police on me."

Steve landed in the psychiatric ward at Hurley Hospital and was prescribed a host of antidepressants. He was kicked out of the Flint school system and didn't bother to enroll elsewhere. He started smoking weed. "I got into the street life," he said. At one point, he was nabbed by the police near the old Baskin-Robbins ice cream parlor on Welch Boulevard, the same place the former pastor of Community Presbyterian had wanted to buy to give kids just like Steve a place to earn money and learn business skills. Steve had an unusually large sum of money for a fifteen-year-old, indicating he was a minor player in the drug trade. He said the police pocketed the cash and let him go. "I had the street mindset that if the police took my money, I should just go steal somebody else's money," he said.

He staked out an ATM with a group of boys, planning to ambush a customer and force him to clean out his account. But no one was using the machine, and they got tired of waiting. Steve spotted a woman walking by with a purse, and he decided to snatch it. The woman resisted and held on before falling hard to the ground and hitting her head. She died in the hospital shortly after Steve was arrested. He faced fifteen years in prison for manslaughter, but the victim's family petitioned the judge to send him to a juvenile facility instead. "I guess they seen something in me," Steve said. "They thought I should get another chance."

Steve ended up far from Flint, in a residential foster care facility in Clarinda, Iowa. He stopped smoking—he had no choice—and threw himself into the program. He earned his high school equivalency diploma, despite never making it to sixth grade. He asked for permission to stop taking antidepressants because he thought they were making his life worse, not better, and the medical staff agreed. He played basketball, baseball, and football. He ran track and cross country. "I did everything I could because what happened to that lady was on my mind so much," Steve said, adding that he still had nightmares about the incident. "I had to do something to take my mind off it. I was sorry for what I did."

Steve did so well in corn country that he was released early in the winter of 2008 and returned to Flint. He felt like he had changed a lot. He was a different person, a better person. He reconnected with his closest childhood pal, a distant cousin whose nickname was Shane. It was like their friendship had never been interrupted. Then Shane was murdered, a victim in the triple homicide behind the old pizzeria not far from Joy Tabernacle. "He was alive one day, and then he wasn't," Steve said. "I couldn't believe it."

Steve started smoking again after the murders, slipping back into his old life. It's common in Flint to celebrate the birthdays of young people who have died as if they were still among the living. That's what Steve had been doing when the state police caught him getting high with some friends in a car in late May. He was celebrating Shane's birthday. They were on Milbourne Avenue, just a few houses up the street from Dave and Judy Starr's place. The police found a gun under the passenger seat where Steve was sitting.

It was enough to earn him six months in county jail, which he served, and ninety days in the New Paths diversion program, which he had stopped attending for some reason. He really couldn't explain why. He also admitted that he'd stopped meeting with his probation officer, as required. "So there's probably a warrant out for your arrest," McCathern pointed out. "We've got to resolve this. You can't just walk away. They not playing when it comes to guns, son. With your past, you look dangerous to them. They don't know the Steve I know. I don't care how emotional you were about Shane, for you to be sitting there with a gun is absolutely ludicrous knowing what God had brought you through and how much you owe society back."

A convoluted discussion ensued as the pastor and Steve tried to remember the name of his probation officer and determine if he had violated the terms of his juvenile probation for manslaughter by failing to fulfill the sentencing for his more recent crimes. It was the kind of discussion that regularly took place around the pastor's desk these days, the same desk where fish fries and youth group activities were once planned in the more sedate days of Civic Park and Community Presbyterian. McCathern would have to help Steve sort out this mess. He ended the discussion by asking Steve to raise his hands in the air. The pastor did the same.

"What do you have to tell me?" McCathern asked sternly.

"That I'm through with all the guns and things," Steve answered softly.

"Now look at your hands," McCathern ordered. "You live by the sword, you die by the sword. You don't want to do that. You have to find a better way."

After Steve had left to do some work around the church, McCathern told me that his story was not all that unusual. Many members of the congregation were trying to rise above a criminal past, while dealing with the loss of friends and relatives who were killed in Flint. The past weekend he had presided over the funeral of a fifteen-year-old girl who had been killed. "The level of suffering in this area is unprecedented," he said. "The sheer volume is unbelievable." He pointed out that one of the workers I had met earlier at his would-be museum was a deacon in the church who had spent thirteen years in prison. Another deacon was required to wear an ankle tether for a previous crime. When a church member named Aaron walked into the office to ask the pastor a question, McCathern announced, "This young man went to prison when he was seventeen years old, but he's doing good now. He's going to Mott College."

I sheepishly asked Aaron how he liked having his life story revealed, however briefly, to someone he'd never even met. "That's all right," he said, shrugging his shoulders. "It's my testimony. It's good for other people to hear it."

I wondered how the pastor could handle being the emotional anchor and troubleshooter for so many people, while dealing with the financial worries that came with running the church. The heating bill alone had to be a challenge for a congregation with such meager financial resources. And his growing list of ambitious long-range projects would cost tens of thousands to implement. I asked him if he ever felt like this was too much for him, if he ever got discouraged. "Oh my God, every day!" he said. "I worry about turning into the so-called angry black man. Many times it's beyond overwhelming. But I don't do this out of my strength. I do it out of God's strength."

I noticed a yellow Post-it note stuck to McCathern's computer when I got up to leave. It was yet another task, another obligation for him to fulfill, but this one was eminently achievable. It was a reminder to buy toilet paper for the church before services on Sunday. "You better get on that," I said, pointing at the note.

"Oh, that will be real trouble if I don't follow up on that one," McCathern said. He was laughing now as he stood behind his desk, a row of abandoned houses, including the Californian's, visible through the window behind him. "That would be a true catastrophe if we ran out of toilet paper!"

He walked me to the door and reminded me that services started at 11:30 on Sunday. As I pulled out of the church parking lot, I could see the workers carrying old wood and drywall from the house that McCathern hoped to transform into the Civic Park Heritage Museum. Like a lot of worthy projects to improve Flint—from fully formed ideas like the shrinking-city plan to my half-baked efforts to buy a house—all he needed to make it happen was money.

26

Thankless Task

I kept my gloves on while I sat in the empty lobby of the mayor's office at 10:30 on a Wednesday morning. The three-block walk from my car in lightly falling snow had been brutally cold. I was shivering despite the dry warmth of city hall, silently vowing to never complain about the weather in San Francisco again. I was eager to see how Dayne Walling's dream of returning home to Flint matched the reality of running the city. With that in mind, he agreed to let me spend a typical day with him.

These "ride-alongs"—as journalists call them—are often the ultimate conceit because no politician will behave "typically" with an audience. Then again, Walling struck me as incapable of true guile. On the rare occasions when he clearly didn't want to answer a question, he talked around it good-naturedly until he wore you down with a numbing barrage of jargon and rambling sentences that meandered and looped back on each other. He did this with the same earnest enthusiasm that he applied to everything. I had learned to simply ask numerous variations on the same question to elicit a more revealing answer.

I was alone in the lobby. The receptionist had been laid off a few months earlier, a casualty of the city's frantic effort to balance the budget. When a distracted-looking man with an armful of file folders tucked under his arm walked into the lobby, he had to angle his head toward the offices behind the desk and call out, "Hello, anyone home?"

A frazzled staffer emerged to tell him that the weekly open house held in the mayor's office was canceled that day. "Can I take a message for the mayor?" she asked. "Well, I've given up on Flint," the man answered, "and I wanted to see if he could give me a reason not to give up on it." He left the lobby with his folders, more disappointed than angry. I wondered if he would get in his car and abandon the city, or if he'd seek out someone else to talk him into staying. These opportunities for citizens to have direct access to the mayor were a holdover from the administration of Mayor Don Williamson, who was known to hand out cash from his own pocket when people presented him with tales of woe. They were less popular now that no money was changing hands.

A few minutes later, Walling was behind the wheel of his gray Chevy Impala with a campaign sticker for himself on the rear bumper. Dawn Jones, a former local TV news reporter who served as his communications director, rode shotgun. I was in the back next to the child's safety seat, surrounded by a smattering of energy-bar wrappers. The snow was still coming down. Old-school slow jams played on the radio.

Walling and Jones were in a good mood, laughing about a comical yet persistent political gadfly named David Davenport, a Flint School Board member who had launched numerous recall campaigns against local politicians, including Walling. One of Davenport's first recall targets had been a city council member he accused of spraying him in the face with insecticide after a contentious council meeting. When that effort failed, Davenport tried to recall six of his fellow school board members, alleging they had violated district policy. A board member repaid the kindness by attempting to have Davenport recalled.

Davenport had set his sights on Walling in February of 2010, just six months after the mayor took office. He complained that Walling's threat to lay off police and firefighters endangered residents. He was joined in his efforts by a one-time Williamson appointee. The former mayor denied that he had a role in the recall effort but told the *Flint Journal* he would gladly run again if Walling were removed from office.

A convoluted process ensued. The Genesee County Election Commission rejected one of Davenport's petitions because he misspelled the word "jeopardize." Davenport threatened to contact the Reverend Al Sharpton and the U.S. attorney general's office to accuse Walling of "genocide" when the police and fire layoffs took place. After the county clerk invalidated thousands of signatures on the recall petition, Davenport and his cohorts filed suit, alleging their constitutional rights had been violated and requesting a preliminary injunction to place the recall on the November general election ballot. A federal judge finally denied the injunction.

"Now he's going to run for mayor next year," Walling said, using the rearview mirror to make eye contact with me.

"Oh God," Jones said, laughing. "I think he's one we can beat."

With the snow starting to stick to the roads, we arrived at the first stop on our schedule—Android Industries. The auto parts maker had laid off hundreds of workers over the past few years, but today the company was announcing a deal to help manufacture a vehicle called the MV-1 specifically for the disabled. It looked like a retrofitted Chevy Tahoe. Though there were a few thousand orders on hand for the vehicle, there were no sales projections beyond that. "We have taken a leap of faith here," said Android's vice president of business development. "If we build it, they will come." The project would add just ten new jobs, but that was nothing to scoff at in Flint. Despite a variety of federal, state, and local incentives to lure new businesses to the area, nothing seemed to work.

The Android facility was a big, scrupulously clean warehouse that was largely empty, a reflection of all the work that used to be done there. Standing on a portable stage accented with poinsettias and a silver vehicle chassis suspended behind it, a succession of company executives and business partners touted "environmentally sustainable coating options" and state-of-the-art "articulating arms." The founder of Android implored the audience to keep the faith, despite the monumental struggles of the auto industry. "We'll grow old in this business together," he said. "Trust me." It was meant to be inspiring but came off as desperate. With each speaker, accompanied by the soothing hum of the heating system, you could feel the energy draining out of the factory. The men on the stage looked depressed—except Walling, who often bobbed his head in agreement as others spoke, a look of engaged optimism on his face. When you're the mayor of Flint, it takes more than a boring media event to break your spirit. Unfazed by being introduced as *Duane* Walling, he gave a short, energetic speech. Afterwards, he eagerly hopped into the backseat of a white display vehicle, seemingly entranced by a rundown on the passive restraint system from a company spokesman. He chatted amiably about the MV-1 with a woman afflicted with spina bifida. He did a few interviews with woefully uninformed TV reporters—giving them background information to help them formulate questions before the cameras rolled—then updated his Facebook page on his Blackberry. "I'm doing my own social media here!" he told a group of men while everyone lined up for the buffet lunch. It was unclear if they were familiar with the concept of social media.

Walling grabbed a cookie and a piece of cheesecake on the way out, finishing off the sweets as we drove back downtown. "I used to add sugar to my Hi-C when I visited my grandma as a kid," he said.

A photo shoot was next on the agenda. Walling had agreed to help a UM-Flint photography student named Sarah with her senior project. She was re-creating a series of classic movie posters with a Flint theme. Through the wonders of Photoshop, King Kong would be perched on top of the Citizens Bank Building in the heart of downtown Flint instead of New York's Empire State Building. Walling would be the stand-in for Fay Wray, trapped in the clutches of the great ape. "She told me to practice my scared face," Walling explained. "I'll have to work on that. I haven't been scared enough in my life to have that down yet."

The shoot happened to be in the William S. White Building on the northern edge of the college campus. The building is named after the current head of the Mott Foundation, who had married Charles Stewart Mott's granddaughter, and located on land once occupied by Auto-World, proving that it's nearly impossible to escape the ghosts of Flint's past. Inside, Sarah greeted the mayor and led him to the studio. She looked the part of a photo student—purple hair, hip glasses, and clothes that looked more San Francisco than Flint. The mayor was in a gray suit with the obligatory U.S. flag lapel pin. It was hard to determine who was more excited about the project. Sarah positioned the mayor in front of a brightly lit green screen and gave him a simple recommendation: "Just look apprehensive."

With his naturally sunny disposition combined with the skills he honed on the campaign trail, Dayne Walling may have met his match with this assignment. He appeared more eager than scared as he raised his hands above his head, like he'd never been happier to be in the clutches of an angry, outsize refugee from Skull Island. It was as if King Kong were a business owner considering relocation to Flint.

"Pretend you've just seen your worst enemy," Sarah offered.

"You want me to whisper some names in your ear, Mr. Mayor?" Walling's communications director asked.

That helped a little, but now Walling looked extremely interested in what King Kong might have to say, like he was empathizing with the monster's unhappy tale of capture and mistreatment.

"Open your eyeballs a tiny bit wider," Sarah suggested.

Now Walling looked like he had just won the lottery. Jesus, this could take all day.

Sarah finally asked the mayor to jump up and down as she snapped his photo. "Do I need to get more air?" he asked, trying to be helpful. Two inches off the ground, the mayor looked mildly distressed but hardly terrified. Close enough. A postpolitical career in Hollywood was not in the cards for Dayne Walling. He's incapable of being something he's not, even if it's just for a gag photo.

We made the short drive back to city hall. The snow had stopped, but any chance of the sun making an appearance that day was long gone. It was midafternoon but felt later. On the edge of the city government complex, just behind police headquarters, we passed a long line of red garbage trucks, their engines idling.

"Why are they doing that?" Walling asked. "I hope it's not a protest or something."

"They picked up my garbage today," Jones responded.

The mayor glanced at the trucks again before we rolled into the darkened, subterranean parking garage. Suddenly he had the worried look that had eluded him at the photo shoot. The mayor had a negotiating session scheduled that afternoon with AFSCME, the union representing all city workers except the police and firefighters. That included the garbage collectors, which may have explained his trepidation. AFSCME had been more amenable in contract negotiations with the city because it appeared to have a better understanding of Flint's dire financial situation, Walling told me. The union had refrained from making inflammatory statements in the press but wasn't above work slowdowns to get its point across.

Overall, negotiations with the city's union workers were going nowhere. So far that year, there had been more than 750 fires in Flint, more than half of them considered arson. It was a dramatic increase over the 496 total fires recorded in 2009. A tentative agreement with firefighters had been voted down by the rank and file in late November. After that setback, Walling had announced the layoff of more than one hundred city workers, including twenty more police officers. Flint's downtown police headquarters would be closed to the public on weekends to save money. It was a frightening new development in a city that had suffered sixty murders that year, one shy of the all-time record, even as homicide rates dropped around the country. San Francisco, despite a population eight times larger than Flint, had forty-nine murders in 2010.

"Are they going to mind me sitting in on the negotiations?" I asked.

"No, because you're not sitting in on negotiations," Walling said, the lighthearted mood of the photo shoot now gone.

"Just thought I'd give it a shot," I said. "Mind if I hang out in the lobby until you're done?"

"Put him in the office of someone who used to work for the City of Flint," Walling instructed Jones.

An hour later, the negotiating session completed, Walling and I drove to the Durant-Dort Carriage Company office, just across from the pink Nash House where I had stayed on my first visit to Flint more than a year earlier. The mayor was attending an event sponsored by the Flint Club, an organization he had formed with three other Flint natives in 2001, when they were all working in Washington, D.C. The goal was to help change the negative perception of Flint. That night's event was a roundtable for UM-Flint students to express their ideas about how to improve life in the city. Surrounded by old-timey brass lamps and memorabilia from the early days of carriage making and the emerging auto industry, the students were mostly positive about Flint. When the moderator asked how many planned to stay in the city after graduation, five of eight raised their hands. "You're kidding me!" he said, genuinely shocked. "Almost everybody!"

But the students weren't shy about pointing out the drawbacks of downtown. Namely, there were still few services available to them. In a brainstorming session, it was determined that the most appealing new business would be a combination Laundromat, tanning salon, and supercheap late-night pizzeria. I was tempted to throw in gun range, but I didn't want to poison the atmosphere. Even with the recent addition of Blackstone's Pub, Wize Guys Pizza, and the upscale 501 restaurant in downtown, Flint nightlife was not exactly geared toward college students. "I've been to a lot of Flint bars, and nobody's dancing, nobody's doing anything," said one young woman. "It looks like they're just there to drown their sorrows, like they're beaten people. There's no life to them. It's just a downtrodden mood."

Back in the car after the event, Walling was enthusiastic. "Those kids show you that Flint is beginning to transform itself into a college town," he said. Then he paused, shook his head, and started laughing. "But that girl wasn't wrong when she described the bars. She had that right. That's Flint!"

Walling dropped me off at my car so I could follow him to his house, a handsome 3,500-square-foot, two-story home with a cozy fireplace off East Court Street. He and his wife bought it in 2006 for $160,000. It's twice the size and half the cost of their previous home in Minneapolis. Walling called it their "dream house," pointing out that they would never need to move because there was a lot of room to grow. Like any good Flintoid, he had a dog—a combination Boxer and Bulldog named Bruno that he picked up at a shelter—who was already earning his keep. A special police detail had been posted at Walling's home earlier in the year when police received "credible threats" against the mayor after he laid off cops during contract negotiations. "There's people in this city who have more to be scared about than Dayne Walling, and they can't get police protection," complained the police union president at the time.

Walling's mom soon arrived with his two sons. She lived just up the street and had been babysitting the boys. Walling's wife wasn't home yet. She was still in Ann Arbor, where she was teaching a class at the University of Michigan as part of a postdoctoral fellowship. "She really loves Ann Arbor, so she spends time on campus at least three days a week," he explained.

The mayor's study is in the basement just off a small rec room, where his sons were soon taking turns trying to execute thunderous dunks on a Nerf hoop. "You can play until 7:30, then it's time for homework," Walling told them. The study was a mixture of a college professor's office and a childhood bedroom. There was a Presidential Physical Fitness Award signed by Ronald Reagan on the wall, along with Flint Art Fair posters and an AutoWorld pennant. I noticed a bowling trophy from the winter of 1985–86 on a shelf. The team was called the Screwballs, and Walling was voted Most Improved.

"I didn't know you were a bowler," I said.

"This is Flint—doesn't everybody bowl?" he answered.

I remembered how excited I had been to finally get my own bowling ball in grade school and not have to use the rentals at various alleys around Flint. My mom took me to the pro shop at Nightingale Lanes, not far from the AC Spark Plug plant. An elderly man measured my hand and showed me the various options in our rock-bottom price range. He asked if I wanted my initials on the ball for a few extra dollars. "It keeps it from getting stolen," he said, knowing exactly how to up-sell in Flint. My mom gave the okay. When the ball was ready, the entire family went along. The same man presented it to me. My brothers and sisters started to laugh, and my mom, who was trying not to crack up, elbowed my brother in the arm. I was confused. So was the man who had fitted the ball. It looked great to me, emblazoned in big letters with my initials: G.A.Y. It was a few years before I got the joke.

Walling's adolescent artifacts shared space with an overflowing collection of urban-planning tomes definitely not meant for mass consumption. "I don't know anyone else who read this except me," he said, holding up a dog-eared copy of a page-turner titled *Cities in Transition: Social Changes and Institutional Responses in Urban Development.* I realized that one of the authors was the father of a girl I dated briefly during my freshman year in high school, before she dumped me for a senior on the hockey team who had a mullet and a driver's license. I decided not to mention this to the mayor. Walling also recommended *The Sustaining Hand: Community Leadership and Corporate Power.* He knew off the top of his head that chapter 12 was devoted to Flint. The mayor provided a quick rundown of half a dozen books, including their theoretical angles and how they dealt with Flint. It was getting late. It had been a long day. But Walling's enthusiasm was ramping up as he discussed a Marxist interpretation of Flint's industrial history.

He pulled open a well-organized file cabinet filled with his academic research. If there was a recommended course of study for becoming mayor of Flint, Walling appeared to have followed it. His honors thesis as an undergraduate at MSU dealt with the environmental and social history of a Flint neighborhood built on top of a General Motors dump. His research project in history as a Rhodes Scholar at Oxford examined the Flint Sit-Down Strike. He wrote extensively about economic development in Flint during the eighties and nineties while earning a master's at the University of London. He completed all the coursework for a PhD in geography at the University of Minnesota, but he never finished his dissertation on community and economic development in midsize cities. Instead, he left school and returned to Flint to run for mayor.

The personal statement that Walling submitted with his application to the University of Minnesota included the typical rundown of academic and professional accomplishments meant to impress without appearing boastful. But it also had an unexpected element—a poem that Walling had written in London when he was a student there. It's not a particularly good poem—it probably drew a few snide comments from the selection committee—but it's heartfelt. It's meant to convey the dichotomies of the capitalist system, a system that bestows great wealth and great poverty, a system that can "undermine our common humanity by isolating each of us." The poem is a reflection of the feelings that animate his "vision for cities, one that is at odds with sprawl, poverty, and other forms of separation."

Stumbling bare legs under a knit skirt,
Dragging plastic bags with boxes of biscuits,
Breathing toothless mouth with spit on her lips,
Searching dark eyes for the familiar gate, and
Passing other people without notice,
The woman walked by.

Striding lean legs under pressed khakis,
Carrying nylon backpack with three new books,
Smiling bright future with the university, yet
Waiting careful mind for wisdom beyond knowledge,
Noticing no one but her,
I walked by.

After reading this in Walling's basement, with his young sons whooping it up outside the door, I asked what it's like for him, after years of study, to finally be running the city where he was born and raised, only to discover that he is effectively the budget cutter in chief, haggling with unions and reducing services to save money. He told me about going to a neighborhood association meeting a few months earlier at Freeman Elementary, where he attended grade school. It was held in the same room where he had participated in a diversity celebration as a kid. All the students wore costumes or brought food to represent their heritage. Walling wore green because he's part Irish. "I remembered that as soon as I walked into the room because it was such a vivid childhood memory," he said. But returning to his old school wasn't exactly a moment of triumph. He had to brief the citizens in attendance on police layoffs, an upcoming increase in their property taxes to cover the cost of a lawsuit settlement left over from the Williamson administration, and the likelihood that a nearby fire station would be closed. "It wasn't easy," he said, then appeared to stop himself from saying more.

The mayor wasn't looking for pity, but it was hard not to feel sorry for him. As we walked upstairs, I heard the closest thing to a personal complaint I was likely to get out of Dayne Walling. "In one way or another, I've been researching this stuff since about 1994," he told me. "It's something I'm just so passionate about. I've been engaged with it for so long. A lot of what I do on a day-to-day basis now doesn't end up being presented in a way that's in-depth. It's all about coming up with short-term solutions. So I'm anxious and willing to finally share what I know about the long-term future of cities, about the future of Flint."

As I walked across the mayor's snow-covered front yard to my car, I could hear Bruno barking inside the house, happy that most of the family had returned home for the night. I wondered if Dayne Walling would ever get the chance to move beyond the latest Flint crisis and get to work on a long-term solution to Flint's woes. There were no guarantees.

27

Joy to the World

When I left the house on Sunday morning to attend church at Joy Tabernacle, the first real storm of the winter was in full swing. The wind was picking up, and dark clouds were dumping heavy snow as I drove slowly down Paradise Drive. A few inches of white stuff already capped the wooden sign with teal-colored palm trees marking the entrance and exit of the Grand Wailea housing development in Grand Blanc, where I was staying with my friend Duane. I guess if you were trying hard to maintain the illusion of Hawaii on a December day in Michigan, you could pretend the sign was dusted with volcano ash.

I was flying back to San Francisco the next day. I was determined, one way or another, to reach some sort of resolution related to my search for a house. As expected, I'd found several more low-priced possibilities in Civic Park that December but no moment of clarity. I'd returned to Flint in the summer of 2009 full of California optimism and brimming with an unrealistic sense of nostalgia. A year and a half later, I'd been thoroughly disabused of the notion that there were any quick fixes for my hometown. The wild optimism I'd felt at Zeitgeist back in San Francisco, fueled by pitchers of pricey microbrewed beer, was long gone. On a mission that demanded practicality, lately I'd found myself daydreaming about how I would save Flint if only I were Bill Gates or Warren Buffet. I'd even blown money on a few Michigan lottery tickets at Paul's Pipe Shop downtown, a rare survivor from Flint's glory days. I was one step from the ultimate delusion: fantasizing that GM would suddenly announce plans to build three new plants in the city and hire seventy thousand workers.

Anxious and uncertain, I fishtailed onto I-475, the highway spur that had wiped out two black neighborhoods to provide speedy access to the Buick factory that no longer existed on Hamilton Avenue. I spotted only a handful of other drivers as the icy interstate carried me from suburbia to whatever urban-planning term might accurately describe Flint in its current amorphous state—a shrinking city, a right-sizing city, a vanishing city? The snowy Sunday morning rendered the landscape all but lifeless. I didn't see a single person on the streets as I passed all the familiar landmarks of my childhood. It was peaceful, but lonely. That changed when I turned left off North Chevrolet onto West Dayton. Joy Tabernacle's beautiful stained-glass windows were illuminated from within. There were several guys vigorously shoveling out the church parking lot as the falling snow covered the stretches they had already cleared. A handful of little kids, puffed up in winter coats, played in the snow mounds piled high around the property. Several cars were crawling toward the church with their lights on.

One of the snow shovelers directed me into a parking space, smiling and using exaggerated arm motions like he was guiding a 747 in for a landing. When I got out, I saw that it was Aaron, the guy I'd met in the pastor's office, introduced to me as someone who had been in prison at seventeen. "Hey, it's good to see you again," he said before he resumed shoveling.

As a Catholic, I had grown up viewing church attendance as an unwelcome obligation that you performed to avoid the guilt and fear that went along with missing Mass. The nuns at Saint Mary's frequently reminded us that failure to show up on Sunday was a mortal sin that could land you in hell if you were unlucky enough to die in a car accident or get murdered before going to confession. Obviously, the sisters didn't coddle their young charges with theological nuance and happy talk, just as the school football coach, who worked in the shop, didn't censure his language at practice. "I want you to rape the fucking ball carrier," he yelled at us one day when somebody missed a tackle. Not the best way to put it, perhaps, but we sure got the idea. Flint had never been a place where you were sheltered too much just because you were a child. But my negative attitude toward church had been heightened by something far less weighty than the eternal fate of my soul. I had to miss the end of the weekly Abbott and Costello movie, a retro indulgence I loved, to attend ten o'clock Mass on Sundays. So I didn't expect to feel much better after a day at Joy Tabernacle.

Looking resplendent in a dark suit and purple tie, Reverend McCathern started things off with a rousing chorus of "Joy to the World," backed up by the organ player and a drummer. My voice is untrustworthy at best, but there were so many people singing, talking, and mingling in the church that I soon found myself belting out the words.

"The last thing you want to do is come to church and be depressed," the pastor announced at the end of the song. He was looking right at me as I stood in a pew ten rows from the front, the only white guy in the church. "The number one prescription in America is antidepressants, yet God has loved us enough to put joy in our hearts!"

He lowered his voice and instantly calmed the mood in the church. "Just be glad to be here. Don't clap. Don't wave your hands. Just smile." He grinned as he surveyed the congregation. "I've got some kind of smile, don't I. Crooked teeth. No teeth. But I still got a smile. Look around at all those silly smiles. It's sure a lot better than all that silly old crying we've all been doing."

The organ revved up with a throaty tremolo, the drums kicked in, and the pastor started building toward a crescendo. "You know how they say, put your hands in the air like you just don't care?" he asked from the pulpit. "Well, I want you to smile like you just don't care!"

If there was a group-therapy session tailor-made for the residents of Flint, past and present, this was it. I was grinning like a fool. "Right here at the corner of Dayton and Chevrolet in Flint, Michigan, we've got joy in our life!" he declared in a booming voice. "Now go to someone and tell them, 'I've got joy!'"

Everyone left the pews, talking and laughing. I forgot to feel awkward and joined in, not that I really had a choice. It's pretty much impossible to opt out of the celebration that is Sunday at Joy Tabernacle. I momentarily stopped agonizing over buying a house. I dismissed my financial worries. I set aside all my concerns about the fate of American cities. This was a chance to forget everything for a while.

Over the next few hours, the emotional temperature of the church rose and fell with the beat of the music. Money was collected. Women passed out in the aisles, attended to by helpers dressed as nurses. Scriptures were read. A girl gave me a Bible so I could follow along. People were healed. More money was collected. New members were welcomed into the church. Testimonials were delivered about drug addicts recovering and utilities being turned on with the help of the Lord. I lost track of how many people hugged me. Near the end of the service, the pastor asked how many in attendance were unemployed and looking for a job. He insisted that they stand up. Nearly the entire church obliged.

"It's like a jungle out there," he said, his voice soft but rising. "Everybody is just scraping by."

He paused and asked, "Do y'all mind if I preach? I mean, can I really preach now?"

"Yes!" the congregation roared back.

"In the midst of this mess, we are blessed!" the pastor yelled, hopping up and down behind the pulpit. "Flint, Michigan, doesn't dictate my joy. General Motors doesn't dictate my joy. God does!"

The pastor stepped away from the pulpit, closed his eyes, and danced on the altar accompanied by the music and the shouting. It was profoundly loud now, louder than any Sunday when this building was home to Community Presbyterian Church. "Put your shoulders back and tell someone we can make it. In the middle of Civic Park, where almost everything is torn down, God is saying, I've got something to give you! When General Motors gets through with it, let me show you what God can do with it!"

I found myself yelling affirmations along with everyone else. It felt good. I knew it was pointless to keep blaming General Motors for everything that was happening on the streets of Civic Park and the rest of Flint. Railing against a soulless corporate monolith wouldn't reduce the unemployment rate or eliminate the abandoned houses, but somehow the pastor tapped into a gut feeling I'd been dismissing since I'd returned to Flint. What the largest corporation in the world had done to my city was morally reprehensible. It was a crime against humanity. I'm not sure this is what the pastor intended, but as I stood in Joy Tabernacle I knew exactly what I wanted to say to General Motors. It wasn't very Christian, but it was certainly heartfelt.

Fuck you, GM.

As we were closing in on the three-hour mark, the service ended. It was probably the closest a lapsed Catholic could come to a religious experience. The pastor looked sweaty, exuberant, and exhausted as he mingled with the congregation leaving the church. When I said goodbye, still awed by everything that had just transpired, I asked him what he planned to do after the service. "Collapse!" he said. "Then I'm going to sit on the couch and watch some football."

I exited through the side door with a few other people. The snow was still coming down, and at least six inches blanketed the parking lot. My

Cavalier looked like a misshapen igloo. I excavated the door handle, unlocked the car, and settled into the driver's seat. I sat in the darkened Chevy, the windows coated in snow, waiting a good five minutes for the heater to fire up.

Without expecting it, I started to cry. It took me by surprise, but there was no stopping it. I was crying for my city. And I was crying for myself.

At that moment, I knew I wasn't going to buy a house in Flint.

Anyone with a calculator and access to my financial records could see that I had no business owning a bungalow in San Francisco, let alone a piece of real estate in a city experiencing a long-running economic catastrophe like Flint. And I had no business dragging Traci down the path to ruin with me, although I sense I would have been single again if I had insisted on following through with my improbable plan. I guess I'd known all this for a while, but I've always had a knack for temporarily rationalizing the irrational.

Now I had to admit that even though I saw myself as some sort of conquering hero—jetting in from the City by the Bay to save the Vehicle City—I wouldn't have been doing my hometown any favors. As another underfinanced absentee landlord, even one with the noblest of intentions, I would have been part of the problem. In fact, the best thing I could do for Flint was buy an abandoned house on eBay and pay to tear it down. But I couldn't even afford that. And talk about depressing. It was one thing for me to recognize the practical merits of Dan Kildee's utilitarian approach. I knew it was a good idea, given the circumstances, but that didn't mean I wanted to actively participate in it. That would have required an act of pure logic, and emotion had always fueled this quest—emotion that was welling up in a jumbled, incoherent way as I sat in the car, trying unsuccessfully to dry my eyes and blow my nose with a crumpled Halo Burger napkin.

Though I'd maintained that this was no midlife crisis—the same claim, I'm sure, made by everyone going through a midlife crisis—I now faced the fear that if Flint slipped away, a part of me went with it. The young me. The kid looking forward to a bright, exciting future. Not some guy with a bad knee who fretted over his mortgage, hustled for freelance writing gigs he wasn't particularly proud of, and wept in a friend's car during a snowstorm.

I realized that I'd seen a house as a way to recapture the sense of belonging I'd never felt anywhere but Flint, the elusive feeling that I'd taken for granted growing up a few blocks away on Bassett Place when my family last lived together under the same roof. Now we were scattered across the country, our life together blasted apart by the economic forces and random nature of modern life that separated so many other American families. Two siblings lived in Washington State. Another lived in North Carolina with her son, a high school freshman whom I hardly knew. My mom was in Florida, alone in her eighties and accessible only by cross-country flights and phone calls. Somehow giving up on my dream of a house in Flint forced me to acknowledge that my family would never truly be together again.

For all my altruistic motives, there was also a strain of selfishness running through my return to Flint. Maybe I just wanted to live in a place where I wasn't constantly being reminded of what I *didn't* have. I longed to be a big fish in a small pond. Even with the violence and despair that defined it now, Flint was a simpler, calmer, more forgiving city than San Francisco, which, despite its many charms, sometimes felt chaotically defined by money, disparity, and neurotic overachievers.

I suppose all this might be considered a breakthrough in the therapy sessions I'd been too cheap to attend, although I'm sure I would have been really pissed off if I'd spent a hundred dollars an hour to feel this bad. I wiped my eyes on my sleeve and tried to distract myself with more practical concerns. This was still Flint in the middle of a blizzard. Getting in touch with my emotions didn't change the fact that I had to make it back to Duane's house in Grand Blanc, and my windshield wipers were frozen in a slab of hardening snow. Of course, I'd forgotten my gloves—stupid Californian! Just as I was digging under the seats to find something to clear the windshield, it was magically swept clean by Aaron, who was taking care of the few remaining cars in the lot. Happy to see a familiar face, I impulsively pushed open the door and got out to talk.

"Thanks for the help," I said.

"Happy to do it," he answered. "I'm the jack-of-all-trades around here."

He paused and added, "You all right?"

"Oh, yeah, my eyes are just watering a little in this cold weather," I stammered. "I'd forgotten what December is like in Michigan. This is my first winter in Flint in twenty years."

"Well, I'm glad I could share it with you," he said.

He turned in a half circle, slowly surveying the stretch of West Dayton Avenue in front of the church. The neighborhood was perfectly quiet. The heavy snow and the muted light managed to mask all the decay. It was hard to tell that many of the houses, owned by people in

Ohio, California, and Alaska, not to mention the Genesee County Land Bank, were abandoned. This easily could have passed for a December day in the seventies with Christmas fast approaching, when Civic Park was still my home and Flint still believed it could recapture all that it once was. It was a beautiful winter scene.

"I don't think I could ever give this up," Aaron said, patting me on the shoulder before he hustled over to another car and began to clear away the snow.

I knew exactly how he felt. A part of me had never left Flint. At the same time, I couldn't deny that there was a large dose of relief in knowing that I was about to walk away. I had a fulfilling life in San Francisco, and another part of me couldn't wait to return. Yet again, Flint was forcing me to deal with two contradictory emotions. I should have been used to it by now. I knew I was doing the right thing, but I couldn't help feeling that I was abandoning the place that made me who I am.

I got back in the car for the drive to suburbia. I needed to start packing for the early morning flight that would take me back to Traci, my love, and the happy little house we couldn't really afford. Back to Sergio, our heavyweight cat. Back to the often trivial concerns that occupy a bustling, creative, prosperous city animated by more money than it knew what to do with. Back to my life in San Francisco, but secure in the knowledge that I would always be a Flintoid at heart.

Epilogue

Summer 2012

It was still drizzling after we ate lunch at McDonald's, so P-Nut and I ditched our plans to paint the exterior of his house on West Dayton Avenue and decided to get started on the interior of the small first-floor sunroom instead. That meant scraping off several decades' worth of old paint and taping the windows. Painting prep is one of the least satisfying home improvement projects, but I was happy to be there. So was P-Nut. He had all the energy and determination you would expect of a twenty-three-year-old first-time homeowner who feels like he's working toward a brighter future. He also had a practical incentive. He was sharing a single room with his girlfriend, Raevyn, and their three young daughters at his father-in-law's home until his two-story Civic Park Saltbox was fit for habitation. He needed more space. Fast. "I want my family to have a real home, so I've been doing something at the house every day," he told me.

P-Nut had already tamed the wild, overgrown yard, cleared the house of debris, pulled up the worn carpet, fixed a few broken windows, and painted the living room a rich red color. The floors still needed refinishing, and some plumbing and electrical work remained to be done, not to mention all the holes in the walls that needed patching. But as abandoned houses in Flint go, this one wasn't too bad. He brought his little girls—who were ages three, four, and six—over on weekends so they could play while he worked. Despite the summer weather, he'd even burned some wood in the fireplace, just because he could. "I'll be saving some money on heat in the winter with all the wood you can find around here," he said as he attacked a windowsill with a putty knife. "It heats up the whole house."

Sherman McCathern was the reason P-Nut and I were working together on a June afternoon in 2012. I'd stayed in touch with the pastor, and during one phone conversation he mentioned that a local real-estate agent had donated a house to the church. In turn, the pastor had given it to P-Nut, a member of the congregation who was trying to turn his life around. McCathern had made the decision after receiving another one of his famous communiqués from God. He had sat P-Nut down for a long talk to ensure that he knew a house was a huge responsibility and would require a lot of hard work to make it a home. The problem now, as usual, was money. They needed funds to fix up the place.

The solution seemed obvious to me. I could donate the money I had set aside for a house of my own in Flint to finance the rehab. This small gesture would have immediate, tangible results. I'd be reaching out to a guy who was roughly the same age I was when I left Civic Park. I'd be doing my part to help the pastor in his uphill struggle to transform the neighborhood. And unlike my earlier plans, this one wouldn't make me an accidental slumlord, saddled with a second home I couldn't afford to maintain. I knew one house wasn't going to magically fix Flint, but I was still determined to assist the city in some way. I didn't like the way I'd left things between me and my hometown. Traci thought it was a great idea, one of my rare epiphanies related to real estate in the Vehicle City.

Reverend McCathern, a survivor well schooled in the art of raising money, happily accepted the offer. "It's providence," he declared, not for the first time. He suggested that I fly out to meet P-Nut and his family, maybe earn a little sweat equity in addition to my donation. So I was back in Flint, a few blocks from my old house, just a short walk from Dave and Judy Starr's place on Milbourne Avenue. It turns out I was no stranger to P-Nut's Band-Aid beige and brown house on the corner. It happened to be the childhood home of writer and former shop rat Ben Hamper. I'd stopped there dozens of times over the years when I carpooled to Saint Mary's with Ben's younger siblings. He had described the old Civic Park in *Rivethead*: "Our neighborhood was strictly blue-collar and predominantly Catholic. The men lumbered back and forth to the factories while their wives raised large families, packed lunch buckets and marched the kids off to the nuns." Obviously, times had changed.

P-Nut was far more organized than I ever was when I tried to fix up my house. He had the painting supplies neatly arranged on a drop cloth in the living room, like a surgeon preparing to operate. He planned to get the entire sunroom prepped and painted in one day. He was wearing unwrinkled jeans and an oversize T-shirt that closely matched the red color he had chosen to paint the walls. His black baseball cap was emblazoned with his nickname in gold script. "Everyone said my head looked like a peanut when I was a little boy and it just stuck," he explained.

While we worked side by side, P-Nut told me his story. He had followed a trajectory similar to many of the young men who had grown up in Civic Park and landed at Joy Tabernacle. His desire to create a home for Raevyn and their kids was driven by the fact that he'd never really had a home of his own. His parents were divorced, and his mother had a drug problem. The courts eventually intervened, and P-Nut was sent to live with his grandparents. His grandfather taught him how to "fix on cars," and he was an accomplished mechanic, skilled enough to get arrested for auto theft when he was thirteen. Seeing over the steering wheel was a bigger challenge than busting the steering column to start the car. He was sent to a juvenile correctional facility in Pennsylvania until he was seventeen. Both grandparents died while he was incarcerated. "I got to come home for the funerals," he said.

When he was released, P-Nut met Raevyn back in Flint, and they rented a house together. He earned a little money working on cars, but not nearly enough to support his growing family. He wasn't above breaking into empty houses in search of anything he could sell, especially copper plumbing and wiring. He was a scrapper, the scourge of Flint's troubled neighborhoods, and his voice got softer when he tried to explain. "It was wrong, but I had kids, no job, and no money," he said. "I didn't want to sell drugs or go out and rob somebody."

In fact, P-Nut and some friends had once targeted the house he now owned—the very house we were working on at that moment. They ran off when a burglar alarm sounded. But P-Nut admitted that his partners had gone back later and stolen the water heater and some electrical wiring in the basement.

Things had gotten worse when the police raided a neighborhood garage where P-Nut was repairing cars. A spare transmission was identified as stolen property. P-Nut maintains he had no idea it was hot, but he did a year in county jail nonetheless. Raevyn could no longer afford rent on their house, so she moved back home with the kids. Visitors under eighteen weren't allowed at the jail, so P-Nut didn't see his daughters while he was incarcerated. "That's when I knew I had to change things when I got out," he said. "I had to take care of my family. I had to do things the right way." His brother was a member at Joy, and P-Nut became active in the church after his release.

Our conversation was soon interrupted when the sound of someone rattling the back door echoed through the empty house, followed by loud pounding.

"Who there?" P-Nut yelled, tensing up.

"You know who there. Let me in!"

It was the voice of Reverend McCathern, and P-Nut hurried over to let him in.

"Why you locking me out?" he asked as he came up the back steps into the living room, followed by Aaron, who had taken in the winter scene with me in the church parking lot that snowy Sunday more than a year earlier when I decided not to buy a house in Flint.

"Security," P-Nut said a little sheepishly.

"Don't make me cut you," I said to the pastor, brandishing my spackle knife.

"Shoot, you don't scare me, son," McCathern said, laughing as he lightly grabbed my shoulder and gave me a push.

Just as the pastor had definite plans for Civic Park, he also had some well-defined ideas about home decorating, and he wasn't shy about sharing them. He suggested a vibrant green for the trim in the small kitchen, holding up a can of Glade air freshener as an example. "Now isn't that a beautiful color?" he asked. "You want each room to be distinctive and different." A discussion ensued about the relative merits of removing a front window to prevent break-ins versus preserving the window and installing security bars. "You need some natural light in here," the pastor explained as he slowly turned to take in the living room. I felt like I was in a home-decor reality show, Flint-style. P-Nut mentioned that he was thinking of a small chandelier for the sunroom, but the pastor wasn't going for it. Instead, he recommended a ceiling fan and "that straw kind of furniture."

"This is like your patio," he elaborated, sweeping his hands forward to encompass the sunroom. "This is where you sit and drink tea."

There was a brief pause before Aaron and P-Nut burst out laughing.

"Okay, I need to step back now, don't I?" McCathern said, shaking his head and looking at P-Nut. "This isn't my house, is it? It's yours."

After a short tour, the pastor and Aaron left. P-Nut and I went back to work for a half hour before Raevyn arrived with the couple's three daughters—Mariah, Kamira, and Jheniya. The little girls had matching braids and appeared to have cornered the market on pink, lavender, and pale blue clothes. They quickly headed for the front yard and were soon racing around the house, yelling and laughing.

By now, we were ready to paint, and Raevyn joined us in the small room with a brush. She was twenty-five, and it turned out that we had gone to the same high school, albeit twenty-one years apart. She told me she'd been skeptical about the house at first, wondering who would just give it away to someone. She also worried about its condition when she learned it had been vacant for a long stretch. Now she was looking forward to moving day. "I'm glad we've been able to fix it up ourselves," she said. "It's good to do something from the ground up. It gives you something to be proud of."

As we painted, talk turned to the future. P-Nut was part of a pilot program that the pastor had brokered with Baker College to help church members get college credit and job training. It was connected with the city's Clean and Green program, so P-Nut and several other members of the congregation got paid for mowing and maintaining dozens of yards and vacant lots in Civic Park. Raevyn was on public assistance, and P-Nut also earned a little extra money fixing cars on the side. The family of five lived on $1,200 a month. P-Nut's goal was to earn his GED and get certified as an automotive technician, building on the knowledge his grandfather had passed on to him before he died. "I know he would have liked seeing me earn a living from the things he taught me," he said.

I wanted everything to work out for P-Nut and Raevyn, but I knew the odds were against them—a young couple with a large family and few resources in a city that faced monumental, perhaps insurmountable challenges. Yet they had not given up yet, and that was an accomplishment all by itself.

And they were not alone. Reverend McCathern and the members of his flock. Mayor Dayne Walling. Dave and Judy Starr and the other diehards on Milbourne Avenue. Dan Kildee. The urban homesteaders of Carriage Town. They were all tough people fighting for Flint in their own ways. And I could fight alongside them in my way. I could keep writing about the city. I could keep coming back and stay connected to the place that meant so much to me. I could donate time and money to the individuals and organizations determined to create a new Flint.

Maybe not the city it was in the fifties, a bastion of the middle class, but a different place that still had pride and dignity.

Instead of viewing my time in Flint as a failure because I hadn't bought a house, I realized as I stood next to P-Nut and Raevyn—looking through the windows at a row of abandoned houses across the street—that it had been a success in all the ways that really mattered. I was part of the city again. I had new friends in my old hometown. And I had a measure of hope for the future.

P-Nut was reaching up to coat the wall above the windows with red paint, and I noticed a series of dates tattooed in black ink on his arms. I asked him what they meant. "These are my daughters' birthdays," he told me, "so I don't forget what I'm here for. So I don't forget my life has a purpose."

Updates

Flint. It's impossible to spin, sugarcoat, or sanitize Flint's fate since I attended church at Joy Tabernacle on that snowy Sunday in mid-December of 2010. A few hours after the service ended, the city recorded its sixty-first murder, tying the all-time record for a single year. That record was broken the next day.

Based on raw numbers, Flint continues to be an extremely threatening place to live. It was ranked the most dangerous city in America by CQ Press in an annual report released in December 2011. The unwelcome distinction was based on FBI statistics for six crime categories, including murder, rape, and robbery. Flint had the highest rate of aggravated assault and the second-highest homicide rate, giving it the top per capita crime rate in 405 cities with at least 75,000 residents. Budget cuts and continued layoffs have pared the Flint police force down to just 132 sworn officers.

With its population continuing to drop, Flint is in a statistical dead heat with Reading, Pennsylvania, for the dubious honor of having the largest share of its residents living in poverty.

There is no way to adequately counter these dry statistics and the human misery underlying them, but Flint demands mental compartmentalization, the ability to absorb bad news while simultaneously ferreting out encouraging signs. Enrollment at the University of Michigan–Flint continues to climb. There are more students at the downtown campus than ever before. Back to the Bricks, an auto cruise that culminates with a downtown street party, draws more than four hundred thousand over the course of a week in August. The polished and pimped-out vintage cars and huge crowds recall the GM parades that rolled down Saginaw Street in the fifties. The City of Flint and the Genesee County Land Bank have used federal stimulus funds to demolish hundreds of abandoned houses and rehab others, including several in Carriage Town. After numerous failed attempts to relocate to the more prosperous suburbs, my high school is biting the bullet and moving to a new home just south of downtown Flint, unleashing a few hundred Catholic school hellions on the city's core. I expect it will be a meaningful learning experience for all involved.

On a more personal note, my grandparents' East Side house on Illinois Avenue is still in immaculate condition, despite the surrounding blight. It has had just three owners over the past century. None were speculators. It's painted a welcoming yellow now, and on a summer day the lawn is lush, the flowerbeds are blooming, and an American flag flies from the metal holder my grandfather installed decades ago. On a recent visit, I met the current owners—an African American couple—and we sat on the front porch and talked. They sounded just like my grandparents as they quietly groused that some of their neighbors could do a better job taking care of their houses. Around the corner, Gypsy Jack's old house is being rehabbed by a group of urban farmers. A few vacant lots are devoted to gardens and a newly planted orchard. There's a pig roaming around somewhere. It's a full-fledged commune known as Peace Mob Gardens, complete with white dudes sporting beards and dreadlocks, along with women in flowing skirts and bandanas. My grandparents left their small Iowa farms to find a new life in the Vehicle City, but I sense they would like knowing that a new breed of farmers has set up shop so close to their old house. They would appreciate young people trying to create a new reality.

Dan Kildee. When his uncle, Democratic U.S. congressman Dale Kildee, announced he would not seek a nineteenth term in office, Dan took a leave of absence from the Center for Community Progress to campaign for the seat. He was elected to Congress in November 2012 and now represents Flint and the rest of Michigan's Fifth District in Washington, D.C.

Dayne Walling. The mayor was easily reelected to a full four-year term in November 2011, despite failing to resolve the labor dispute with

Flint's police and fire departments. Walling didn't have much time to celebrate. With the city facing massive budget deficits, the State of Michigan appointed an emergency financial manager with broad powers to run the city less than a month after the election. The role of the mayor and city council members was severely curtailed while the financial manager implemented a series of cuts, layoffs, and tax increases in an attempt to balance the budget. The financial manager, who is granted the power to force concessions on city workers, imposed contracts with the equivalent of a 20 percent wage reduction on police, firefighters, and other municipal employees. The State of Michigan determines when fiscal control of the city will be returned to Mayor Walling and the city council. The labor contracts and the emergency financial manager law itself are being challenged in the courts.

Michael Freeman and Perry Compton. They continue to improve their home on University Avenue in Carriage Town. A local housing organization purchased the empty house they owned across the street—the same place I considered rehabbing with them—and it has been restored to mint condition. Michael now works at the Center for Community Progress. He was recently elected to the Mott Community College Board. Perry joined forces in 2010 with David White, the archivist at Kettering University considered the original urban pioneer in Carriage Town, to open Witherbee's Market. It was the first grocery store in the downtown core in decades, but it was short-lived. Unable to pay rent and cover the debt payments associated with renovating the building, they closed the market just over a year after it opened.

Rich. The friend whose optimism fueled my dream of buying a house in our hometown continues to sell real estate in San Francisco and struggle with his role as a Flint property owner. He reluctantly sold the gutted house he owned on University Avenue. He also put the duplex he owns in Carriage Town up for sale, but pulled it off the market when there were no offers. He has no plans to sell the pink Nash House.

Dave and Judy Starr. The Starrs still live on Milbourne Avenue. They have no plans to move, but many of their neighbors have given up. On a block with twenty-one houses, only eight are occupied. Dave had a recurrence of lung cancer in 2012 and is undergoing treatment. Despite the setback, he continues to make progress on his backyard pond and waterfall.

Sherman McCathern. The pastor of Joy Tabernacle Church is still energetically ministering to his flock under trying circumstances. Just before Christmas 2012, a large portion of the church roof collapsed. No one was injured, but services were being held in the basement until an insurance settlement could be reached. Though he has been unable to do much work on the Civic Park Heritage Museum due to lack of funds, McCathern has enlisted more church members eager to further their education in the pilot program he helped create with Baker College. After his initial skepticism, he now endorses Dan Kildee's shrinking-city model and is unfazed by the dwindling number of residents in his neighborhood. "I accept that we're going to have to tear down some of these houses," he said. "It's like we have to purge Civic Park before we can bring it back."

P-Nut and Raevyn. After making numerous repairs, the couple moved into their home on West Dayton Avenue with their three daughters.

Gordon Young and Traci Vogel. We still reside in our 700-square-foot San Francisco mansion with our two cats, Sergio and Purdy. We've managed to make a small dent in our mortgage. We plan to donate a portion of any profits from this book—yes, more unrealistic thinking, but you never know—to various Flint organizations working to help the city, including Joy Tabernacle Church, Saint Francis Prayer Center, Whaley Children's Center, and the P3 Campaign to relocate Powers Catholic High School.

Acknowledgments

My profound thanks to all the Flint residents who cooperated with me on this book, especially Sherman McCathern, Dan Kildee, Dayne Walling, Michael Freeman and Perry Compton, and Dave and Judy Starr. You put up with my interview requests, phone calls, emails, and frequent visits for more than three years. You welcomed me into your homes and put up with me at work. I can't tell you how much I appreciate it.

This book would not have been possible without the assistance, advice, and encouragement of my good friend Rich. He has made a huge financial and emotional investment in Flint, often with little reward or thanks. His efforts have made the Vehicle City a better place.

Rich's sister, Berniece, welcomed me into her home and made me feel like a part of her family on my visits to Flint. Her warmth and kindness buoyed me during some very stressful times. (The toilet paper she bought me also helped.)

I am grateful to everyone who offered their friendship, insight, and a place to crash during my numerous trips to Flint. Thanks to Susan Miller and Mark Sanford, Ellen and Jim Perry, Jan Worth-Nelson and Ted Nelson, and Duane Gilles.

Special thanks to Jane Hogan, Tom Pohrt, J Willy, Darnell Ishmel, Dave McDonald, Jim Holbel, Shawn Chittle, Stephen Rodrick, and Kara Tambellini for their great stories about Flint and their entertaining reminders of why it's such memorable place.

My profound appreciation goes out to Howard Bragman for all his inspiration and advice. He also provided one of the greatest lines describing our hometown in the book.

Thanks to Jeff Gerecke for believing in the idea of a book about Flint.

The groundbreaking work of historian Andrew Highsmith was invaluable in understanding Flint's racial dynamics and the legacy of Charles Stewart Mott. His research illuminates an aspect of the city's history that has long been misunderstood and neglected. It had an emotional impact on me personally. He graciously elaborated on his work in time-consuming interviews and email exchanges. A revised and expanded version of Highsmith's insightful dissertation, "Demolition Means Progress," is forthcoming from the University of Chicago Press. It is essential reading for anyone who truly hopes to comprehend the forces that animate the Vehicle City. Although Highsmith was not raised in Flint, he moved to the city and bought a home—the ultimate sign of dedication—while conducting research. Without a doubt, he is an honorary Flintoid.

The journalist and historian Kim Crawford guided me through the fog of confusing and contradictory information surrounding Flint's alleged founder, Jacob Smith, with patience and good cheer. His compelling book, *The Daring Trader*, is the definitive treatment of the colorful fur trader who set up shop on the banks of the Flint River and shaped the city's history for decades to come.

Gerry Godin, the prolific author of the fascinating All Things Buick blog, was a friend and guide as I rediscovered Flint. His tours of the city—not to mention lunches at Angelo's Coney Island and some great stories—helped me feel at home again in the place where I was raised.

I am indebted to the hardworking and underappreciated reporters and editors at the *Flint Journal*. In an era of budget cuts and layoffs, they tackle the challenging task of covering the city on a daily basis, usually with little thanks or encouragement. I consulted and cited the work of numerous staff members, but I want to especially thank Ron Fonger, Andrew Heller, Laura Misjak, Scott Atkinson, and Kristen Longley, as well as David Harris, who has the daunting task of covering crime in the city. Editor Marjory Raymer was extremely helpful and kindly put up with numerous annoying inquiries while she was running a busy newsroom.

The travel, research, and reporting for this book would not have been possible without generous donations from the readers of Flint Expatriates. The project was also supported by a Presidential Research Grant awarded by Santa Clara University, a Hackworth research grant awarded by the Markkula Center for Applied Ethics at Santa Clara University, and a College of Arts and Sciences Dean's Grant awarded by Santa Clara University. Assistance was also provided by the Communication Department and the Center for Student Leadership at Santa Clara University.

I'm indebted to Lisa Davis, who walked me through the process of writing this book, offering much-needed guidance on everything from structure to word choice, when she wasn't calmly talking me through my frequent panic attacks. I owe you one. Reed Malcolm, Dore Brown, and the other editors at the University of California Press deserve particular praise for all their guidance and assistance.

Novella Carpenter, Connor Coyne, and Mick Normington read the book in manuscript form and offered incisive feedback when it was needed most. They also put up with my numerous follow-up calls with good cheer. Don Richards generously offered his assistance when it came time to separate fact from fiction related to Flint's history. Terry Schwarz and Frank J. Popper provided expertise on the shrinking-city phenomena. Douglas Weiland, executive director of the Genesee County Land Bank, was an invaluable source for information on anything and everything related to urban planning in Flint. The staff at the Alfred P. Sloan Museum expertly answered my arcane questions about Flint's geographic boundaries. Robert Burack, Jennifer Welch, Kurt Wagner, and Eric "Squirrel Boy" Francis helped research one of the more unexpected episodes in the book. Thanks to Jack Shafer and Michael Newman, who helped get this all started at *Slate*.

Ben Hamper, author of the quintessential Flint book, *Rivethead: Tales from the Assembly Line*, reminded me that a city wouldn't be much fun if there was nothing wrong with it.

I promise a round of drinks for Max, Michael, M.G., Carlo, Keith, and the rest of the Zeitgeist gang. Thanks for all the great ideas, some of which were actually useful. The same goes for my friend Meredith Arthur, whose enthusiasm and advice often kept me going.

My love and appreciation go out to my mom, Patricia Young, who made life in Flint such a memorable adventure. More than anyone else, she understands the city and why I wrote this book. Thanks for giving me, Matt, Katie, and Marty an exciting life.

Finally, my love and thanks to Traci, who is an honorary Flintoid if there ever was one. I don't know what I would do without you. I promise not to talk about Flint more than once a day from here on out.

Notes

PROLOGUE

Source: Some of the material in this prologue originally appeared in an article I wrote for *Slate* headlined "4 BR, 3.5 BA, Grm Ftr.: Why I want to buy a house in Flint, Mich." It was posted on June 18, 2009, at www.slate.com/articles/news_and_politics/dispatches/2009/06/4_br_35_ba_grm_ftr.html.

City rankings: Richard Eisenberg and Debra Wishik Englander, "The Best Places to Live in America," *Money*, August 1, 1987; Kurt Badenhausen, "In Pictures: America's Most Miserable Cities," *Forbes*, January 30, 2008, www.forbes.com/2008/01/29/detroit-stockton-flint-biz-cz_kb_0130miserable_slide_4.html; and Kurt Badenhausen, "In Pictures: America's Fastest-Dying Cities," *Forbes*, August 5, 2008, www.forbes.com/2008/08/04/economy-ohio-michigan-biz_cx_jz_0805dying_slide_4.html; Joshua Zumbrum, "In Pictures: The Best and Worst Cities for Recession Recovery," *Forbes*, June 10, 2009, www.forbes.com/2009/06/09/recession-economy-cities-business-beltway-recovery-cities_slide_12.html; and Klaus Kneale, "The Best and Worst Cities for New Jobs," *Forbes*, September 17, 2009, www.forbes.com/2009/09/17/cities-hiring-firing-careers-leadership-newjobs.html.

Jobless rate: Melissa Burden, "Genesee County and Flint Unemployment Rates Edge Up Slightly in July," *Flint Journal*, August 27, 2009. Prosperity in auto manufacturing centers like Flint and Detroit had earlier helped lift the economic fortunes of the entire state. "In 1955 Michigan's per capita income was 16 percent above the U.S. average—among the highest in the world—and by 1960 the state probably had the world's broadest middle class," according to *Michigan in Brief: 2002–2003*, a reference document about Michigan state government and public policy sponsored by the Michigan Nonprofit Association and the Council of Michigan Foundations, www.michiganinbrief.org/. For information on Flint's poverty levels, see Sabrina Tavernise, "Reading, Pa. Knew It Was Poor. Now It Knows Just How Poor," *New York Times*, September 26, 2011.

Figures and projections on school enrollment: "Facilities Advisory Committee's Report to the Flint Board of Education," December 17, 2008, p. 27.

Camry banned from UAW property: Ron Fonger, "New UAW Boss Standing Behind Ban on Foreign Cars on Union Property," *Flint Journal*, August 19, 2010.

CHAPTER 1. PINK HOUSES AND PANHANDLERS

Sources: Some of material in this chapter originally appeared in two articles I wrote: "4 BR, 3.5 BA, Grm Ftr.: Why I Want to Buy a House in Flint, Mich.," *Slate*, June 18, 2009, www.slate.com/articles/news_and_politics /dispatches/2009/06/4_br_35_ba_grm_ftr.html; "Faded Glory: Polishing Flint's Jewels," *New York Times*, August 19, 2009.

Gone to grade school at Saint Mary's: I attended a lot of schools in Flint. I started out at Homedale Elementary on the East Side when my entire family briefly lived with my grandparents. After we moved into a house of our own, I enrolled at Civic Park Elementary. When Civic Park closed for renovation following a massive fire, I entered the Catholic school system at Saint Michael's near downtown. Despite the protests of students and parents alike, the diocese decided to close the school when I was in third grade, and I transferred to Saint John's, where the inner-city kids from Saint Mike's weren't exactly welcomed with open arms. I eventually headed back to the East Side and attended Saint Mary's for sixth through eighth grade before heading to Flint Powers Catholic High School.

CHAPTER 3. BOURGEOIS HOMEOWNERS

Pollan builds a hut: Michael Pollan, *A Place of My Own: The Architecture of Daydreams* (New York: Penguin, 2008), 215–17.

"Look at what our hands have made!": Pollan, *A Place of My Own*, 173–74.

"Gravy on your french fries": Ben Hamper, *Rivethead: Tales from the Assembly Line* (New York: Warner Books, 1991), 15.

CHAPTER 4. VIRTUAL VEHICLE CITY

Fake IDs: When I was fifteen, I possessed a comically bad fake ID. On the advice of my girlfriend, I used makeup to conceal the final digit of the 1966 birth year on my Michigan license, the first step in bumping my age up to twenty-one. I then took a piece of Scotch tape and lifted a zero out of the phone book, stuck it inexpertly where the final 6 had been, and used a razor blade to cut away the excess tape. I didn't have a light touch, and I cut an imperfect square into the license around the new number. Those grooves, coupled with the elevation caused by the makeup and tape, created a 3-D effect that drew the eye directly to the altered date. It looked like I had spray-painted a tiny zero on a piece of Plexiglas and stuck it to my license with Bondo. My altered license worked like a charm. Flint was not the kind of place that would deny someone the right to drink simply because they were underage, and I had many rivals for the "Worst Fake ID" championship. One girl I knew, who was black, managed to secure the ID of another friend's eighteen-year-old sister. There was only one problem: the sister was white. When my African American friend nervously presented her fake ID at a bar for the first time, the bouncer did a double take, then calmly said, "Nice tan. Go on in."

Brawl at Chuck E. Cheese: Shannon Murphy, "Case Closed: No Charges in Fights at Chuck E. Cheese," *Flint Journal*, February 3, 2008; Elizabeth Shaw, "Brawl Breaks Out at Chuck E. Cheese in Flint Township," *Flint Journal*, January 28, 2008; Bryn Mickle, "Chuck E. Cheese in Flint Township Is More Peaceful Place after Banning Booze Eliminated Fights," *Flint Journal*, January 9, 2009.

"Hope that city someday returns to its former glory": Anonymous, March 19, 2008 (9:25 P.M.), comment on "Lay Me," Flint Expatriates, March 17, 2008, www.flintexpats.com/2008/03/lay-me.html#comments.

"I grew up a fat, Jewish, gay guy in Flint": Howard Bragman with Michael Levin, *Where's My Fifteen Minutes? Get Your Company, Your Cause, or Yourself the Recognition You Deserve* (New York: Penguin, 2008), 201.

"I'm leaving this town": Patricia Young, "Sentimental Journey," Flint Expatriates, November 7, 2007, www.flintexpats.com/2007/11/sentimental-journey.html.

"I love Flint": Misty Gower, "'I Love Flint': Gordon Young's Web Site Connects Expatriates through All Things Vehicle City," *Flint Journal*, August 13, 2008.

"Dismal cascade of drek": Ben Hamper, email message to author, June 28, 2009.

"The state shaped like a welder's mitt": Hamper, *Rivethead*, 15.

CHAPTER 5. BAD REPUTATION

Flint's bad reputation: "Riding Along with the Cops in Murdertown, U.S.A." was the headline of a story by Charlie LeDuff that ran in the April 15, 2011, issue of the *New York Times Magazine*. Dan Barry called Flint "the toughest city in America" in a *New York Times* story headlined "Amid Ruin of Flint, Seeing Hope in a Garden," which ran on October 18, 2009.

Not one of a hundred acres was farmable: Henry Utley, Byron M. Cutcheon, and Clarence Burton, *Michigan: As a Province, Territory, and State, the Twenty-Sixth Member of the Federal Union*, vol. 2 (New York: Publishing Society of Michigan, 1906), 253–54.

"Nothing but Indians, muskrats and bullfrogs": J.W. Leonard, *Industries of the Saginaws* (East Saginaw, Mich.: Courier, 1887), 10. Carl Crow, *The City of Flint Grows Up* (New York: Harper & Brothers, 1945), 9.

"Many tall tales came out of the woods": Crow, *The City of Flint Grows Up*, 10.

Jacob Smith: For the portrait of Jacob Smith, I drew on a variety of sources, including numerous newspaper articles; Willis F. Dunbar and George S. May's

Michigan: A History of the Wolverine State (Grand Rapids, MI: William B. Eerdmans, 1995); and *Picture History of Flint,* edited by Lawrence R. Gustin (Grand Rapids, Mich.: William B. Eerdmans, 1976). Separating fanciful legend from historical fact is no easy task when it comes to Jacob Smith. Local histories often repeat dubious stories about the fur trader's daring escapes from hostile Indians and overstate the amount of time he actually spent in the area that would become Flint. The best source for accurate information on Smith and the region's early history is Kim Crawford's *The Daring Trader: Jacob Smith in the Michigan Territory, 1802–1825* (East Lansing: Michigan State University Press, 2012). Crawford, a former reporter at the *Flint Journal,* dispels the myths that swirl around Smith to present a compelling and meticulously researched portrait. He also elaborated on his work in a telephone interview and a series of email exchanges in April 2012.

Locating a trading post on the Flint site: Gustin, ed., *Picture History of Flint,* 21.

Smith on the Cass payroll: Crawford, *The Daring Trader,* 166–69.

"A very careless man in his business affairs": Crawford, *The Daring Trader,* 211.

Smith's death: Gustin, ed., *Picture History of Flint,* 21–22.

"Wilds and untrod solitudes": Alexis de Tocqueville, *Journey to America,* ed. J.P. Mayer, trans. George Lawrence (New York: Anchor, 1975), 370.

"Bears for watch dogs": Tocqueville, *Journey to America,* 378–79.

"The tide of emigration is rapidly increasing": Gustin, ed., *Picture History of Flint,* 31.

"And Flint they are": Gustin, ed., *Picture History of Flint,* 10.

"Lumbering was rough business": Crow, *The City of Flint Grows Up,* 18.

Peak as a lumber town: Gustin, ed., *Picture History of Flint,* 51.

$1 million annually: Crow, *The City of Flint Grows Up,* 22.

150,000 vehicles annually: Sidney Fine, *Sit-Down: The General Motors Strike of 1936–1937* (Ann Arbor: University of Michigan Press, 1989), 101.

Permanent office on Broadway: Gustin, ed., *Picture History of Flint,* 82.

"Vehicle City": Fine, *Sit-Down,* 101.

"Piles of rotting sawdust": Crow, *The City of Flint Grows Up,* 24.

CHAPTER 6. THE ROAD TO PROSPERITY

Billy (William C.) Durant: For the brief portrait of GM's founder, I relied on various newspaper articles and several books, including Ronald Edsforth's *Class Conflict and Cultural Consensus* (New Brunswick, NJ: Rutgers University Press, 1987); and Willis F. Dunbar and George S. May's *Michigan: A History of the Wolverine State* (Grand Rapids, MI: William B. Eerdmans, 1995). William Pelfrey's *Billy, Alfred, and General Motors: The Story of Two Unique Men, a Legendary Company, and a Remarkable Time in American History* (New York: AMACOM, 2006) was particularly helpful in capturing the spirit and personality of Billy Durant.

GM was incorporated in New Jersey: Pelfrey, *Billy, Alfred, and General Motors,* 126.

Durant and his wife survived on handouts: Pelfrey, *Billy, Alfred, and General Motors,* 276.

Ten million cars: Andrew Highsmith, "Demolition Means Progress: Race, Class and the Deconstruction of the American Dream in Flint, Michigan" (PhD diss., University of Michigan, 2009), 40.

"In the worst areas": Edsforth, *Class Conflict and Cultural Consensus,* 66–67.

Family farm: My mother now owns the farm originally purchased for my grandmother's younger brother. She has rented it to an independent farmer for decades and uses the income to augment Social Security payments and a small pension from McLaren Hospital. After all these years, a piece of property paid for with money made in Flint during better times is still supporting my family, a bit of the Vehicle City prosperity that has endured.

Flint families on relief: Highsmith, "Demolition Means Progress," 47–48.

High mortality rates: Highsmith, "Demolition Means Progress," 93.

Flint Sit-Down Strike: Though I consulted several sources, my description of the strike is drawn primarily from Sidney Fine's definitive work on the subject, *Sit-Down: The General Motors Strike of 1936–1937* (Ann Arbor: University of Michigan Press, 1989). This engaging work is a must-read for those hoping to understand the dynamics of the early labor movement in Flint.

"The tide of battle ebbed and flowed": Fine, *Sit-Down,* 4–5.

"An industrial marvel": Highsmith, "Demolition Means Progress," 42.

GM employment figures: Highsmith, "Demolition Means Progress," 42.

"The Flint economy . . . can be described in a single word": Highsmith, "Demolition Means Progress," 41–42.

Charles Stewart Mott: For the portrait of Flint's greatest benefactor and his foundation, I relied on a variety of sources, including Fine's *Sit-Down* and Pelfrey's *Billy, Alfred and General Motors.* But the most comprehensive and insightful examination of Mott is found in "Demolition Means Progress: Race, Class, and the Deconstruction of the American Dream in Flint, Michigan," a 2009 dissertation (and forthcoming book from the University of Chicago Press) written by historian Andrew Highsmith. It is an in-depth investigation of how Mott's philanthropic activities profoundly influenced Flint and furthered Mott's political and social agenda. With more than $2 billion in assets, the Charles Stewart Mott Foundation continues to have a major impact on Flint, funding everything from Italian glass exhibitions at the art museum to community policing initiatives that help the city avoid laying off more cops.

Reputation for thrift: Al Rothenberg, "The 'Skinflint' of Flint," *WardsAuto,* May 1, 1996, http://wardsauto.com/news-amp-analysis/skinflint-flint-cs-mott-gave-away-millions-he-watched-his-pennies.

"Very truly yours, C. S. Mott": Douglas Martin, "Stewart R. Mott, 70, Offbeat Philanthropist, Dies," *New York Times,* June 14, 2008.

"The virtues of self help": Highsmith, "Demolition Means Progress," 95. For more on Mott's political views, see Highsmith, "Demolition Means Progress," 95–99.

Workers deserved to be shot: Highsmith, "Demolition Means Progress," 107.

Mott's philanthropy: Highsmith, "Demolition Means Progress," 100–101.

Enrichment courses: Highsmith, "Demolition Means Progress," 100–106, 121–24.

Flint College and Cultural Center: Lawrence R. Gustin, ed., *Picture History of Flint* (Grand Rapids, MI: William B. Eerdmans, 1976), 236.

CHAPTER 7. BAR LOGIC

"No Ho Zone" sign: According to Marjory Raymer's August 4, 2008, story in the *Flint Journal*, "Sherrie Lynn Palmer, a budding artist, made the sign featuring drawings of eyes watching the street and a dog chasing a prostitute. Russ Palmer, 57, got the idea for the sign after seeing a report on the ozone level."

"Cost less than a new Cadillac": John Law, "Escape to Detroit," Laughing Squid, August 15, 2008, http://laughingsquid.com/escape-to-detroit/.

"Now is the best time ever to buy in Detroit": John Law, August 28, 2008 (1:47 A.M.), comment on "The First of Thousands?" Flint Expatriates, August 22, 2008, www.flintexpats.com/2008/08/first-of-thousands.html.

CHAPTER 8. DOWNWARD MOBILITY

Sources: Much of the information in this chapter is based on the house-hunting tour I took with Jennifer Tremain and Ryan Eashoo, along with numerous interviews I conducted with them and other Flint real-estate agents. I also spent significant time scouting houses on my own in various Flint neighborhoods. For specific details on the houses, I turned to MLS listings and City of Flint property tax records. Some of the material in this chapter originally appeared in an article I wrote for *Slate* headlined "4 BR, 3.5 BA, Grm Ftr.: Why I Want to Buy a House in Flint, Mich," June 18, 2009, www.slate.com/articles/news_and_politics/dispatches/2009/06/4_br_3_5_ba_grm_ftr.html.

Michael Moore and the hall of fame: Getting into the Davison High School hall of fame is apparently tougher than winning an Oscar. Michael Moore has been rejected a handful of times over the years, despite Ryan Eashoo's efforts. "Would you want him as a role model?" Don Hammond, a selection committee member who opposed the filmmaker's induction, asked in a January 14, 2005, Associated Press story that ran in *USA Today*. "Would you want your son or daughter to be like him?"

Williamson resignation: Mary Ann Chick Whiteside, "Don Williamson," *Flint Journal*, October 8, 2007; Shannon Murphy, "Timeline: Don Williamson's Reign as Flint Mayor Marked by Success, Controversy, Disputes," *Bay City Times*, February 9, 2009.

CHAPTER 9. BLACK AND WHITE

Flint's racial history: I drew on a number of sources to learn about my hometown's racial dynamics and create a brief portrait of Floyd McCree. In addition to numerous *Flint Journal* articles and interviews with residents, I consulted Willis F. Dunbar and George S. May's *Michigan: A History of the Wolverine*

State (Grand Rapids, MI: William B. Eerdmans, 1995); Steven P. Dandaneau's *A Town Abandoned: Flint, Michigan, Confronts Deindustrialization* (Albany: State University of New York Press, 1996); and Ronald Edsforth's *Class Conflict and Cultural Consensus* (New Brunswick, NJ: Rutgers University Press, 1987). Nora Faires and Nancy Hanflik's *Jewish Life in the Industrial Promised Land 1855–2005* (East Lansing: Michigan State University Press, 2005) deals primarily with discrimination against Jewish residents, but it also touches on the treatment of African Americans in the city. The most comprehensive and useful source was "Demolition Means Progress," a dissertation and forthcoming book by historian Andrew Highsmith, which I have cited earlier. It is the most complete look at how race intersected with economics, demographics, politics, and urban planning in Flint. It also reveals the deeply embedded institutional racism that permeated Flint, despite the close personal relationships uniting many black and white residents.

Most liberal cities: The Bay Area Center for Voting Research, "The Most Conservative and Liberal Cities in the United States," 2006.

Don Williamson conviction: Mary Ann Chick Whiteside, "Don Williamson," *Flint Journal,* October 8, 2007.

Klan had "substantial political popularity": Dandaneau, *A Town Abandoned,* 192.

GM housing segregation: Highsmith, "Demolition Means Progress," 59.

Crowded North End housing: Highsmith provides an extensive analysis and description of the deplorable housing conditions endured by many African American residents. See "Demolition Means Progress," 318–30.

In Flint, "the North End" is often used as a euphemism for the predominantly African American sections of the city. It is a fluid designation, shifting with demographics as well as the racial sensibilities of the person employing the term. When I was young, it roughly referred to the neighborhoods around the Buick factory complex and on either side of Saginaw Street as it ran north from downtown. When I returned, it had grown to encompass any area north of the Flint River. For some, the entire city was deemed unlivable because of its racial makeup—Flint and the North End were one and the same. It is still a convenient way for whites to indicate black neighborhoods without explicitly identifying them as such.

Twenty-two people living in a five-room house: Highsmith, "Demolition Means Progress," 328.

Third most segregated city: Highsmith, "Demolition Means Progress," 63–64.

Segregated cemeteries: Highsmith, "Demolition Means Progress," 65.

"A cramped and dark coat closet": Highsmith, "Demolition Means Progress," 169.

School district boundaries and segregation: Highsmith thoroughly details the extent of segregation in the local school system. In 1960, Flint had thirty-five public elementary schools. Twenty-one schools had fewer than twenty black students, while eight had substantial black majorities. See Highsmith, "Demolition Means Progress," 155.

"GM Crow must go": Highsmith, "Demolition Means Progress," 196–98.

Few black sales clerks: Highsmith, "Demolition Means Progress," 187–88.

Race-based classifieds: Highsmith, "Demolition Means Progress," 184.

Growth in the African American population: Highsmith, "Demolition Means Progress," 326.

McCree becomes first African American mayor: Highsmith, "Demolition Means Progress," 338.

"Essentially a symbolic position": Highsmith, "Demolition Means Progress," 338.

McCree and the fight for open housing: Highsmith offers a highly detailed account of the material I summarize. See Highsmith, "Demolition Means Progress," 317–61.

Commission dragged its heels: Highsmith, "Demolition Means Progress," 348–49.

Detroit riots: Highsmith, "Demolition Means Progress," 351.

McCree resigned: Highsmith, "Demolition Means Progress," 353.

Protests against housing segregation lead to passage of measure: Highsmith, "Demolition Means Progress," 354–57. For more detail on the protests, see Highsmith, "Demolition Means Progress," 356.

Klan opposition to open housing: Highsmith, "Demolition Means Progress," 357.

Referendum defeated by forty-three votes: Joe Lawlor, "Flint Made Civil Rights History 40 Years Ago," *Flint Journal*, February 10, 2008.

First city in America to implement an open housing ordinance: Lawlor, "Flint Made Civil Rights History."

"It's just wonderful": Lawlor, "Flint Made Civil Rights History."

"I wonder if it's all for naught": Lawlor, "Flint Made Civil Rights History."

McCree loses to Rutherford: James A. Sharp Jr. became the first popularly elected African American mayor of Flint when he defeated James Rutherford in 1983. Sharp served one term and was defeated in 1987 by Matt Collier, who is white.

IMA Auditorium dances: Adrienne Oliver and Patricia Young, interviews with author, June 2009.

"Now that hurt": Adrienne Oliver, interview with author, June 2009.

CHAPTER 10. THE FOREST PRIMEVAL

"Let's just bulldoze it": Rush Limbaugh's broadcast discussing Flint's shrinking-city plans aired locally from noon to 3 P.M. on WWCK 1570 on June 16, 2009.

Turf grass study: David Runk, "Flint Study Asks: How Does Well-Kept Grass Matter?" *Boston Globe*, December 26, 2009.

"Tree larceny": Shannon Murphy, "Charges Filed in Thefts of Black Walnut Trees Last Year in Flint," *Bay City Times*, April 15, 2008.

"Returned . . . to the forest primeval": David Steitfeld, "An Effort to Save Flint, Mich., by Shrinking It," *New York Times*, April 21, 2009.

Misconceptions about shrinking-city plan: Even urban planners, schooled in managing growth, have been caught off guard by the shrinking-city trend. "Most planners lag in grasping the widespread existence and impressive implications of shrinking cities," according to a team of planners writing in the journal *Progress in Planning.* "They are only beginning to comprehend it and find ways to respond to it. In particular, they have to overcome their aversion, usually induced by the growth-oriented wider culture in which they operate, to the very idea of shrinkage. They believe it means a pessimistic, unhealthy acceptance of decline." See Justin B. Hollander et al., "Planning Shrinking Cities," *Progress in Planning* 72 (2009): 223–32.

Depopulating cities in Germany: In Europe between 1990 and 2000, forty-nine cities shrank in Great Britain, forty-eight in Germany, and thirty-four in Italy. At the same time, nearly one hundred Russian cities got smaller, and an aging citizenry and strict immigration policies caused the population in many Japanese towns to dip. See Tann vom Hove, "Not All Cities Will Benefit from Rising Urbanization," *City Mayors: Habitat 2008,* November 22, 2008, www.citymayors.com/habitat/habitat08-urbanization.html.

Factors that can lead to a city's decline: Deborah E. Popper and Frank J. Popper, "The Road to Right-Size Cities," *Yes!* November 16, 2010.

More cities in the developed world shrank than grew: Despite increases in the world population, many cities continue to shrink because people are migrating to vast, sprawling megaregions. The largest include Hong Kong-Shenzhen-Guangzhou, China, home to about 120 million people; Nagoya-Osaka-Kyoto-Kobe, Japan, expected to reach 60 million people by 2015; and the Rio de Janeiro–Sao Paulo region with 43 million in Brazil. See John Vidal, "UN Report: World's Biggest Cities Merging into 'Mega-Regions,'" *Guardian,* March 22, 2010.

U.S. cities shrinking: Justin B. Hollander et al., "Planning Shrinking Cities," *Progress in Planning* 72 (2009): 223; Justin B. Hollander, *Sunburnt Cities: The Great Recession, Depopulation and Urban Planning in the American Sunbelt* (New York: Routledge, 2011), 4.

"We can no longer be sure that we are the city of the future": J. Patrick Coolican, "Lessons Las Vegas Can Learn from the Rust Belt," *Las Vegas Sun,* October 11, 2009.

CHAPTER 11. THE NAKED TRUTH

Saint John neighborhood and urban renewal: A variety of sources informed this section. I conducted a series of personal interviews with Adrienne Oliver and my mother, Patricia Young, both of whom frequented the Saint John neighborhood in the 1950s. Dan Kildee discussed the legacy of urban renewal at length in several interviews. The most comprehensive treatment of Saint John and other urban renewal projects in Flint can be found in Andrew Highsmith's dissertation and forthcoming book, "Demolition Means Progress." Highsmith also elaborated on his work in an extensive telephone interview on July 20, 2011, and in a series of follow-up emails.

By 1960, Saint John was 95 percent African American: Highsmith, "Demolition Means Progress," 420.

Epicenter of black life: Highsmith, "Demolition Means Progress," 421–22.

"When sunlight did arrive": Highsmith, "Demolition Means Progress," 423.

Largest rat population: Highsmith, "Demolition Means Progress, 422.

Proposed construction of Interstate 475: Highsmith, "Demolition Means Progress," 426–27.

The Urban League and NAACP supported the plan: Highsmith, "Demolition Means Progress," 428–31.

"Most racially segregated": Highsmith, "Demolition Means Progress," 473.

Highsmith's Urban League lecture and house in Mott Park: Andrew Highsmith, telephone interview with author, July 20, 2011.

CHAPTER 12. THE TOUGHEST JOB IN POLITICS

Source: Some of this material originally appeared in an article I wrote for *Slate* headlined "Can Anyone Run This Place? The Depressing Yet Inspiring Race for Mayor of One of America's Most Troubled Cities," August 3, 2009, www.slate.com/articles/news_and_politics/dispatches/2009/08/can_anyone_run_this_place.html.

"Tonight we celebrate": Kristen Longley, "Walling Plans to 'Go to Work' for Flint after Definitive Mayoral Victory over Clack," *Flint Journal*, August 5, 2009.

"I think we . . . sometimes don't support our own": Scott Atkinson, "Brenda Clack Concedes in Mayoral Race," *Flint Journal*, August 4, 2009.

Walling took five black precincts: Longley, "Walling Plans to 'Go to Work.'"

Budget deficit of American cities: Tad Friend, "Contract City," *New Yorker*, September 5, 2011, p. 35.

CHAPTER 15. BURNING DOWN THE HOUSE

"He doesn't care about the city": Laura Angus, "Flint to Lose 69 Police Officers, Firefighters Face Layoff Thursday," *Flint Journal*, March 25, 2010.

"Thank God it's not summer yet": Laura Angus, "Flint Had 51 Suspected Arsons in Two Weeks," *Flint Journal*, April 7, 2010.

"I can't solve the city's problems": "Burton's Fire Chief to Flint: 'We're Not Responding,'" *Flint Journal*, April 2, 2010.

"Someone has it out for Carriage Town": Laura Angus, "Rash of Fires in Flint Thought to Be for 'Perverted Political Purpose,'" *Flint Journal*, March 26, 2010.

"This is a series of coordinated criminal attacks": Angus, "Rash of Fires."

"You can read between the lines": Angus, "Rash of Fires."

Residents howled in protest: Kristin Longley, "Weekly Trash Pickup to Begin Next Month after Flint Mayor Dayne Walling Said He Won't Veto Budget," *Flint Journal*, June 15, 2010.

"Moving in a positive direction": Kristen Longley, "Mayor Dayne Walling Orders 5 Percent Pay Cut for Himself and Staff; Calls for Union Concessions," *Flint Journal*, November 4, 2009.

"We've tried to negotiate in good faith": Laura Misjak, "Mayor, Police Chief Will Talk about Consequences of Possible Layoffs," *Flint Journal*, February 11, 2010.

Unfunded liability: Eric Scorsone and Nicolette Bateson, "Case Study: City of Flint, Michigan," report prepared for Michigan State University Extension,

September 2011, p. 44, available at http://expeng.anr.msu.edu/uploads/files/42/
MSUE_FlintCaseStudy-2011%202.pdf.

Public safety costs: Spending on public safety by the City of Flint covers
working and retired police and firefighters, the city's 911 system, the city attorney's office, and the Sixty-Eighth District Court.

"Like putting a Band-Aid on a bazooka wound": Kristen Longley, "City of
Flint to Lose 80 Police, Firefighters with Layoffs," *Flint Journal*, February 17,
2010.

"A level higher than it was when I was elected": Laura Misjak, "$6.7 M Grant
Expected to Help Flint Rehire 39 Firefighters," *Flint Journal*, April 7, 2010.

Threefold increase in arson: David Harris, "Flint's East Side Bears Worst
Arson Scars: 'They Burned the Whole Block,'" *Flint Journal*, January 8, 2011.

CHAPTER 16. EMOTIONAL RESCUE

Jan and Ted's meeting in Tonga: Peace Corps volunteer Deborah Gardner
was murdered in Tonga on October 4, 1976. She was stabbed twenty-two
times. A fellow volunteer named Dennis Priven was charged with murder in
Tonga but found not guilty by reason of insanity. He returned to the United
States and was set free. Journalist Philip Weiss chronicled the murder and its
aftermath in *American Taboo: A Murder in the Peace Corps*, published in 2004
by HarperCollins. Jan Worth's novel based on her Peace Corps experience is
called *Night Blind* and was published in 2006 by iUniverse.

CHAPTER 17. GET REAL

Sources: The material in this chapter is based on a series of personal interviews with Dan Kildee and Dayne Walling, as well as their statements at the
Michigan Summit in East Lansing, Michigan, on June 12, 2010. Some of the
material appeared in the profile of Kildee I wrote for *Slate*: Gordon Young,
"The Incredible Shrinking American City: What Dan Kildee Wants America
to Learn from the Sorry Tale of Flint, Mich.," *Slate*, July 16, 2010, www.slate.
com/articles/news_and_politics/dispatches/2010/07/the_incredible_shrinking_
american_city.html.

"Why do you ask, Dan?": I heard this anecdote during a June 18, 2010,
interview with Matt Schlinker, a close friend of Dan Kildee's going back to their
days on the Northern High School hockey team, at his home. Schlinker also
worked on several of Dale Kildee's election campaigns. He lives off East Court
Street, not far from Dayne Walling, Dale Kildee, and the house where I stayed
during the summer of 2010. Even this well-maintained, upscale neighborhood
has empty houses. After the interview, Schlinker walked me over to the vacant
house next door to his home to show me how he had doctored the plywood
securing the front door to look more realistic by spray-painting in small windows and a doorknob, complete with shading and shadow. It was trompe l'oeil,
Flint style.

Pennsylvania land-bank bill: The 2010 land-bank bill failed in Pennsylvania,
but a revamped version was under consideration in 2012.

Jane Avenue between Minnesota and Iowa Avenues: There were twenty incidents of arson on this block of Jane Avenue alone in 2010. "They burned the whole block," said Allen Willard, a fifty-three-year-old who lived in the only occupied dwelling on the block. "I used to wake up at 2 or 3 A.M. I'd open my eyes, and I'd see flames [reflecting] on my bedroom wall. A house a week started going down." David Harris, "Flint's East Side Bears Worst Arson Scars; 'They Burned the Whole Block,'" *Flint Journal*, January 8, 2011.

CHAPTER 19. FADING MURALS

One of the country's first subdivisions: Donald Richards, "The Way It Was," *East Village Magazine*, December 1981, p. 9.

Response to substandard living conditions: Highsmith, "Demolition Means Progress," 58.

"I can send out a surveying crew in the morning": Richards, "The Way It Was," 9. William Pitkin, a New York landscape architect, is generally credited with the street layout and plat of Civic Park, but he relied primarily, if not exclusively, on design and survey work already completed by Charles Branch, a surveyor and former county road engineer hired by Charles Stewart Mott. According to Donald Richards, a Flint historian who interviewed and corresponded with Branch extensively, Pitkin only came to Flint twice and never visited the Civic Park site. Although Pitkin is named on the historic-site marker for Civic Park, Branch eventually received recognition from the Civic Park Community League and other organizations for his work after Richards wrote about his unheralded contributions. Richards, "The Way It Was," 9–10.

New homes completed in seven hours: Tomblinson, Harburn, Yurk & Associates Incorporated Architects and Planners, and William Kessler & Associates, consulting architects, "Civic Park Home Preservation Manual," 1981, pp. 1–4.

CHAPTER 20. GUN CLUB

"Dayton Family": After my tour with Dave and Judy Starr, I tracked down Raheen "Shoestring" Peterson of the Dayton Family through his record label. He's thirty-eight and raising three teenage kids. He lives in Texas now but makes frequent visits back to Flint to visit his grandparents, who still live on Bonbright Street. After chronicling, if not celebrating, some of Flint's roughest areas in song for so many years, he admitted he no longer felt comfortable in the city. "I don't go to any of the old stores or places I used to go because there's too many people getting killed," he said. "There's too many young guys standing around. There's no police on the street. It's not a safe place." I suggested that Flint wasn't exactly a peaceful city when he was younger, but he quickly countered that there's no comparison. "It's real bad now. Real, real bad," he said. "To tell you the truth, when we was doing the music and talking all that gangsta and ghetto shit, them was the good times. Now that I'm older, I look back and realize Flint was good back then compared to now."

CHAPTER 21. BARGAINING WITH GOD

Community Presbyterian Church: "Several Presbyterian families in the area first met in December 1919 for a Christmas party, and by 1921 the group had grown so large that a formal Presbyterian church was organized," reads the green and gold Michigan Historic Site marker located in front of the church. "The congregation's first building was an old construction barracks located at the corner of Hamilton and Chevrolet. The basement of the present Gothic-inspired edifice was completed in 1924, and the sanctuary in 1927."

"The dog was never really the same after that": The High family bought their home on Greenway Avenue from Michael Brown, who became interim mayor of Flint when Don Williamson resigned to avoid a recall in 2009, setting the stage for the election of Dayne Walling. Before the Browns lived there, it was the childhood home of Jon Scieszka, who went on to write the popular children's books *The True Story of the Three Little Pigs* and *The Stinky Cheese Man and Other Fairly Stupid Tales.* He became the country's first National Ambassador for Young People's Literature in 2008, a position described by the *New York Times* as "a kind of children's book version of the Library of Congress's poet laureate program." He now lives in Brooklyn.

"Two white students apparently were shoved": Ed Hayman, "Northwestern Again Has Racial Violence," *Flint Journal,* February 15, 1972.

Cabell suicide: David V. Graham, "Assistant Principal at Beecher Is Dead," *Flint Journal,* February 24, 1972.

Suicide note: David V. Graham, "Cabell's 'Letter to Beecher' Describes His Frustrations," *Flint Journal,* March 6, 1972.

Antibusing movement: Patricia Zacharias, "Irene McCabe and Her Battle against Busing," *Detroit News,* May 4, 1997.

Pontiac Northern: Pontiac Northern High School is now known as Pontiac High School.

Sale of Community Presbyterian: The details of the sale of Community Presbyterian and the church's history are based on numerous interviews with Sherman McCathern, Rick McClellan, Timm High, and Andrea Drapp, the business manager of the Presbytery of Lake Huron.

Celebration at Joy Tabernacle: Jennifer Kildee, "The Torch Has Passed: Flint's Joy Tabernacle Church Moves into Community Presbyterian Church Building," *Flint Journal,* October 30, 2009.

CHAPTER 22. PSYCHO KILLER

David Motley's body: Laura Angus, "Flint Homicide Victim Found in Yard Identified as David Motley," *Flint Journal,* May 24, 2010.

"He was in no condition to be fighting or running": David Harris, "Families of Serial Killer Victims Searching for Charges for Closure," *Flint Journal,* October 8, 2010.

Murder rates: Marjory Raymer, "A Chronology and Map of Flint's 2010 Homicides," *Flint Journal,* December 13, 2010.

"I think that he's hunting": Laura Misjak, "Genesee County Serial Killer Asks for Victims' Help before Stabbing," *Flint Journal,* August 9, 2010.

"Now that we have a very good description": Mike Brunker, "Will Layoffs Hamper Cops Hunting Serial Killer?" MSNBC.com, August 7, 2010, http://news.ca.msn.com/top-stories/msnbc-article.aspx?cp-documentid = 25122619.

Abuelazam: David Harris, "One Year after Serial Killer Attacks, Law Enforcement, Victims Want Justice," *Flint Journal*, August 8, 2011; staff and wire reports, "Suspect in Serial Stabbings Caught, Police Say," *USA Today*, August 12, 2010.

"Now everyone can breathe a sigh of relief": Alan Gomez and Larry Copeland, "Stabbing Spree Suspect Agrees to Return to Mich.," *USA Today*, August 15, 2010.

CHAPTER 24. HOME ON THE RANGE

San Francisco handgun ban: Justin Berton, "SF Groups Mobilize to Deny Permit to Gun Shop," *San Francisco Chronicle*, September 8, 2010.

CHAPTER 26. THANKLESS TASK

Williamson known to hand out cash: Mary Ann Chick Whiteside, "Don Williamson," *Flint Journal*, October 8, 2007.

"If we build it, they will come": Kris Turner, "Flint Auto-Parts Maker Android Looks to Disabled-Accessible Vehicle for Profit, Job Creation," *Flint Journal*, December 9, 2010.

Increase in arson: David Harris, "Flint's East Side Bears Worst Arson Scars: 'They Burned The Whole Block,'" *Flint Journal*, January 8, 2011.

Police protection for Walling: Laura Angus, "Mayor Dayne Walling Had Police Detail on Two Occasions at Home after Receiving Threats," *Flint Journal*, March 31, 2010.

Walling's academic research: Dayne Walling, "The Nicest Neighborhood Park: Contamination, Community, Conflict, and Change in Windiate Park, Flint Michigan" (honors thesis, Michigan State University, 1996); Dayne Walling, "Politics and Labour in Flint, Michigan USA, 1936–1937" (thesis, University of Oxford, 1998).

EPILOGUE

"Our neighborhood was strictly blue-collar": Ben Hamper, *Rivethead: Tales from the Assembly Line* (New York: Warner Books, 1991), 10.

UPDATES

Flint crime rates: Kathleen O'Leary Morgan et al., eds., *City Crime Rankings 2011–2012: Crime in Metropolitan America* (Thousand Oaks, Ca.: SAGE, 2011).

Residents living in poverty: Sabrina Tavernise, "Reading, Pa., Knew It Was Poor; Now It Knows Just How Poor," *New York Times*, September 26, 2011.

Sources and Further Reading

Bragman, Howard, with Michael Levin. *Where's My Fifteen Minutes? Get Your Company, Your Cause, or Yourself the Recognition You Deserve.* New York: Penguin, 2008.

Crawford, Kim. *The Daring Trader: Jacob Smith in the Michigan Territory, 1802–1825.* East Lansing: Michigan State University Press, 2012.

Crawford, Margaret. *Building the Workingman's Paradise: The Design of American Company Towns.* New York: Verso, 1995.

Crow, Carl. *The City of Flint Grows Up.* New York: Harper & Brothers, 1945.

Dandaneau, Steven P. *A Town Abandoned: Flint, Michigan, Confronts Deindustrialization.* Albany: State University of New York Press, 1996.

Diamond, Jared. *Collapse: How Societies Choose to Fail or Succeed.* New York: Penguin Books, 2005.

Dunbar, Willis F., and George S. May. *Michigan: A History of the Wolverine State.* Grand Rapids, MI: William B. Eerdmans, 1995.

Edsforth, Ronald. *Class Conflict and Cultural Consensus: Making of a Mass Consumer Society in Flint, Michigan.* New Brunswick, NJ: Rutgers University Press, 1987.

Faires, Nora, and Nancy Hanflik. *Jewish Life in the Industrial Promised Land 1855–2005.* East Lansing: Michigan State University Press, 2005.

Farley, Reynolds, Sheldon Danziger, and Harry J. Holzer. *Detroit Divided.* New York: Russell Sage Foundation, 2002.

Fine, Sidney. *Sit-Down: The General Motors Strike of 1936–1937.* Ann Arbor: University of Michigan Press, 1989.

Flinn, Gary. *Remembering Flint, Michigan: Stories from the Vehicle City.* Charleston, SC: History Press, 2010.

Flint, Anthony. *This Land: The Battle over Sprawl and the Future of America.* Baltimore, MD: Johns Hopkins University Press, 2006.

Gallagher, Winifred. *The Power of Place: How Our Surroundings Shape Our Thoughts, Emotions, and Actions.* New York: HarperCollins, 2007.

Gluck, Peter R., and Richard J. Meister. *Cities in Transition: Social Change and Institutional Responses in Urban Development.* New York: Franklin Watts, 1979.

Goldberger, Paul. *Why Architecture Matters.* New Haven, CT: Yale University Press, 2009.

Green, Hardy. *The Company Town: The Industrial Edens and Satanic Mills That Shaped the American Economy.* New York: Perseus, 2010.

Gustin, Lawrence R., ed. *Picture History of Flint.* Grand Rapids, MI: William B. Eerdmans, 1976.

Hamper, Ben. *Rivethead: Tales from the Assembly Line.* New York: Warner Books, 1991.

Herron, Jerry. *AfterCulture: Detroit and the Humiliation of History.* Detroit: Wayne State University Press, 1993.

Highsmith, Andrew R. "Demolition Means Progress: Race, Class and the Deconstruction of the American Dream in Flint, Michigan." PhD diss., University of Michigan, 2009.

Hollander, Justin B. *Sunburnt Cities: The Great Recession, Depopulation and Urban Planning in the American Sunbelt.* London: Routledge, 2011.

Jones, Bryan D., and Lynn W. Bachelor. *The Sustaining Hand: Community Leadership and Corporate Power.* Lawrence: University of Kansas Press, 1993.

Kidder, Tracy. *House.* New York: Houghton Mifflin, 1999.

Kotlowitz, Alex. *Never a City So Real.* New York: Crown, 2004.

LaRose, Lawrence. *Gutted: Down to the Studs in My House, My Marriage, My Entire Life.* New York: Bloomsbury, 2004.

Marcus, Clare Cooper. *House as a Mirror of Self.* Berwick, ME: Nicolas-Hays, 2006.

Pelfrey, William. *Billy, Alfred, and General Motors: The Story of Two Unique Men, a Legendary Company, and a Remarkable Time in American History.* New York: AMACOM, 2006.

Pollan, Michael. *A Place of My Own: The Architecture of Daydreams.* New York: Penguin, 2008.

Ritivoi, Andrea Deciu. *Yesterday's Self: Nostalgia and the Immigrant Identity.* Lanham, MD: Rowman & Littlefield, 2002.

Rozycki, Paul. *A Clearer Image: The Seventy-Five Year History of Mott Community College.* Flint, MI: Mott Community College, 1998.

Ruhlman, Michael. *House: A Memoir.* New York: Penguin, 2005.

Stoll, Steven. *The Great Delusion: A Mad Inventor, Death in the Tropics, and the Utopian Origins of Economic Growth.* New York: Hill and Wang, 2008.

Sturken, Marita. *Tourists of History: Memory, Kitsch, and Consumerism from Oklahoma City to Ground Zero.* Durham, NC: Duke University Press, 2007.

Terkel, Studs. *Hard Times: An Oral History of the Great Depression.* New York: Pantheon, 1970.

Thompson, Heather Ann. *Whose Detroit? Politics, Labor, and Race in a Modern American City.* Ithaca, NY: Cornell University Press, 2001.

Tocqueville, Alexis de. *Journey to America.* Edited by J.P. Mayer. Translated by George Lawrence. New York: Anchor, 1971.

Weesner, Theodore. *The Car Thief.* New York: Random House, 1972.

Worth, Jan. *Night Blind.* New York: iUniverse, 2006.

Index

Carriage Town (Flint, MI): arson in,
135; author's house hunt in, 114–16,
120–25; author's temporary residence
in, 1–2, 8–12, 76, 94–95, 106, 108;
crime rate in, 108–9; as diverse
neighborhood, 109–10; as gentrified,
107–8; historic integrity of buildings
in, 124–25; infighting in, 123; revival
of, 1, 60, 106–7, 108–10, 111–14, 240,
243, 244; as shrinking-city movement
epicenter, 106
Carriage Town Neighborhood Association,
109, 123, 135
Cass, Lewis, 38–39
Center for Community Progress, 150, 243
Central High School (Flint, MI), 75, 98, 100
Character Inn (Flint, MI), 110
Charles Stewart Mott Foundation, 8,
49–50, 72, 74, 120, 214, 222, 254n
Chevrolet, Louis, 44
Chevy in the Hole, 48, 63, 131
Chippewa tribes, 37–39, 41
Christine (Civic Park resident), 78–79, 144,
160
Chuck E. Cheese brawl (Flint, MI; 2008),
31–32
Civic Park (Flint, MI): abandoned lots in,
176, 177, 234–35; author's family home
in, 125, 144, 162–64, 252n (ch. 1);
author's house hunt in, 144–45, 160,
195, 199–200, 229; author's visit to,
164–66, 175–79; churches in, 181, 262n
(ch. 21); crime in, 172, 173; economic
decline of, 172; history of, 160–62,
262n (ch. 19); Milbourne Avenue Block
Club, 168, 169–71, 179; revival of,
165–66, 189, 210–13; white flight from,
172–73, 181–82. See also Community
Presbyterian Church (Flint, MI); Joy
Tabernacle (Flint, MI)
Civic Park Community League, 262n (ch.
19)
Civic Park Heritage Museum (planned),
211, 212, 218, 245
Civic Park School, 144, 163, 166, 252n
(ch. 1)
civil rights movement, 73
Clack, Brenda, 67, 70, 96, 102–5
Clack, Floyd, 102
Clarinda (IA), 216
Clean and Green program, 240
Cleveland (OH), 86, 150
Clinton, Bill, 27–28
Clinton, Hillary, 28
Clio (MI), 135

code enforcement, 88–89
College Cultural District (Flint, MI), 63–64
Collier, Matt, 258n (ch. 9)
community education, 49–50
Community Presbyterian Church (Flint,
MI), 168, 181–82, 184–85, 189, 214,
262n (ch. 21). See also Joy Tabernacle
(Flint, MI)
Compton, Perry, 112–14, 115, 121,
125–27, 128–30, 135, 244
Coney Island (Flint culinary specialty), 82,
158
Copa nightclub (Flint, MI), 30–31, 66, 109,
157
CQ Press, 242
crime, 172, 191–96, 214–17
Crow, Carl, 41

Dance Ministry, 102
Davenport, David, 220–21
Davidson (MI), 135
Davis, Miles, 98
Davison High School (Davison, MI), 66,
256n (ch. 8)
Dayton Family (hip-hop band), 178–79,
262n (ch. 20)
Delarie (Civic Park resident), 165–68
Democracy in America (Tocqueville), 39
"Demolition Means Progress" (Highsmith),
71–74, 97–99, 254n, 257nn
Detroit (MI), 37, 38, 73, 86, 134, 138, 150,
251n
Devil's Night, 134
DeVynne (singer), 103
diversity, 109–10
dog executions, 126, 128
domestic violence, 126
Donovan, Shaun, 81, 152
Dorsey, Ira ("Bootleg"), 178
Dort, J. Dallas, 43
Dort Music Center (Flint, MI), 50
Douglas, Derek, 152
drug houses, 10, 109, 139
Duane (author's childhood friend), 201–2,
234
Durant, William C., 43–44, 49, 110
Durant-Dort Office Building (Flint, MI),
8, 224
Durant Hotel (Flint, MI), 153

East Court Street, 63, 156–59
East Side (Flint, MI), 75–76, 153–55,
156–59, 261n (ch. 17)
East Village Magazine, 145
eBay, 61, 115